FOR DAVID, LOVER
BOATS MADE FROM
TREES . . .
BARRY

SPLINTER FLEET

SC648

SPLINTER FLEET

The Wooden Subchasers of World War II

Theodore R. Treadwell

NAVAL INSTITUTE PRESS
Annapolis, Maryland

Naval Institute Press
291 Wood Road
Annapolis, MD 21402

Library of Congress Cataloging-in-Publication Data
Treadwell, Theodore R. 1916–
Splinter fleet : the wooden subchasers of World War II / Theodore R. Treadwell.
p. cm.
Includes bibliographical references and index.
ISBN 1-55750-817-8 (alk. paper)
1. Submarine chasers—History. 2. World War, 1939–1945—Naval operations—Submarine. 3. World War, 1939–1945—Naval operations, American. I. Title.

D783 .T74 2000
940.54'51—dc21

00-029211

Printed in the United States of America on acid-free paper ♾
07 06 05 04 03 02 01 00 9 8 7 6 5 4 3 2
First printing

Unless otherwise noted photos are from the author's collection.
Frontispiece: Heading Out by Matt Hirsheimer

To the brave young men who served in the Splinter Fleet—
and especially to those who did not return.

Though shattered planks 'neath oceans lie,
Their souls in peace shall never die.

Contents

Foreword

Having also, like the author, commanded a subchaser during World War II, I wholeheartedly embrace this book for its enlightenment about a class of American warship that has too long been overlooked. We have all heard much about PT boats, submarines, destroyers, and other ships of that great war, but the exploits of the little SC subchasers have gone largely unnoticed and are all but forgotten. Indeed, so little has been written about these vessels that they are virtually unknown. Few of us know what subchasers looked like, why they existed, and what they actually did.

Splinter Fleet makes up for all that by showing us what kind of ships they were and why they were—as the Patrol Craft Sailors Association reminds us—"too good to be forgotten." Originally intended as a stopgap deterrent against German U-boats, they proved to be highly useful for other wartime missions. Many were used in amphibious operations as landing control and communication vessels. As such, they were the first ones to arrive close inshore, facing enemy mortar fire and air attacks while directing waves of landing craft into the beach. Some were used for highly dangerous shallow-water minesweeping prior to the landing. Others were converted into gunboats, steaming up hostile rivers behind enemy lines to provide counter support to ground troops in Pacific jungle warfare. In all of these activities they were exposed, vulnerable, and expendable.

When not thus engaged, subchasers continually were called upon to escort, patrol, and search the seas for submarines, derelict mines, enemy barges, and other suspicious and dangerous objects. Much of their duty consisted of dull, dreary voyages at three-knot speeds, plodding in the wake of the bigger ships as they escorted floating dry docks, supply barges, and other service vessels. Often on the fringe of the big, spectacular battles, they fought their mini-battles, not only against the enemy but against nature. They sailed in the most violent weather under the most uncomfortable kind of living conditions.

Most of the young men who manned the subchasers were landlubbers, unaccustomed to the ways of the navy and the sea, but they soon showed how quickly they could learn and how well they could fight. With typical American aplomb and humor they sailed into harm's way, accepting the bad with the good, enduring their discomforts and casualties with a minimum of complaints. Some paid the highest price and were never to return. Their skirmishes with the enemy were fought in the shadows of the major, highly publicized battles and received little or no attention from newsmen. Yet the accomplishments of the intrepid men of the "Donald Duck Navy" reflect the highest traditions of courage and valor.

This book tells some true stories of how the little ships and their men fought kamikazes, torpedo bombers, midget submarines, coastal barges, and other enemy vessels. It shows how they coped with typhoons, icing, groundings, fire, collisions, rogue whales, and other hazards of the deep. Fortunately there was a mixture of fun and laughter too, which helped offset the dangers and discomforts.

Today, those who served on the wooden subchasers look back on those years with tremendous pride and a sense of accomplishment. They shared a kind of disciplined informality and camaraderie not found elsewhere in the navy. I can personally attest to this, and there is absolutely no doubt in my mind that my experience as a subchaser sailor helped mold and strengthen my character. In addition it was a tremendous learning experience. I learned how to get over seasickness. How? By hating it so much I quit being seasick. I also learned how to play winning poker. Finally, although I was very young, I learned how to appear older than I was by smoking cigars.

Unrecognized and unheralded, the little subchasers deserve better. Here is a well researched, enduring testimony of their accomplishments that is not only welcome but long overdue.

Pierre Salinger

Preface

This book was originally meant to be a personal journal of my life in the South Pacific aboard a World War II subchaser, the sole intention being to entertain my grandchildren, using as reference some letters and pictures sent home and saved by my family that had been gathering dust in the attic for over fifty years. In the process of recollection, however, I began to realize that, although I had served two years on a subchaser, I really knew very little about them and their place in naval history. Along with this, I discovered that the role of the subchaser was so vague and ill-defined that it needed to be explained.

The word *subchaser,* so common during the war years, has been virtually forgotten. As a topic it cannot be found in any encyclopedia. A search of the Web is not very helpful except for the most ardent researchers. And recently, a navy veteran of the Vietnam War confessed to me that he had never heard of a subchaser. He isn't alone. Hardly anyone born after 1945 has heard of subchasers or knows anything about them—what they were, and what they were supposed to do. Yet during the war years they were a household word, particularly during the Battle of the Atlantic, when they took the brunt of the U-boat war.

Inquiring further, I learned that a good number of men who had served on the little "spitkits" had experienced adventures far more interesting and colorful than my own. Some of their personal accounts are startlingly clear and credible, while others are dimmed by time, requiring verification. To help sort fact from fiction it was necessary to do a lot of investigating and spend many hours of research at the Naval Historical Foundation and the National Archives II in Washington, poking through once classified material, war diaries, action reports, and various other documents.

Ship's logs, with endless notations regarding courses and speeds, magnetic versus gyrocompass readings, wind, sea conditions, and the like, are indispensable, but looking for story material in them can be quite tedious. Page after page of "steaming as before" or "moored as before" appear in monotonous repetition. But persistence reveals a few references to the daily drama that plays on every ship, whether under way or in port. The resulting narratives are an attempt to present life aboard the subchaser as truthfully and factually as possible.

The first three chapters, which present the history, background, and nature of subchasers, may seem unexciting to lay readers, but they are necessary, even at the risk of providing more information about the Splinter Fleet than one ever needs to know. Subsequent chapters recount a few subchaser adventures that I consider to be unusual and worthy of retelling.

No attempt is made here to document the histories of all 438 subchasers built and commissioned during the war. For anyone interested in the bare facts about each SC—where and when built, when launched, commissioned, and decommissioned, how disposed of, and so on, a good source is the eight-volume edition of the *Dictionary of American Fighting Ships,* which can be found in many public libraries. A second excellent source, with considerable information about SCs, their ordnance, postwar disposition, and so on, is *Allied Coastal Forces of World War II,* volume one, by John Lambert and Al Ross.

Early in my research efforts I learned about an organization called PCSA—the Patrol Craft Sailors Association—formed in 1986 by eight navy PC veterans for the purpose of keeping the traditions and histories of navy patrol craft alive. PCs were considerably larger than SCs and were steel-hulled. They were often referred to as subchasers—which indeed they were—but more often they were called "PCs." When those grand old PC salts organized PCSA, they did not forget their little brothers, the wooden SCs. Fortunately for me, they wisely decided to invite SC veterans to join them, with the result that the PCSA membership roll includes men who served on 272 different SC subchasers in World War II. PCSA very kindly made their names available to me, and I have been able to interview many of these men face-to-face or by phone or correspondence, reaping a rich store of experiences and adventures heretofore untold anywhere. I am deeply grateful to PCSA and its recently retired membership chairman, Joseph F. Kelliher, for providing this source. (Appendix C contains more information about PCSA.)

In the early days of this project, a PCSA member, Robert W. Daly Sr., who is a naval historian of considerable merit, shipped to me all his files pertaining to SCs, explaining that, having served on a PC, he intended to concentrate on PCs and leave the SCs up to me. His generous and forthright sharing of information during these years of labor has been most helpful and appreciated. To all those PCSA men who contacted me with stories and pictures, I am most grateful and hereby express my deepest thanks. Whether they found room in this volume or not, they are all included in its spirit.

There has been a resource in the preparation of this book without whom it could never have been written. Dan M. Treadwell, who happens to be my eldest son, became interested, then engrossed, in this project during its early stages. The result has been hundreds of hours of his time—a willing, unflagging, and tenacious effort—in Washington, D.C., fleshing out and copying ship's logs, war diaries, official action reports, photographs, and countless other related materials. His talent for archival research and his ability to extract salient points from voluminous data have produced an amazing wealth of information about subchasers of both world wars. Without his diligence and loyal support, for which I am deeply grateful, this book would have foundered as ignobly as those unlucky subchasers that met similar fates. My youngest son, Ted R. Treadwell III, truly a computer "guru," proved invaluable by opening my mind to the intricacies of file management and the rich world of the Internet. (How in the world did all the great writers do it without a computer?)

Many other people—more than I have room to mention here—contributed their time or talents to this effort with individual research, stories, experiences, referrals, or expertise. I am especially grateful to the following persons for their invaluable assistance: Worthington Adams; A. H. Angelini; Joseph W. Barr; George Baxter; Cdr. Niels Otto Boerresen, Royal Norwegian Navy; Dr. Robert Browning, USCG; Eugene P. Burns; Bruce Carey; Richard Chiasson; E. J. Comeau, PCSA; Robert L. Cory; J. Henry Doscher; Jack Garamella; Charles A. Gardner; William D. Goldfarb; Eunice L. Gourdon; Kent Halverson; Vera Hart; Matthew S. Hirsheimer; Bernard M. Hollander; Daniel V. James; John W. Jamison Jr.; Roy Johns; Gary W. Kohs; Capt. Bruce P. Keller; Jean Kyte; David Lawrence; Cassia Leet; Rick Lindsey; Albert L.

McNomee; James E. Milholland; Edward Moore; John T. Moore; James Myers; Sandy Orsted; Howard Pierce; Frank A. Pilgrim; William Prechtl; Scott Price, USCG; George Puente; Paul and Maria Purdum; Leo J. Ranjo; Henry Reents; Henry C. Rivers; William W. Robinson; Alden A. Rosser; S. Sandvold, Curator, Royal Norwegian Naval Museum; Capt. George R. Schneider; Sandy Smith; Vernon Smith; Edward P. Stafford; Ted Stone; Donald S. Stroetzel; Capt. Lawrence P. Treadwell Jr., USN (Ret.); Abe Taubman; Burney Tucker; John Tully; Bob Wallstrom; Wayne L. Werner; James Wise; Conrad S. Young; Barry Zerby; Franklyn Zinn; Jerry Zweifler.

I also want to thank Paul Wilderson, among others on the editorial staff of the Naval Institute Press, and my copy editor, Jeanne Pinault, for their patience and helpful assistance.

Lastly, I thank my loving wife Elizabeth for her understanding and support during the six years it has taken to complete this book.

SPLINTER FLEET

Prologue

Within a few weeks after the United States declared war against Germany in 1941, U-boats sank over twenty merchant ships off the East Coast in full view of the unprepared and defenseless U.S. Navy. By the summer of 1942 the U-boats had sunk more ships and taken more lives than were lost at Pearl Harbor. Something had to be done, and quickly.

In 1942 and early 1943, little wooden ships designated "SC" for subchaser were among the first vessels to be sent out to challenge the German U-boats in what history has called the Battle of the Atlantic. Too small, too slow, and too poorly armed to survive confrontation on the surface with a U-boat, their very presence nevertheless kept enemy subs below the surface, rendering the subs ineffective.

The submarine emergency was very similar in the beginning months of both world wars. In World War I, when the first subchasers were commissioned, their primary duty for the entire war was to search and destroy enemy subs. In doing so they achieved a degree of glamour and heroics, especially for their work in the Mediterranean, but this quickly faded away when that war ended. Resurrected with the same urgency in 1941, with U-boats sinking shipping at will, the new subchasers faced the same conditions up and down the Atlantic coast. They were thrust into the brutal fury of another war despite a serious lack of experienced officers and men, inadequate armament, often no radar, sonar that wouldn't work properly, and compasses that defied proper calibration.

But the green officers and crews quickly learned the ways of their little wooden vessels and the ways of the sea, accepting both with magnificent strength and tenacity despite the pounding discomfort, the gut-wrenching seasickness, the loneliness and stress, and the sometimes dreadful situations they encountered. The men were very young, some of them mere boys still in high school. Some had hardly begun to shave. Nevertheless, given the extraordinary task at hand and the uniquely uncomfortable vessel in which they were assigned to perform it, they quickly became men. Thrown together as strangers, they quickly bonded, relishing the sharing of adventures and misfortunes in the Splinter Fleet. And at war's end, despite the hardship and the rigors, few of them would have traded their duty for that of any other ship of the navy, nor their personal character-building experience for all the world.

Though they were sturdy little vessels, it was obvious from the beginning that SCs were inadequate in size and armament for the real task, which was to track down U-boats and sink them. Nonetheless, as a deterrent and nuisance to U-boats they were much more effective than the "hooligan navy" of private sailing yachts and fishing vessels that had been pressed into service during the months prior to open warfare. They were maneuverable, had better armament and considerably longer cruising range, and were manned by twenty-four men and three officers trained—if hastily—and ready to fight.

When larger, more suitable ships became available to fight the subs in combination with aircraft, the role of SCs changed from emergency countermeasure to more useful purposes in the new kind of amphibious war we were fighting. Their shallow draft, quiet operation, low hull lines, maneuverability, and overall dependability made them the "little ships that could," workhorses as control vessels in countless invasions. Throughout the war, they provided harbor patrol and antisubmarine screens and escorted hundreds of convoys all over the world. They were constantly in harm's way as they fought dive-bombers, mortar fire, and enemy attacks from Casablanca, Bizerte, Anzio, Sicily, and Palermo to the bloody beaches of southern France and Normandy. In the Pacific they fought their way from the steamy shores of the Solomons and New Guinea through Arawe, Cape Gloucester, Biak, Saidor, Leyte, Kwajalein, Eniwetok, Saipan, Guam, Iwo Jima, and Okinawa, taking in their stride dive-bombing, machine-gun strafing, mortar fire, kamikaze attacks, and typhoons and other natural disasters. They recovered dead and wounded from sinking ships, rescued downed pilots, attacked submarines, fought off enemy planes, swept mines, shot up barges, and laid smoke screens, spilling blood all the way. Their skirmishes with the enemy were short, vicious, and for the most part unnoticed and unheralded.

They performed innumerable thankless and unseen tasks—unrecognized, unknown, and sometimes unremarkable except that all these things were necessary for winning the war.

Although one Associated Press writer referred to them as "snarling little things loaded with death and destruction,"[1] in truth the wooden-hulled SCs were an anomaly—the dwarf mutants among warships, the ragtag kid brothers with the hand-me-down design left over from World War I, the lowest of low in the navy's pecking order. Spawned to be expendable, the subchaser was thrust upon the high seas to face the underseas wolfpack, simply because the nation was in dire need and there was no other weapon available. If the navy's war had been a pickup ball game, the SC subchaser would have been the last player chosen—and reluctantly at that—by the team captains. But it wasn't a game and the navy had no choice. It was a time of national emergency and the tiny ships were needed now.

Aside from having a wooden hull, the SC subchaser of World War II was distinguished as the smallest commissioned warship in the navy. Whenever I ask a layperson whether he or she knows what a subchaser was, the most common reply is, "Wasn't it something like a PT boat?" The answer, of course, is an emphatic "No!" The length of an SC was 110 feet, while PT boats were only eighty feet long. PT boats were commissioned collectively in squadrons, whereas SCs were commissioned individually, making them the smallest commissioned warships in the navy. Subchasers were not the high-speed vessels that their name implies. Their normal cruising speed was twelve knots, and although the ones equipped with pancake diesels and variable pitch propellers could reach flank speeds of twenty-one knots, even this was slow when contrasted with the speed of a PT boat, which could reach forty knots or better.

Compared to the SC's normal complement of three officers and twenty-four enlisted men, a PT had two officers and twelve enlisted. Both vessels were made of wood, but SCs used conventional plank construction, whereas PT boats were fabricated out of marine plywood. Moreover, each type of vessel had a different mission in life. SCs were designed to search and destroy underwater submarines, while PT boats were designed for high-speed surface warfare.

Subchaser personnel tended to be different, too. The officers and enlisted men who served aboard SCs were mostly reservists, unaccustomed to the rigid ways of the navy and lacking the finer points of ship discipline and formality. Dress codes aboard subchasers were for the most part nonexistent. The general appearance of the men was scruffy, matching the appearance of the ship itself. Several SCs would nest together in port, often alongside a supply ship, while taking on water, fuel, and provisions and all looking quite messy, with wet bedding and laundry strung out on improvised clotheslines for all to see. Men in dirty jeans, cutoffs, and skivvy shirts busied themselves loading, sorting, chipping, scraping, painting, cleaning guns, and performing other tasks about the ship. Crates of provisions, machinery, ordnance, spare parts, and other gear were stacked at random to be stored or put to use. The scene in port was always that of disarray—bedraggled, disheveled-looking vessels, alive with working men looking not much better than hoboes.

On such tiny ships personal contact was close from top to bottom. Although protocol was often lacking and certain officers were occasionally guilty of being on too familiar a footing with enlisted men, there was a strength of spirit, a camaraderie, a unity of purpose and teamwork that was almost without peer on other ships. Every man on a subchaser, including the officers, had to wear many hats. Pharmacist's mates were assigned battle stations at 40-mm guns. Yeomen stood watches at sea with everyone else. Gunner's mates manned the helm. Electrician's mates prepared meals when ship's cooks were seasick. Third officers were responsible for supply, communications, engineering, and medical services. Executive officers were personnel managers, gunnery officers, and administrators. Commanding officers were navigators, disciplinarians, the morale force, and the point at which the buck stopped, bearing the full brunt of responsibility for the ship's safety. But under way the commanding officer stood four-hour watches like everyone else. Under such circumstances the influence of the captain was greatly magnified, and the ship and her crew tended to be as the captain was—good, bad, or indifferent.

At sea the subchasers were rough-riding bucking broncos. Their narrow beam and shallow draft produced an unceasing roll that could make even experienced sailors queasy. In heavy seas, this roll combined with a violent pitching motion to preclude any real rest or sleeping. Seasickness was common among subchaser men, particularly on the first day out after being in port several days. The standard cure for seasickness was to say little about it, forgo eating, and stand the watches no matter how uncomfortable. The retching would continue, but with an empty stomach it was less messy.

Many, if not most, of the officers were recent college graduates, with only ninety days of basic training and an additional sixty days of specialized training at SCTC (Subchaser Training Center). The "ninety-day wonders" and their free-wheeling, slatternly looking crews almost deliberately ignored the ways of the regulation navy and settled for their own set of rules, thus indelibly stamping themselves the "Donald Duck Navy." But there was something about the SCs that permanently won over most of the men who served on them.

Now in his seventies, Albert Angelini, a former pharmacist's mate on SC 744, still claims that his service on the subchaser was and continues to be a highlight of his life.[2] And many ex-subchaser men who saw service on other, larger ships say they are most proud of their subchaser days. "Of all my navy service as an enlisted man during both World War II and the Korean War, I am most proud of my subchaser days," says Francis R. Walsh of SC 505. [3]

Career navy men, on the other hand, looked upon the SCs with disdain. In their eyes subchasers weren't really navy. Small in size and short on tradition, they offended even more by their informal, non-navy, hastily trained reservist officers and crews. Once when my ship, SC 648, was operating in the Pacific, we found ourselves short an electrician's mate and requested a replacement from the Bureau of Personnel. We got a career navy electrician's mate who had served twelve years on submarines and wanted a change of scenery. He proved to be an extremely competent electrician's mate, and everyone was very happy with the change—everyone, that is, except the electrician's mate. After two weeks on the 648, he asked to be transferred back to submarine duty. When I asked him why, he politely replied that he felt safer on submarines. Failing in several attempts to dissuade him, I reluctantly gave permission for the transfer. Many years later one of my old crew members told me the true reason for his transfer request: It seems he was embarrassed to be on a ship that was so untypical of the navy. Duty on an SC, he felt, wouldn't look good on his service record. He couldn't bring himself to tell me he was ashamed of being on a subchaser.

Throughout this book the terms "SC," "Spitkit," "110-footer," "Subchaser," "Donald Duck Navy," and "Splinter Fleet" are synonymous and refer only to the small, wooden SC subchasers. A confusion in terminology took place early in the war when the term "subchaser" was often used to designate the PC, which was also an antisubmarine vessel but larger than the SC and made of steel. The navy designated the first group of SCs as PCs in order to distinguish them from their World War I counterparts. This designation was changed in 1942 after the 173-foot PCs came into full production, so that "SC" signified only the 110-foot wooden-hulled subchasers and "PC" signified only the 173-foot steel-hulled patrol craft. But in photographs of some of the earlier SCs the letters "PC" can be seen painted on the hulls.

There are other vessels that some purists will say should be included under the term "Splinter Fleet." One of these was the 136-foot YMS minesweeper, also built of wood. But YMS's were classed as "District Craft" instead of "Minor Combatant Types" in the navy's principal ship recognition document for its own fleet.[4] Another hull closely allied to the Splinter Fleet was the APc, small coastal transports used as navigational guides in some smaller landings and often as command ships for LST or LCI flotilla commanders. The APcs were wooden-hulled and slow, many of them built in Maine like fishing draggers, and, being somewhat lowly themselves, were sisters-in-kind with the SCs. Nevertheless it shall be left to others to labor the point while we single out the SC subchaser as the heart and soul of the "Splinter Fleet." These, the smallest commissioned warships of the United States Navy, were the "Spitkits," and these alone lay first claim to being known as the "Donald Duck Navy"—a dubious distinction in the eyes of some, yet a proud one for others.

The title for this book is taken from a poem written in 1942 by a gunner's mate named Oris E. Moore. "Oh-Eee" was aboard the battleship *Pennsylvania* when Japan struck Pearl Harbor on 7 December 1941; the *Pennsylvania* was in dry dock and survived the attack unscathed. His second claim to fame was a flowing beard with which he was so closely identified that, after getting it shaved off during a particularly lively liberty, he was challenged upon attempting to reboard the ship. In any event, after a leave in the states, Moore was transferred to Subchaser Training Center in Miami and was subsequently assigned to SC 1016. SC 1016 operated out of Colón, Panama, in the South Atlantic, making the "Aruba Run" many times through the Caribbean. It was during the height of German U-boat activity, and in addition to her escort and patrol duty the 1016 was often called upon to pick up survivors of torpedoed transport ships.

One of his shipmates remembers Oh-Eee sitting on an ammunition ready box in front of the pilothouse one fine afternoon, scribbling "The Splinter Fleet" on yellow legal paper. The poem has become legend for all men who served on the 110-foot wooden subchasers.

The Splinter Fleet
by Oris E. Moore

They sing the praises of the battleship,
The carrier is queen of the sea,
The cruiser is tops on the sailor's lists
For a fighting ship is she.

The destroyer sails the sea with pride,
The submarine's work is neat,
But we are the legion of forgotten men,
The sailors in the SC fleet.

We are indeed a motherless child,
Along, long way from home.
Our base is any port we make,
For our destiny is to roam.

No concern is shown for the work we do,
No thought for the way we live,
Like sardines we're packed in wooden crates
Which usually leak like a sieve.

We bounce around like a piece of cork,
No rest is to be had at sea,
The duty is tough and never ends
But the life we live is free.

Our chow all comes from a box or can,
Nothing fresh ever comes this way,
We do our laundry in the propeller wash,
It's a system that's here to stay.

We comb our hair with a ki-yi brush,
Take showers in the water from the sea,
Our trademark is ruggedness,
Yes, a salty bunch are we.

Our stay in port is never long,
For we have work to do,
We have forgotten the comforts of civilian life,
And are happy where the water is blue.

Wooden ships with iron men,
Is a tradition centuries old,
We live up to that in the Splinter Fleet,
When on convoy and patrol.

Our purpose is like the Concord light,
A continuous vigil at sea,
Protecting ships from submarines,
To keep our country free.

1

World War I Subchasers

The First Generation

The class of vessel known as the "subchaser" originated during World War I. In 1916 the United States was still neutral, but there was little doubt that sooner or later she would be dragged into Britain's war against Germany. German U-boat submarines had been torpedoing merchant ships daily with little regard for locale, flags, neutrality, or international rules. Desperate to provide countermeasures, the British hastily designed a lightly armed eighty-foot motor launch designated "ML" and contracted with the United States for the construction of five hundred and fifty of them.

Although highly maneuverable, the MLs were too small to be effective. Their cruising radius was too short, and in heavy seas they were almost useless as an antisubmarine weapon. Not until two German submarines visited the United States for a brief port call in the summer of 1916 and audaciously sank five ships shortly thereafter was the U.S. Navy galvanized into action. Spurred by a young assistant secretary of the navy named Franklin D. Roosevelt, the navy undertook its own design for an effective antisubmarine vessel.

Steel was scarce, as was the capacity of big shipbuilding yards, already fully contracted to build destroyers and other larger ships. Roosevelt invoked naval architects to come up with a suitable design for a subchaser made of wood. The idea was to build them quickly in small boatyards, using people with the necessary skills in wooden-boat construction to get the job done.

No history of subchasers would be complete without mentioning the name of the man who was responsible for the design. Albert Loring Swasey, naval architect, a graduate of MIT, came from a family rich in the lore of the sea and saltwater sailing. A boating enthusiast at the age of nine, he performed his first service to the navy during the Spanish-American War. In 1898, he took a leave of absence from his studies at MIT and went to Newport News Shipyard to work (at $7.50 per week) on warship design. He subsequently became a partner in Swasey, Raymond & Page, a yacht designing firm, where he acquired a reputation for some notable yacht designs, one of which was an express cruiser named the *Houp-la,* the fastest boat built at the time and a forerunner of the ML. In 1915, with a weather eye on the war clouds over Europe, Swasey organized a civilian-manned squadron of nine boats to act as a patrol for spotting possible submarine activity in American waters. This activity came to the attention of Roosevelt, who promptly wrote Swasey a letter of commendation for his initiative. Shortly after that, the nine yachts were assigned navy crews and ordered to active duty.

2 April 1917, at the age of 40, Swasey was commissioned as a lieutenant commander in the Naval Reserve and was appointed superintending constructor for the navy's Bureau of Construction and Repair in the New York district. It was here that he was given the responsibility for designing a subchaser that would have the seaworthiness and the endurance necessary to be effective against the U-boats. Swasey designed a triple-screwed vessel, 110 feet long with a fifteen-foot beam, powered by three Standard six-cylinder, 220-horsepower gasoline-driven engines.

Although the popular view was that a subchaser should be very fast, Swasey disagreed, maintaining that extreme speed was not worth the price in the sacrifice of seaworthiness, cruising range, and comfort. Despite a storm of criticism from big- and small-ship men alike, who had anticipated speeds of at least thirty or forty knots, he went ahead with preparations to have the boats built with a top speed of seventeen knots and a cruising range of one thousand miles. He designed a bow flare similar to that of a big whaleboat with its hull cut off at the waterline aft—a design unsurpassed for sea work since the time of the Vikings.

The propulsion system consisted of three 220-horsepower Standard six-cylinder gasoline-driven engines connected to three screws, each with thirty-nine-inch propellers. Designed for a complement of two officers and twenty-five enlisted men, the vessels had a displacement of eighty-five tons.

SC 26, a World War I subchaser *National Archives*

The armament consisted of two 3-inch 23-mm guns and two machine guns. Later on a depth-charge projector, or Y-gun, was substituted for the after 3-inch gun, and it proved to be the most effective antisubmarine weapon of all. There being no electronic sonar in those days, the vessels were equipped with underwater hydrophones for detecting engine and propeller noises.

In late March 1917 the first contracts were let for construction. By the time the war ended, 440 Class SC-1 subchasers had been completed and placed into service. They were built at navy yards and by experienced craftsmen in thirty-four small boatyards on both coasts and the Great Lakes. Most were completed in less than a year. One hundred were sold and delivered to France. An additional 121 craft manned by American crews crossed the Atlantic under their own power, refueling at sea from tankers accompanying or being escorted. The subchasers in Europe operated in the approaches to Britain and France and in the Mediterranean; those in the United States combined with destroyers in operations off the East Coast against the U-boats.

The gallant little subchasers of the First World War ranged far and wide, completing missions as far north as Archangel, Russia, inside the Arctic Circle. Many SCs were captained by enthusiastic amateur yachtsmen with Ivy League backgrounds, establishing an air of informality and relaxed discipline that continued on the SCs of World War II. The small size of the ships and the nonconformist ways of their men earned them the labels "Cinderellas of the Fleet" and "Splinter Fleet." Officers and crews were a close-knit group, almost to a man recruited from the Naval Reserve. They were a hardy lot. At sea the conditions aboard the little boats—with constant pounding, rolling, and pitching—were grueling, definitely not for the fainthearted. The opinions of historians about the performance of the World War I subchasers are quite contradictory. One source boasts that the SC was the most important weapon of World War I, crediting them with destroying "40 percent of all the U-boats sunk in the war."[1] Another claims that they "achieved no fewer than 19 kills" in the Mediterranean.[2] Still another source took a diametrically opposite view: "The submarine chasers never fulfilled the hopes placed in them . . . the chasers never achieved a single kill."[3] Indisputably, they had been designed before the difficulties of antisubmarine operations had been fully realized. Nevertheless, their effectiveness as an antisubmarine deterrent cannot be denied.

In an operation in 1918 known as the "Otranto Barrage," a dozen or so American subchasers helped keep the U-boats bottled up in the Adriatic, unable to escape to the open sea to press their attacks. By denying the Germans the offensive power of their U-boats at this critical stage, the Otranto Barrage was perhaps the greatest single contribution of the subchasers in World War I. Then, on 2 October 1918, eleven SC-1s blew up enemy mines in the Austrian harbor of Durazzo, thus playing a significant role in the only general naval engagement by the American navy in the war.

Subchasers disappeared rather quickly after World War I, too specialized to be retained in large numbers. One hundred were transferred to France. Fifty-three hulls were transferred to the U.S. Coast Guard, who used some for chasing rumrunners during the Prohibition years, although to a limited extent, for they proved too slow. A handful were converted for oceanographic and special survey work. The navy kept some for training in shiphandling at the Naval Academy. The midshipmen called them "bumper boats," and though they were an effective introduction to the rough ways of the sea, the seasick future admirals being trained on them no doubt acquired a lifelong aversion to them. Other SCs were placed in the Great Lakes region for use by the local naval reservists for training.

The navy used a handful of World War I subchasers in World War II: SC 64, stationed in the Azores during the first war, served from April to December 1942 and then was converted to a water barge and sold in March, 1943; SC 102, the only World War I subchaser equipped with a Y-gun, served

USCG *Belleville,* formerly SC 258, circa 1942 *Courtesy of Scott T. Price*

five years in the second war before being transferred to the War Shipping Administration for disposal in March 1947; SC 330, which had been at Gibraltar in 1918, served in the second war from 1 January 1940 to 18 April 1945; SC 412 saw service from 1 April 1941 to 2 July 1945; SC 437, pressed into service in October 1940, served five years before being decommissioned 28 June 1945.

The Coast Guard operated four World War I subchasers during World War II: SC 229, which it named *Boone* and designated WPC (number unknown); SC 231, which it named *Blaze* and designated WPC-336; SC 238, named *Bowstring* and designated WPC-365; and SC 258, named *Belleville* and designated WPC-372. Fifty-three World War I subchasers were still in existence after World War II, all of them registered with the Coast Guard, some still on the registered list as late as 1981.[4]

Some World War I subchasers had interesting postwar careers. SC 428, for example, was acquired by the City of Baltimore and used as a fireboat. Others were purchased to serve the private sector.

SC 127 was purchased in 1924 by Elizabeth O. Douglas of Rowayton, Connecticut, and for several years was known as the Douglas Houseboat Studio, the home and studio of commercial and marine artist Harold W. Douglas and his wife. In 1928, the vessel was purchased by Louis A. Round Jr. of New London, Connecticut. Recently discharged from the U.S. Coast Guard, he christened her the *Elizabeth Ann* after his new bride. Shortly thereafter, the *Lizzie Ann* began running the twenty-mile ferry and cargo route between Stonington, Connecticut, and Block Island under the house flag of the Interstate Navigation Company. Room was made on her foredeck to carry one car. As the years went by her routes were changed, but she continued to ply the waters of Narragansett Bay as a ferry and mail boat, making the run year-round in the severest of weather conditions. She was taken out of service on March 3, 1951, for a long overdue major overhaul. On April 21, 1951, while being refurbished at a boatyard in New London, she caught fire and was destroyed. Her untimely end, after thirty-four years of faithful service, was not befitting a ship of her stature, but the capriciousness of the sea has not always been kind.[5]

An even unkinder fate was that of SC 168, purchased in Brooklyn in 1923 by Seymour Lasker for conversion into a private yacht named *Sunbeam.* With a crew of three, Mr. Lasker set out from New York for Chicago by way of the Erie Canal. While crossing Lake Erie they made a serious navigational error that brought them to Chippewa on the Niagara River, a few miles above the falls. Realizing their error just before sundown, they tied up the *Sunbeam* and went into town for some entertainment, planning to resume their journey the next morning. During their absence the ex-subchaser somehow broke free of her mooring and began drifting down river. When she reached a site just southwest of the Toronto Power Company generating station, approximately one thousand feet from shore, she became stranded on the rocks and heeled over on her side. When Mr. Lasker surveyed his problem, he decided that the recovery costs were prohibitive and sold the vessel for one dollar "as is" to William "Red" Hill, who planned to haul the vessel off the rocks by using shore-stationed cranes. However, the Niagara Parks Commission required a cash bond in advance to cover any damage to park land. The bond was more money than Mr. Hill had hoped to make from the recovery, so he dropped his plans.

Winter ice gradually broke up the subchaser, until finally nothing was visible of the hull. Since 1961 the reef on which the vessel was stranded comes into view in the winter season. It is said that the boilers, propeller shaft, and other heavy equipment of the vessel are still visible during low-water periods.

2

World War II Subchasers

The Second Generation

The ascendancy of Adolf Hitler, threatening the involvement of the United States in a second world war, revived urgent interest in an antisubmarine shipbuilding program. By 1938 history began repeating itself with astonishing similarity to the events of 1916. Germany was at war with Britain and France, and their U-boats were again roaming the seas at will, sinking tens of thousands of tons of Allied shipping. Franklin D. Roosevelt, now president, called for an all-out construction program for subchasers as a stopgap. There being only one antisubmarine vessel on the entire East Coast (USCG cutter *Dione*), the navy again had to make do with hastily recruited YPs, minesweepers, motor launches, sailing vessels, and a "hooligan navy" of privately owned yachts and trawlers. Alfred Loring Swasey, by then semiretired, was commissioned to come up with a suitable design for a new subchaser, once again to be made of wood, since steel—as in the earlier war—was reserved for bigger ships. The hull length of 110 feet and the use of some fifty small boatyards around the country matched the subchaser building program of the earlier war.

In 1939 a competition for a suitable subchaser design was arranged between Luders Marine Construction Company of Stamford, Connecticut, an experienced World War I boatbuilder, and Electric Boat Company (Elco) of Bayonne, New Jersey, maker of PT boats. This led to an experimental subchaser built from each design, the SC 449 and SC 450. Of these, the Luders

SC 449 became the design of choice. Launched in May 1940, she was commissioned that September, the prototype of all 438 SC subchasers built during the war. The SC 449 played an unspectacular role as a training ship during much of the war until January 1945, when she became the guinea pig for a top secret experiment (described in chapter 20).

A third design, SC 453, was powered by two new "pancake" type diesel engines, capable of driving the ships at speeds up to 21 knots. The pancake-equipped SC became the prototype for the World War II wooden subchaser, but only 243 SCs received pancake engines. The remaining 195 were powered by General Motors straight-8 diesels (8-268A 500 hp). Although these had top speeds of only fifteen knots, they performed the same duties as the pancake-equipped SCs. The SCs with pancake engines had variable-pitch propellers and were easier to maneuver than those with the 286A diesels. In addition, the pancake engines were lighter in weight, reducing the stern draft by eighteen inches. The reason all subchasers were not equipped with pancake engines and variable pitch propellers was a matter of urgency. Production of pancake engines could not meet demand at a time when vessels to fight the U-boat war were a critical need.

One might inquire why the size and general configuration of the second-generation SCs were so similar to those of their antecedents. At first glance the newly designed SCs looked hardly different from those of World War I. Both hulls were 110 feet long, and each had a distinctive rub rail running two-thirds the length of the vessel, three feet above the waterline. Both had guns mounted forward and aft, with a stubby little pilothouse amidships. The flared "whaleboat" bow and a low silhouette were common to both. But the second-generation design, officially designated the SC-497 class, was two feet wider at the beam than the SC-1 class.

Another major difference was the means of propulsion, the earlier version being triple-screwed with gasoline engines and the newer version twin-screwed with diesel engines. The pilothouses on the new chasers were made of cast aluminum instead of wood. The newer ones were equipped with sophisticated sonar gear, rocket depth-charge launchers (mousetraps), and 3-inch/50 or 40-mm guns forward instead of the old 3-inch/23 cannons. Most were equipped with radar, although many of them were not so equipped until the war was almost over. The major differences between the two generations of subchasers was not so much in the hulls as it was in the greater sophistication of electronic gear on the later vessels.

SC 745, a World War II subchaser, Southwest Pacific, 1944. The ship's pet dog stands at the peak of the bow.

To a yachtsman's eye, the lines of a subchaser's hull were rather pleasing, with a graceful flare at the bow and a fluid fore-to-aft sweep worthy of admiration—were it not for the homely, tugboatlike pilothouse jutting up amidships and a deck hopelessly cluttered with guns, ordnance, and other gear.

The nomenclature for SCs has been confusing. In World War I the SCs were identified by the letters "PC" followed by a number. "PC 225" was, for example, actually SC 225. At the start of World War II the same numbering series was continued, with the result that the first vessels built were initially listed as PCs. Then in October 1942 the nomenclature was changed to "SC" to differentiate the 110-foot wooden-hulled subchasers from the larger 173-foot steel-hulled patrol craft, which were more accurately designated "PC." But many SCs slid down the ways after that with the letters "PC," later to be changed by the crews to SC.

World War II SCs—the SC-497 class—had a normal complement of three officers and twenty-four enlisted men, a cruising radius of fifteen hundred miles, and speeds from fifteen to twenty-one knots, depending upon the type of drive. Typical SC armament consisted of eight rocket-propelled "mousetrap" depth charges mounted on the bow, a 40-mm or 3-inch/50 cannon forward of the pilothouse, three 20-mm Oerlikon antiaircraft guns aft, and fourteen or more 300-pound depth charges on racks or rails and K-guns toward the stern. Many SCs mounted an additional .50-caliber machine gun on the flying bridge or at the fantail. An assortment of small arms, including Thompson submachine guns, completed the arsenal.

Although the United States was not officially at war until 7 December 1941, keels for eighty-four SCs had already been laid before that date. The average construction time from keel-laying to launching was six months, but many were built in less time. Elizabeth City Shipyard, Elizabeth City, North Carolina, set a record when on 6 April 1942 it launched SC 704 only thirty days after laying the keel.[1] Most of the forty-nine boatyards where they were built were small, family-owned enterprises employing highly skilled craftsmen, some of them having built SCs during World War I.[2] Details for quality construction were meticulously spelled out in quaint, wooden-boat terms reminiscent of nineteenth-century whaling or clipper ships. The hull planking

> must be long-leaf yellow pine. Planking butts shall be carefully laid out so as to have as wide a distribution as practicable and so as not to conflict with butts or scarphs of planksheer, clamps, shelf and other longitudinals. Planking to be caulked with oakum and cotton, payed with paint, and filled with putty. The decking to be of Douglas fir or white pine edge grain, the mast of Sitka spruce, hollow, built up construction. The stem to be of white oak, side 7 [inches], built up and molded with deadwood apron and knee. A mahogany steering wheel with four complete turns of wheel to throw rudder head to port or starboard. The hawse pipe to be of trumpet type, fitted at stem head to form a fair mooring eye.[3]

The boatyards adhered as closely as they could to specifications but often used woods or materials most readily available in their individual areas. As it turned out, it didn't matter; there wasn't a "lemon" in the entire subchaser fleet. Thanks to the craftsmen who put them together, every one of the 438 subchasers built for World War II proved to be strong, tough, sturdy, seaworthy vessels, as any man who ever sailed on one will tell you.

That they were seaworthy, buoyant, and safe in almost any sea, however, offered little comfort to the sailors who for months on end endured cramped quarters, poor ventilation, damp or moldy bedding, water shortage, and the incessant—often violent—pitching and rolling. If the bedding wasn't wet, it was damp. If it wasn't damp, it was moldy. There was never enough time or sunshine when in port to air bedding thoroughly, particularly in the Atlantic and other waters in the Northern Hemisphere. Noxious diesel fumes from exhausts on each side of the hull at the waterline bathed the ship in a sharp, sickening, odoriferous aura, recalled with extreme distaste by all SC veterans.

The cutaway drawing and list of ship particulars of SC 648 are typical of most World War II subchasers. (See figure 1.) The illustration barely hints of the crowded and uncomfortable conditions existing on SCs for the twenty-seven men who lived aboard. The forward compartment, a space about eighteen feet long by ten feet wide, was the living quarters for sixteen men. The men slept in tiered pipe bunks that were folded against the bulkhead when not in use. Men who wanted to sleep had to put up with others in the lighted compartment who were playing cards, talking, or as was often the case, arguing. Eight men occupied the after crew's quarters, sharing their space with the ship's company during mess, which was prepared three times daily (when the cook wasn't seasick) in the cramped galley. In addition to his folding pipe berth, each man had a shelf and a small locker for all of his gear and personal possessions. His private world was not much bigger than a refrigerator.

No one knows for sure which generation of sailors suffered the rougher ride, since both were uncomfortable even in moderate seas. The heavy roll combined with a violent pitching motion, resulting in a harsh, incessant, corkscrew pounding that permitted neither sleep nor rest for anyone. In both wars creature comforts on the subchasers consisted of cramped, often damp or downright wet quarters, no bathing or washing facilities, and long periods when there was a scarcity of fresh water and palatable food. Meals at sea were plain, scanty, and cold, since ship's cooks, as a group, were notoriously prone to seasickness. On rough trips it was almost every man for himself.

In the early days of the war the sole purpose of the SCs was to hamper, deter, and slow down the U-boat offensive in order to give the United States time to build destroyers, destroyer escorts, and antisubmarine aircraft to wage all-out war against the U-boats. The wooden subchasers and their larger sister ships, the 173-foot steel-hulled PCs, were intended to serve more as stopgaps than as offensive weapons. Armed with depth charges, the SCs and PCs screened merchant convoys with their underwater sound gear, keeping the U-boats submerged and on the defensive, unable to launch their torpedoes.

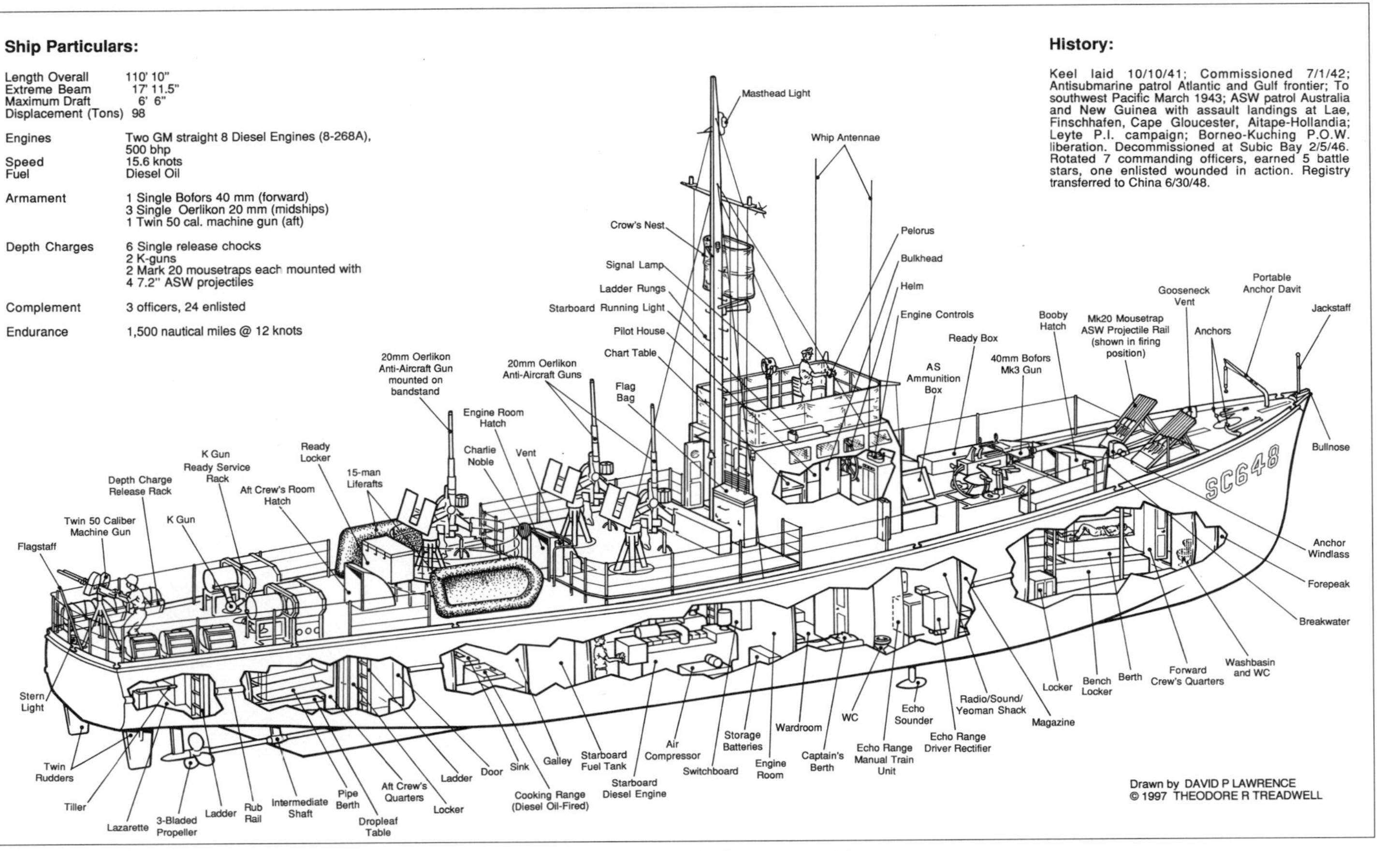

Figure 1. USS Subchaser SC 648

While most SCs at some time during the war were equipped with radar, a few had none until the war was almost over, making necessary the constant use of a lookout in the crow's nest while under way. The photo (below) of six subchasers nested together in Milne Bay, New Guinea, in 1943 shows four of them with radar domes atop their masts. SC 648, nested between SC 749 and SC 637, has no dome and would not get radar until early 1945.

The deck of an SC was as crowded as the compartments below. The only open space was the quarterdeck immediately aft of the pilothouse, a space approximately eight by seven feet surrounded by a disarray of flag bag, ready lockers, ventilators, Charley Noble (galley stack), antiaircraft guns, and the engine room hatch. One had to be nimble to avoid obstructions while making his way about the ship, whether topside or below decks. It helped to be of medium or small build. Jim Moyer, a big, burly sonarman on the 648, was forever banging some part of his body into a projection or sharp object, resulting in an eruption like "Ow! This goddamned ship was built for midgets!" and sending his shipmates into convulsions.

The speedy construction and deployment of SCs in 1942 was a good beginning, but everyone knew that the little ships were no match for the

Six subchasers are nested alongside their tender in Milne Bay, New Guinea, 1944.

U-boats, especially if they ran into one on the surface. Still, they were a big improvement over fishing trawlers and private motor yachts because of their greater maneuverability, longer cruising radius, and heavier armament. A surfaced sub could outshoot, outrun, and outmaneuver a subchaser, but no U-boat commander would be foolish enough to surface in the presence of a subchaser unless he was certain no other ships were nearby, which was rarely the case. By keeping submarines submerged and thereby unable to take periscope aim, SCs proved to be an effective deterrent. A submerged U-boat was forced to operate solely on batteries, draining its only source of power. The SC could track with its sonar and make repeated depth-charge attacks while notifying other ships and radioing for backup.

Of course, in the unlikely event it surfaced, the submarine could retire to a comfortable distance and take its time shooting the subchaser out of the water. The navy's standing rule was that the SC was to ram at flank speed any surfaced enemy submarine it might encounter, a rule fraught with high risk and considerable danger—most likely death—to the subchaser. A ninety-five-ton wooden ship ramming a steel-plated submarine, ten times heavier and fully armed, would be like crashing full speed into an immovable steel jetty on which men were shooting at you point blank with cannon and machine guns. The 4-inch deck guns on the U-boats had considerably more power and range than either the 3-inch/50 or the 40-mm guns of the SC. Every man who served on a subchaser knew these facts, and while he assumed a "come what may" attitude, he felt much more comfortable when his ship was escorting a convoy in company with other escorts.

SCs continued convoy and patrol work throughout the war, even when larger destroyer escorts and destroyers became available in quantity. The Battle of the Atlantic did not begin to change in our favor until the spring of 1943, when destroyer escorts and destroyers teamed with vigilant and aggressive air patrols to form killer groups that methodically searched for and destroyed the U-boats. As deterrents, SCs more than proved their value. But unlike the SCs of World War I, which were used solely for antisubmarine patrol, the new generation of SCs would be used for many other purposes suitable for their size and capabilities. As control vessels in amphibious landings, shallow water minesweepers, smoke layers, air-sea rescue ships, ferryboats, antisub patrol and other missions, the SCs were invaluable.

From landings in the Mediterranean at Palermo, Salerno, Anzio, and Southern France, they proved themselves gutsy and indispensable. At Normandy they were invaluable. In the Pacific they were used as control boats in assaults at Lae, Finschhafen, Hollandia, Cape Gloucester, Leyte, Guam, Saipan, Kwajalein, Eniwetok, Iwo Jima, Okinawa, and countless other bloody beaches. Their shallow draft and maneuverability gave rise to the conversion during the war of seventy SCs to SCCs—subchaser control vessels.[4] The conversion provided additional radio equipment and sleeping quarters for extra radio and radar personnel who came aboard during amphibious operations. These communication teams not only directed the assault waves on D-Day but remained aboard, sometimes for as long as two weeks after the invasion, to serve as a communications and traffic-control center between beach and landing boats.[5]

One veteran SC sailor wrote recently: "We went to sea on a wooden ship as the smallest combatant ship in the U.S. Navy. We went everywhere the big ships went and to many places the big ships were unable to go. . . . [t]hose of us who served . . . knew we had truly gone to sea and performed our duty."[6]

The tales that can be told about the SCs are like those of *Mr. Roberts* and *McHale's Navy,* and they are legion. That subchasers and their men were not exactly "regular Navy" was all too true, yet they managed to prevail, riding out the war in grubby splendor and humble fortitude.

3

Subchaser Training Center

As the United States entered World War II, concurrently with the program of construction of subchasers, the navy faced the huge task of recruiting and training men to operate them. Few people today realize the magnitude of the job they faced, or how much they accomplished in those first few desperate months after Pearl Harbor. Caught completely by surprise, the navy sprang into action immediately by recalling warrant and chief petty officers who had recently retired. Many of them did not have to be recalled. They re-enlisted the day after Pearl Harbor. They were the specialists—the chief boatswain's mates, signalmen, machinist's mates, yeomen, gunner's mates—whose lifetime careers had been devoted to the navy. They were the ones who could give hands-on training to the green landlubbers enlisting in droves all over the country.

In addition, instructors and professors from leading colleges and universities were offered commissions in the Naval Reserve. They knew nothing about the navy, ships, or the sea, and they admitted it. But once they were given the rudiments of codes, communications, diesel engines, operation of sonar gear, radar, navigation, damage control, antisubmarine tactics, aircraft recognition, electricity—the subject didn't really matter—they knew how to make up a teaching manual and teach from the book. I have had much schooling during my life, but some of my finest instructors were men in the navy who admitted they didn't really know the subject but merely knew how to teach it.

Subchasers needed officers as well as enlisted men. The navy offered commissions to students in their final year at college and graduate schools with active duty deferred until June 1942 to allow them to get their degrees before donning their uniforms. It was a smart tactic, enabling the navy to get a jump on local draft boards, some of whom were selecting draftees strictly by lottery, a flawed system whereby a potential Ph.D., M.D., or electrical engineer could wind up in the army as a buck private. The recruitment strategy paid off. All across the country, thousands of fourth-year and graduate students at colleges and universities eagerly signed up to become commissioned officers in the United States Naval Reserve, ready to report for active duty upon completion of their studies that June. Most of these were sent to officer training schools for ninety days of rigorous physical and classroom training, emerging at the end of this period as "ninety-day wonders."

In March 1942, Cdr. Eugene F. McDaniel, a thirty-eight-year-old Annapolis graduate, was given the job of setting up and running a naval training center in Miami called SCTC, the Subchaser Training Center. McDaniel, a thin, lanky, bespectacled Virginian who looked more like a college professor than a sailor experienced in submarine warfare, was a man of decisive action, a doer. He had a fiery, fanatical hatred for the enemy, particularly all Nazis. Having served thirteen years on destroyers in the Atlantic, he never forgot the time when, before the United States was officially in the war, his ship had answered an SOS to pick up seamen off a torpedoed British ship. He found their lifeboats, all right—unarmed, riddled by machine-gun slugs, and full of blood and bodies.

The first thing he did when he got to Miami was to get a lifeboat, spatter it with about forty bullet holes, splash realistically painted blood stains around its insides, and set it up as "Exhibit A" outside the entrance to the training center. Every Monday he would personally address each incoming class, using the lifeboat as illustration. He began by telling the men that there was no time to consider their individual desires. They were there to learn a tough job, and quickly. Each man in all likelihood would face a situation where he alone would be responsible for ten Allied ships and their crews. The speech would wind down with a blistering diatribe of hatred for the Nazis and the Japanese. Pointing to the lifeboat he would exhort, "See what they do? Deliberately and callously machine-gun defenseless sailors as they float

Lt. Cdr. E. F. McDaniel, commanding officer, SCTC, at his desk, 1942
National Archives

in their lifeboat. The Nazis are nothing but inhumane, ruthless murderers, and you and I will put a stop to it." His fiery denunciation was something no one who heard it would ever forget.

When McDaniel arrived on the scene in March 1942, SCTC occupied the old Clyde Mallory pier, commonly known as Pier Two. The building, which overlooked Biscayne Bay, was noisy and poorly ventilated, and the classrooms, separated by thin partitions, were hardly ideal. He had only four officers to help him. They had to find places for the first class of twenty students to eat, sleep, and study. The staff worked around the clock outlining courses, arranging classes, deciding on curriculum, and teaching, some of which McDaniel did himself.

Their objective was clearly defined: The subchasers and PCs, and later the destroyer escorts—more than fifteen hundred ships—had to be manned with men and officers properly trained to perform their duties of escort and patrol. The pressure was intense; submarines were roaming the East Coast at will, sinking ships in alarming numbers. Subchasers under highest priority were coming off the ways from scores of shipyards. Crews had to be trained and ready as fast as the ships were launched.

The navy had picked the right man, for McDaniel knew how to reduce red tape to a minimum. When channels of communication with Washington were too slow, he acted upon his own, at times stepping on toes but getting the job accomplished. He was helped by the tremendous sense of urgency everyone felt.

After SCTC hit its stride, a typical week for officers would be as follows:

> Monday: Four hours of classroom instruction in antisubmarine warfare (ASW), one hour for lunch, one hour of medical instruction (on many SCs the captain was the ship's doctor unless a pharmacist's mate formed part of the roster), three more hours on ASW.
>
> Tuesday: Two hours of medical instruction, two hours of sonar and ASW, followed by an exam. In the afternoon, out to sea on an SC or a YP for seamanship drills.
>
> Wednesday: Two hours' instruction in communications; one hour of sonar and ASW; medical exam; four hours of sonar and ASW in afternoon.
>
> Thursday: Docking practice aboard an SC; ASW and radar instruction.
>
> Friday: Five hours of ASW; radar exam; two hours of navigation instruction.
>
> Saturday: All day at sea with drills in gunnery, communications, shiphandling, and "tentative command."

An entire week at SCTC was spent on instruction in various types of ordnance, including mousetraps, depth charges, ammunition, pyrotechnics, fire control doctrine, etc. Loading drills were conducted on 40-mm, 3-inch/50, and 20-mm guns and .50-caliber machine guns; battery control drills and small arms instruction were included, all thoroughly interspersed with exams. The only time off for officers-in-training was on alternate Sunday afternoons.

Toward the end of their six-week course, the trainees were given a three-to-five-day cruise to familiarize them with an understanding of enlisted functions while under way. Student officers stood deck watches, manned the helm, trained the guns, operated sound gear, and saw duty as quartermaster and in the engine room. Each student was instructed to bring aboard "1 small hand bag, 2 bath towels, 1 set shaving gear, 1 soap, 1 comb, 3 khaki uniforms (wear one) without coat, 1 skivvies, 2 handkerchiefs, 2 sox, 1 toothbrush and powder, 1 notebook and pencil."[1]

Thanks to Commander McDaniel, in its four years of existence SCTC became a legendary model as a training center. The reserve officers who survived the rigorous six weeks of intensive training would never forget it. The Miami facility set standards that were followed by dozens of naval training centers all over the country. The SCTC type of operational training, developed and proven effective for ASW vessels, proved to be valuable for other

Instruction in knot tying, SCTC, 1942 *National Archives*

ships. Some officers trained at SCTC were assigned to other classes of ships like destroyer escorts (DEs) and destroyers (DDs). By 1945 SCTC had become Miami's biggest business, overflowing into ten hotels on Biscayne Boulevard and extending into a dozen piers on the waterfront.

Over twenty-five thousand officers and fifty-seven thousand enlisted men were trained at SCTC, including officers from Russia, Brazil, Cuba, and France. A total of 598 U.S. Navy ships and 79 foreign ships were shaken down by this activity.[2]

No one knows exactly how the term "Donald Duck Navy" originated, but at some time during its existence SCTC used memo pads printed with an unofficial logo depicting an imitation Donald Duck sporting a Y-gun and depth charges. To this day old SC and PC salts talk about having been members of the Donald Duck Navy, some with pride, others grudgingly. On one point they all agree. If the Donald Duck Navy had an "Annapolis," it was SCTC, and its commandant was Cdr. Eugene F. McDaniel.

4

The Battle of the Atlantic

When war was declared in December of 1941 at least five German U-boats were operating freely off the east coast of the United States—a coast, for all practical purposes, undefended. Adm. Adolphus Andrews, Commander, Eastern Sea Frontier, had at his disposal four yard patrol boats (YPs), four subchasers, one Coast Guard cutter, three World War I "Eagle" boats, and 103 aircraft, only five of which were combat ready. This tiny force was to protect a 28,000-square-mile area extending from the St. Lawrence River down to North Carolina. Defense forces in the Gulf of Mexico and the Caribbean were in no better shape.

The U-boats found our merchant fleet sailing unescorted and with their lights on at night. There was no radio discipline; shore stations operated as if in peacetime, broadcasting time signals and weather reports. Shoreside cities blazed with lights at night. The U-boats, hardly believing the bonanza offered them, roamed up and down the coast with impunity, sinking everything in sight. Within a period of ten days, they sank twenty-five ships totaling 200,000 tons. Not one U-boat was damaged, much less sunk.[1]

It became a time of feverish activity for the navy, having suddenly found itself in a shooting war on two fronts, with Japan in the Pacific and Germany in the Atlantic. Keels for new second-generation SCs were just being laid. Excerpts from the personal diary of the NOIC (Naval Officer in Charge) Inshore Patrol at Norfolk[2] reflect the seriousness of the situation:

> 7 Dec '41—News of Jap attacks on Pearl Harbor and Declaration of War. Ordered double patrol at NOB piers.
>
> 11 Dec '41—War with Germany & Italy. Need minelayer.
>
> 12 Dec '41—Air raid warning. Complete blackout all night.
>
> 20–23 Dec '41—Problems. False reports of subs. Sweeping for Churchill's vessel. 9 patrol boats to Annapolis. Confusion re mine field. Working on anti-torpedo harbor defense.
>
> 13–14 Jan '42—Reports of 18 enemy subs approaching coast. One sinking 60 miles south of Block Island. All vessels on patrol or standing by.
>
> 17 Jan '42—SC 437 at Little Creek laying mine field entrance Chesapeake Bay. Last mine laid 1200.
>
> 18–19 Jan '42—Enemy subs off coast. Two sinkings & two attacks off Wimble Shoals. Much confusion, repetition, false alarms. Several vessels sent SOS's & reported attacks not verified.
>
> 20–21 Jan—Boats to Wimble Shoals where sub contacted. Can't communicate by radio, arranged visual code.
>
> 21–27 Jan—Hectic. Subs off Hatteras.
>
> 30 Jan—SS *Rochester* torpedoed 90m east of Cape Charles—sent *Roe* to rescue.
>
> 31 Jan—Inspected USCG *Rush.* Pitiful fighting subs with such small slow vessels. *Roe* brought in *Rochester* survivors. Went out again.
>
> 1 Feb—*Tacoma Star* torpedoed. Searched, no results.
>
> 3 Feb—Unsuccessful search for *Amerikaland* & *Tacoma Star.* No results. *San Gil* sunk midnight in 4th Naval District waters.
>
> 5–6 Feb—Two ships sunk off coast. *Dione* reported sub contact. Depth charged.
>
> 8–10 Feb—Several sinkings—DDs for temp duty. Necessity for training program.
>
> 11 Feb—All retired officers to be examined physically for sea duty. *Adamant* & SC 102 collision, SC sunk.
>
> 15–16 Feb—Tanker sunk off Cape Henry. *Calypso* got 42 survivors.

18 Feb—*Dione* got *Paramount* in tow off Ocracoke—CO & crew had abandoned. Taken to Morehead City.

24 Feb—Raised SC 102.

27 Feb—Subs near Hatteras—one sinking reported.

28 Feb—USS *Jacob Jones* (DD) sunk—11 survivors picked—details scarce—Hit in bow, later in stern—believed depth charges exploded.

1 Mar—*Dallas* had contact with sub. Sent *Calypso* to help.

2 Mar—*Dallas* in . . . dropped 46 depth charges . . . *Calypso* on spot. Bad nor'easter, gale & rain.

15 Mar—Two sinkings during night. *Cole* & *Dupont* on scene 5 hrs. later. Got nearly all survivors.

17 Mar—Two sinkings Diamond Shoals—1 grounding, much confusion.

19 Mar—Red hot day. *Dickerson* arrived 1100—hit by 5" shell from unknown tanker, exploded in pilothouse. Killed 3, wounded 6, captain died on arrival navy yard. Got *Hamilton* & *Osprey* for Sec 3. *Roper* repairs completed. To Cape Lookout area—*Tourmaline* in with survivors, out again. 4 sinkings in Hatteras area. Cdr. Miles got telegram son killed in Far East—was on *Sacramento* in Dec.

28 Mar—*Green* picked up & delivered 13 survivors of *Equipoise*.

Mar—SS *City of New York* sunk off Hatteras. *Roper* searching. Survivors supposed to include 40 women & children.

31 Mar—*Roper* got 70 survivors and *Acushnet* 23 from *City of New York*. Tug & 3 barges sunk by sub torpedo & gunfire.

1 April—Tanker *Tiger* torpedoed last night. YP patrol picked up survivors. *Jackson* ordered to scene. *Roper* complained re reception of survivors *City of NY*—confusion—delay.

2 April—Coal vessel sunk off Winter Qtr. Shellfire.

3 April—Vessel shelled by sub near West Quarter. Getting damaged vessels in.

6 April—*Norwich City* . . . Unable sight sub which he says was on surface. Too slow.

7 April—*Landown* sunk S. of Hatteras. Much confusion.

9 April—2 vessels sunk in night.

11 April—One vessel sunk off Cape Lookout after daylight. *Ulysses* sunk. *Manley* got 290 survivors to Charleston.

13 April—*Roper* reported sub on surface during night—gunfire—survivors.

14 April—*Roper* returned Cape Henry. 29 bodies from German sub. *Empire Trust* sunk in daylight off Diamond Shoals.

17 April—Many subs reported off coast . . . no sinkings.

21–23 April—Still no sinkings . . . plane reported 11 subs on surface heading west about 200 miles east of Jersey coast.

24 April—Report of 11 subs believed to be blackfish or whales. No results. No sinkings.

13 June—In answer to requisition 10 patrol vessels, told by ComEasternSeaFrontier to get yachts or trawlers.

18 June—YP-389 sunk off Hatteras. 2 subs reported off Cape Henry.

It wasn't until late in 1942 that SCs finally began coming off the ways and were quickly being commissioned for escort and patrol duty, working out of several bases along the East Coast. It was a time of testing and training for green officers and crews of the Splinter Fleet, unaccustomed to the navy and the seafaring life. It was a time in which an incorrect appraisal of a situation, a missing link in communication, an abuse of authority, or just plain inexperience could lead to an abrupt perception of reality. Getting used to the ways of the regular navy was part of every reservist's education, and often his only teacher was experience itself.

New officers quickly learned the hard facts of life. Jules J. Jordy, Lt. (jg) USNR, in command of SC 638 based in Norfolk, ordered sonar from Philadelphia, something his ship badly needed for locating, tracking down, and destroying U-boats. Two weeks later, still with no sonar, after spending the morning in a fruitless search for the gear around the base, he returned to his ship and was intercepted by the quartermaster, who informed him that he was wanted in Operations immediately. Jordy knew there was a convoy forming up for a trip to Charleston and that they needed an escort, but there was no way the SC 638 could be a proper escort without sonar. A good officer and a man of decision, he marched over to Operations to tell the captain in charge that he couldn't go.

The captain was waiting for him. "Jordy, here's your TF plan, departure is set at 1500. You ready?"

"Sir, we don't have sonar gear and I don't expect it for another week or so."

The captain looked at him. "Do the Germans know that you don't have sonar?"

Launch of SC 1007, Fellows & Stewart Inc., Terminal Island, California
National Archives

"No, sir."

"Then what in hell are you waiting for? Get out there and escort those ships down to Charleston."

He did.[3]

The experience of obeying orders, no matter what, came as a severe shock to some civilians who had become officers. A day or so after newly commissioned Ens. Jonas M. Berkey reported aboard SC 1039 as third officer, the ship was ordered out into the Caribbean on patrol. As soon as it left the breakwater and entered the rough sea, Berkey, on the flying bridge, became seasick. In order to give his new officer some navigating experience, the captain told Berkey to go below to figure their position. Berkey, forgetting that he was no longer a civilian, answered he could not do that because he was sick. The captain's reaction was an immediate and blistering lecture, both personal and specific, including the threat of a court-martial unless Berkey obeyed orders. In less than a minute, the pain of seasickness was nothing compared to Berkey's fear of the captain and a court-martial. He went dutifully below to the chart room and figured their position, after which he stood a four-hour watch in constant agony from seasickness. His temporary feeling of hatred for the captain gave way to profound respect in the days to follow, for he had suddenly learned the meaning of military obedience and the strength of authority—albeit the hard way. Having been forced to work successfully even though in pain gave him a new self-confidence. Later, when he became captain of the ship, he used the same method to impress the meaning of military obedience to his men.

"Those were tough days," writes Daniel V. James, former commanding officer of SC 1002:

> Wooden ships that small were never intended to be on the high seas for extended periods making like make-believe warships. Having a signalman who didn't know code was not much different than having a C.O. with a similar level of competence and experience. We were anything but an all-star team. Rather, the Navy considered us losers to begin with—but better than nothing. We gave as good as we got. But what a way to grow up! We were close to the unforgiving sea, and took every wave in style, wet bunks and all. We learned to cope not only with the elements but with ourselves as well.[4]

The rough and sometimes grisly work of searching for and rescuing survivors of torpedoed or mined ships or collisions was unrelenting. In the bitter cold of early morning on 7 January 1943, all standby SCs stationed at Cape May, New Jersey, were ordered out to search for survivors of an escort vessel that had been run down by a merchant ship the night before. After a few hours' search, SC 1354 found seventeen men floating in the freezing water, all wearing their lifejackets, but none alive.[5]

A couple of weeks later SC 1354 was assigned to escort a U.S. submarine from Delaware Bay to New York Harbor—a routine business if all submarines had not been vulnerable to attack from trigger-happy U.S. merchant ships, ever on the alert for U-boats. Too, SCs looked like submarines in certain seas, and here was a *real* submarine being escorted by a ship that *looked* like a submarine. Both vessels flew the biggest American flag they could find, and SC 1354 manned her signal lamp continuously, placing herself between the submarine and any ships spotted and signaling furiously to advise the other ship that they were friendly. Even so, one merchant ship they passed was at general quarters with guns trained on them and alarmingly failed to respond to the signaling; fortunately, though, the merchantman held its fire.

Beginning in May and June 1942, the Caribbean was being overrun by German U-boats. It began when six U-boats entered the Caribbean through the Florida Straits, and the Windward and Mona passages, after successfully operating in more northern waters between New York and Cape Hatteras. In May the first of four SC subchasers arrived at San Juan, Puerto Rico. SC 1279 and her men were greeted as "saviors" of Puerto Rico by the citizens of San Juan, who did not know that the 1279's sonar was inoperative because of missing parts, aside from her having no radar.

These deficiencies were corrected within a couple of weeks, and an opportunity to test their effectiveness suddenly appeared when they were escorting a merchant ship to Guantanamo Bay, Cuba. Without warning, there was a sudden explosion on the cargo vessel, and within a matter of minutes she sank. Simultaneously, the 1279 picked up a strong submarine contact and made a depth-charge attack, dropping seven charges. They waited for the seven underwater explosions, but heard only two. Five depth charges had failed to roll off, inexcusably rusted and "frozen" to the racks—due to the failure of the gunner's mates to pay more attention to maintenance. Everyone aboard the sunken merchant ship was either in a lifeboat or wearing a life jacket, and all were rescued without injury, but the incident taught SC 1279 a lesson in preparedness that her men never forgot.[6]

One Saturday, late in the afternoon, the captain and the executive officer and a third of the crew of the 1279 went ashore in San Juan for a few hours of liberty, leaving the third officer, Ens. William Kruse, in charge of the ship. Late that afternoon the base NOIC, a stocky, red-faced navy commander, arrived in person at the gangway, very much out of breath. He informed Kruse that a sonar contact on an enemy submarine had been reported in the vicinity of the entrance to the San Juan harbor. He ordered Kruse to get the 1279 under way immediately and to track down and destroy the enemy sub. When Kruse told the commander his captain and executive officer and a third of the crew were not aboard, he turned a deaf ear. He ordered Kruse to get the ship under way without delay. "Official orders will follow," the commander said abruptly, as he turned around and departed.

Kruse decided that orders were orders. He had never conned a ship in his life, but he did the sensible thing. He called the crew together and told them the situation. Fortunately he had men on board who knew how to light off the engines, others who could handle lines, and a good quartermaster standing by while he gave orders to the wheel and engine room. Although he had never moved a subchaser in, out, or away from anything before, he got the 1279 turned around in available but limited space and gingerly headed out. It was late afternoon.

Kruse was so preoccupied with moving the vessel away from the pier, dodging other craft, and cautiously heading down the channel that they were almost at the harbor entrance before he and his quartermaster began asking themselves questions. If the 1279 was indeed the only ASW vessel in San Juan, how did that commander hear about the enemy contact? Who had detected the sub and where? Kruse ordered the radioman to contact the base and try to find answers. The base replied that the contact had been made by a YP that had recently installed sonar. The YP had been out earlier in the day and had made a strong contact in the vicinity of a sea buoy at the channel entrance.

Kruse and his men knew the sea buoy was located over a large underwater rock formation that the 1279 had used for sonar detection and practice runs only a day or two before. After making several runs on the rock, always checking for movement, then sweeping a larger area beyond the rock, parts of the puzzle began to come together with unanimous agreement among crew members and Kruse. The YP had made a "loud and clear" contact, all right, but it was on the rock, not a U-boat. Earlier that day the YP had gone to sea with the attack instructor to test their newly installed sonar equipment. The instructor made the contact and was so certain it was a sub that he quickly headed for San Juan to report it.

Kruse and company searched in vain for two days and two nights. When they finally returned to the base, it took almost the same length of time to convince the base commander that the instructor had misjudged the contact. He had failed to apply Basic Rule No. 1 for sonar contacts, which was to come back to center bearing and check for movement.

This tale has a sad footnote. The CO and XO never served another day on the SC 1279. The day the commander had ordered the vessel out was also the skipper's birthday, and he and the executive officer went ashore to celebrate. After imbibing more than they should have, they wandered into an area at the Normandie Hotel in San Juan that was off limits to anyone but a French admiral and his staff. The admiral was having a party of his own within these limits, and the 1279's skipper and his exec barged into the party more than a little inebriated and quite disorderly. As a result they were placed in the brig. A court-martial was held, the skipper was relieved of command of the 1279, and the exec was assigned to the base YP as junior officer—the same YP that had originated the false report about the enemy submarine contact. Kruse reports that eventually the skipper received another command but that the exec committed suicide. If the incident prompted that tragic end, it is all the more ironic that he was only tagging along on the CO's spree.

The subchasers, with their green officers and crews, were pressed into duty for which they were not fully prepared, but the slaughter inflicted by U-boats was so relentless and so damaging that every means possible had to be put to use. Shakedown cruises for many subchasers were working assignments in convoy escort duty, lasting seven days or longer. The rough ocean conditions, no water-making capability, cramped and uncomfortable quarters, and poor ventilation all added up to a miserable introduction to the sea for youngsters away from home for the first time in their lives.

Still, some stories had happy endings. Ed Sullivan, on the first patrol of SC 507 out of Staten Island off the New Jersey coast, was sitting on the rail with his buddy Fogerty, who was facing outboard. They each had only two months in the navy. Sullivan suddenly noticed Fogerty's jaw drop, eyes widen. Fogerty gasped "Torpedoes!" Spinning around, Sullivan saw two wakes streaking directly at them only thirty yards away. Their hearts in their mouths, the tyros watched, transfixed, scared beyond belief. Suddenly the bubbling wakes turned 90 degrees in unison and began playing in their bow wake, dorsals curving gracefully as they broke water. Two porpoises were innocently engaged in their age-old play with a ship at sea.[7] One didn't have to be new or green to be startled by the phosphorescent wake of porpoises at play; mariners often failed to recognize them as such at first sighting and commonly broke formation, changed courses and speeds, and tried evasive tactics until they realized their error.

Not long after this incident Sullivan, Fogerty, and the 507 found themselves engaged in the real Battle of the Atlantic. On the night of 26 February 1942, rudely awakened shortly after midnight by the sounding of general quarters, they scrambled topside for their battle stations. Less than a thousand yards on their port beam they could see a ship broken in half, engulfed in bright orange and red flames that flickered high into the night sky. In the most horrendous disaster yet to strike the American merchant fleet, the tanker *R. P. Resor* had been torpedoed by German U-boat 578. The commanding officer of the 507, Lieutenant Taylor, intensified their sonar search in an effort to make contact with the enemy sub. They spotted a life raft with three men in it. They launched the wherry, but the oil was so thick on the surface that the wherry could make no headway. Taylor had to back the 507 into the heavy oil to come alongside the raft. The survivors were so heavy with oil it took four men to drag them aboard. Two of the three men survived, out of a total of fifty men on the *R. P. Resor.* When a coast guard cutter arrived a few hours later, they transferred the survivors and the dead man and resumed their patrol. The ship burned for two days off the Jersey coast, clearly visible to crowds who thronged the seashore to watch. A few days after she sank, a story in the newspaper reported that the coast guard had been the first on the scene—incorrectly, since it was SC 507 that arrived first.

New officers frequently found themselves in situations requiring decisions for which they had no prior experience. SC 983 was in dry dock having its seams recaulked after being split open from underwater depth-charge explosions. The third officer was ordered to stay with the ship while the other two were ashore on leave. His most important duty was to sign off the daily work order as each job was completed. One day he was called to the rear of the ship where workmen were using a huge wrench and a sledgehammer to tighten the massive nuts that held the propeller shafts. The young officer had never seen the screws before—or anything else on the undersides, for that matter. The shipwrights wanted him to tell them when the nuts had been properly torqued. He looked at the foreman and said, "What do you think?" The foreman returned his look with an understanding smile and said, "I think they are pretty damn tight now." He took a deep breath, crossed his fingers, and signed.[8]

With little experience to go on, officers in the "Donald Duck Navy" could not always count on conventional personnel assignments, either. At one time SC 998 had on its roster three chief boatswain's mates, one first-class boatswain's mate, one coxswain, and no seamen. Before this was straightened out, no work was done except by the coxswain and the third officer. The topheaviness resulted from ship movements to three or four ports in different sea frontiers after requisitioning replacements. At each port a new chief boatswain would report aboard. Another time the same SC had three officers exactly reversed in role and rank. The commanding officer was an ensign, the executive officer was a lieutenant (jg), and the third officer was a senior grade lieutenant. Fortunately none of the officers let it bother them and the situation was eventually straightened out.[9]

In some situations, resourcefulness had to serve where experience failed. Early in April 1942, SC 540 was placed in commission in Benton Harbor and ordered to report to New Orleans by way of the Mississippi. Having no charts, the 540 relied on road maps picked up from gas stations along the route. Along the way they tied up each night to avoid the hazards of what one man described as "logs, trees, houses and barns floating down the Big Muddy."[10] SC 437, making the same trip some months before, put another spin on it. They tied up every night and went ashore for liberty. At every stop, crowds would gather to greet them, so rarely had anyone in those parts seen an "honest to God" warship.[11]

No amount of experience can prepare a sailor for everything that can happen on a ship. SC 656 was in a group escorting a convoy of tankers from Galveston when she was relieved by another subchaser and ordered to proceed independently to the naval operating base (NOB) Key West. On the way the weather began to deteriorate, and the commanding officer, Lt. Edward O'Donnell, anxious to make Key West before conditions got worse, increased the ship's speed, resulting in considerable pitching and rolling. The violent motion of the ship sheered a toggle pin on one of the depth-charge racks, causing the charge to fall to the deck, where it commenced rolling from gunwale to gunwale. The crew managed to secure the charge, but it represented a serious explosion hazard if its detonator had been damaged. Determining that the safest procedure would be to drop the charge overboard, the captain had a couple of his men erect a temporary platform on the fantail so that he, the captain, could execute this maneuver. Just when everything was in position and the captain had stationed himself to shove the charge over the side, a large wave slapped him overboard. Startled, the crew sprang into action. The officer of the deck ordered all engines stopped. However, by the time life rings had been tossed, the captain was being carried out farther and farther from the ship. Each wave became an eternity in which the captain could be seen on the top of one wave only to disappear into the trough of another.

SCs were equipped with a wherry with a lightweight outboard motor, and two men of the 656 wasted no time preparing to lower it. They were on the weather side and the wherry kept smashing against the side of the ship. One man, Charlie Adler, was already in the wherry when suddenly a large wave struck, tearing it free from the ship. White-faced, Charlie attempted to start the outboard but gave up after several tries and began rowing in an attempt to reach the captain. The crew members watched as Charlie, seemingly rowing in air on the crest of a wave, then completely disappearing in the trough of the next, made little headway.

The OD was finally able to maneuver the ship toward the captain, who had managed to get hold of one of the life rings. A cargo net was lowered, and he clambered up to where they could grab him and bring him aboard. He was

Depth charges and K-gun on a subchaser *National Archives*

sputtering mad, calling his crew a "bunch of goddamned fools" while they were recovering Charlie and the wherry. After a trip below to his cabin to change into dry clothes, Lieutenant O'Donnell reappeared and called everyone to quarters. He apologized for losing his composure and told the men they had done a remarkably creditable job under very difficult conditions.

Henry Rivers, the boatswain's mate who tells this story many years later, says it is not intended to be derogatory; in his opinion, Lieutenant O'Donnell was one of the finest persons with whom he served during five and a half years in the navy.[12]

No sailor dreads anything more than a collision at sea, and subchaser men were especially aware of the threat of collision. Because of their small size,

Depth-charge explosion

SCs were very difficult to spot in heavy seas. As mentioned earlier, in some conditions they rode so low in the water that they looked startlingly like submarines and this, of course, was an open invitation for an attack from friendly ships. Near Alligator Reef off the Florida coast one night, PC 1123 mistook SC 1470 for a submarine, rammed it, and cut it almost in half. She was only doing what she had been trained to do. Her aggressive attack was her best defense against what she perceived to be a surfaced sub.[13]

In a similar incident with a better ending, SC 989 was escorting a convoy one bright moonlit night from Key West to Guantanamo, maintaining position off the starboard bow of the convoy. The radioman overheard a message from one of the ships to all others in the convoy, announcing that there was a submarine off the starboard bow. The ships had mistaken the 989's low silhouette for a submarine and were talking about blowing it out of the water. The men on the beleaguered 989 spent a good portion of the night frantically trying to convince the convoy who they were.[14]

The collision that Marion C. Bonham tells about was characteristically unpredictable. He had no sooner come aboard SC 1330 as its new executive officer when the ship was assigned to escort several vessels taking the Duke of Windsor, who was the governor of the Bahamas at the time, and his entourage back to the Bahamas after a visit to the United States. The convoy consisted of a large group of ships. Among the escorts was an eighty-three-foot Coast Guard patrol vessel, USCG 83421. At some time during the first evening out, John Winter, commanding officer, relieved Bonham of the watch and told him to go below and get some sleep. The weather was good, sea calm, visibility good.

Bonham had just taken off his pants, ready to jump into his bunk, when he felt the ship hit something, making a loud crashing sound. Pulling his pants back on, he rushed topside to observe the bow of the CG 83421 close aboard and perpendicular, with men clinging to it. The 1330 had plowed straight into it.

No ships were allowed to turn on their running lights and no searchlights were used during the rescue. Tight security had to be maintained, for there were U-boats in the area and the Prince of Wales was an important personage. The 1330 went alongside the unlucky vessel, pulled the men off, and brought them on board. All were saved, and none were happy. Although damage to the 1330 was relatively slight, the CG 83421 was cut in two about ten feet from the stern. A board of inquiry was held, but the cause of the collision was not clear and no one was ever blamed or held responsible for it.

Lieutenant Winter remained in command of the 1330 to participate with valor at Utah Beach in the Normandy invasion a year later.[15]

A collision nightmare came true at 2130 on the night of 2 March 1943. Escorting a convoy southbound off Cape Hatteras, SC 682 was patrolling her assigned station on the starboard quarter of the convoy. Conditions were poor, with a heaving cross sea and a northeasterly wind, intermittent squalls, and rain. Visibility had closed to about four hundred yards. The watch on the 682 was startled when, almost simultaneously, a broad line of running lights suddenly showed from ships unexpectedly approaching from the opposite direction. In those days of complete blackouts, nothing but the gravest emergency would cause ships to light their running lights. The lights were only six thousand yards ahead and closing fast. The unthinkable had happened. Two convoys, one southbound and the other northbound, were in the same shipping lane and on a collision course. Disaster was imminent.

Unable to determine what, if any, avoidance course her convoy was making, the 682 maintained her own course of 197(T [true]). Suddenly a white flare fired by one of the northbound vessels was seen dead ahead. General quarters was sounded. Two lights were observed burning brightly near the waterline of what turned out to be a non-navy tug in trouble, the *Wellfleet*, while another larger vessel was lying to near the scene. John Gay, commanding officer of the 682, changing courses and speeds to avoid another northbound vessel, finally reached the scene and circled the *Wellfleet*, which appeared to be in a sinking condition. They could see a sizable hole at the waterline on the starboard side, and she was listing about 20 degrees. Clouds of steam billowed from a broken line. Signaling, the 682 asked if she needed assistance, to which the reply was affirmative.

The ship lying to about two hundred yards away was the merchant tanker *Edward L. Doheny*, and it was she who had struck the tug. The *Doheny* was in the act of lowering a boat when she signaled the 682 to ask if she could remove the men from the tug. In raging seas and sizable waves, Gay spent the next twenty-five minutes in a masterpiece of shiphandling during which all seventeen men of the *Wellfleet* were transferred onto the 682 with no injuries and only minor damage to the 682. Detaching herself from the convoy, she proceeded to Morehead City, North Carolina, where she landed the men from the tug.

A survival story should have a happy ending, but, tragically, it would not be so for SC 1024, a sister escort in the 682's convoy. At the time the two convoys headed into each other on their collision courses, SC 1024 had been on her station, which was on the port quarter of the southbound convoy, some distance abeam the 682—both subchasers in the same relative position with respect to the convoy but on opposite sides.

Not until she arrived in Morehead City did the 682 learn that SC 1024 was missing. An air-sea rescue search was under way in the vicinity of the two-convoy collision. The search continued for several days but nothing—not a single trace—was ever found. SC 1024 had been swallowed up in the tumultuous sea, disappearing from the face of the earth without anyone knowing what happened to her.[16]

Although the disappearance of the 1024 remains a mystery, another collision of ships among those two ill-fated convoys is the likeliest explanation. A tanker, SS *Cities Service Fuel,* or a merchant ship, SS *Plymouth,* in the northbound convoy, could have been involved, but exactly how is not clear. Each of the bigger ships reported that they thought they had hit something.

One can only imagine the horror of a giant steel bow cresting high on a wave and plunging down directly onto the subchaser in the trough below, driving it into the depths. Or perhaps, like a one-two punch, the big ships struck the 1024 in rapid succession, the first ship crushing the tiny subchaser into a helpless mass, followed by the second ship dealing the knockout blow, plunging her into oblivion. Whatever happened, the 1024 was hit so hard, so quickly, and so completely that she was destroyed and obliterated forever. By the time anyone on the tanker or merchant ship realized they might have hit something, it was all over. There were no survivors, no flotsam, no debris. Thirty miles off Cape Hatteras, SC 1024 and her twenty-five men vanished forever. The men of SC 1024 gave their lives for their country in a sudden, savage, inexplicable moment—as much a mystery now as then—on the high seas.

Nothing appeared in the papers about the missing subchaser until nine days later, when the *New York Times* published its weekly list of war casualties. The country was at war, and information of this type was routinely withheld because the military considered it too sensitive. Included in a little squib in the *Times*'s weekly list of missing military and naval personnel from New Jersey appeared the name, "IRWIN, HERBERT, Jr., lieutenant, reserve; wife, Mrs. Sheila Saxton Irwin, Summit." Lieutenant Irwin was the commanding officer of SC 1024.

There being no proof of any drowning, the name of every man aboard SC 1024 had to be carried on the rolls of the Bureau of Naval Personnel as "missing" for one year, to conform with the Missing Persons Act. The legal uncertainty could only have prolonged the distress of their families. As a tribute to their sacrifice, and with deepest respect, the names of these men are listed below.[17]

Herbert M. Irwin Jr., Lieutenant, USNR, Commanding Officer
Warren Williams, Jr. Ensign, USNR, Executive Officer
George H. Guy, Ensign, USNR, Third Officer
John W. Ahern, Machinist's Mate 2c, USNR
Thomas E. Bailey, Gunner's Mate 2c, USN
Adam Belich, Seaman 2c, USN
Curtis L. Bucklin, Motor Machinist's Mate 2c, USN
Gaetano Carusone, Ship's Cook 3c V-6, USNR
Chester J. Chapman, Radioman 3c V-6, USNR
Charles R. David, Fireman's Mate 1c, USN
Albert H. Dow, Radioman 2c V-3, USNR
John A. Gilliam, Machinist's Mate 2c, USN
Harold V. Haner, Chief Boatswain's Mate (AA), USN
Joseph T. Lewandowski, Yeoman 3c V-6, USNR
Charles F. Liney, Apprentice Seaman V-6, USNR
Robert W. McCommons, Gunner's Mate 3c V-6, USNR
Bennie F. McCurry, Seaman 2c, USN
Paul Olivieri, Apprentice Seaman V-6, USNR
George A. Pearson, Fireman's Mate 1c M-2, USNR
George A. Perkins, Quartermaster 3c V-6, USNR
Louis B. Rieffel, Sonarman 3c V-6, USNR
Ellis E. Rudy, Sonarman 3c V-6, USNR
Ray C. Spicer, Mess Attendant 2c V-6, USNR
William H. Stopp, Electrician's Mate 2c V-6, USNR
Joseph E. Taylor, Sonarman 3c V-6, USNR

5

Her Maiden Voyage

SC 709 was commissioned on 16 November 1942 at Elizabeth City Shipyard, Elizabeth City, North Carolina, a happy ship—a clean, tight ship with two good officers and an excellent crew. Her commanding officer was Lt. William C. French Jr., USNR, a graduate of Northwestern University and a product of SCTC Miami. The executive officer, Ens. Albert D. Jordan, was also trained at SCTC. The 709's complement of enlisted men was unusually experienced and capable, half of them with ratings of first class or better. She had a chief boatswain's mate—a precious commodity on subchasers—and several members of the crew were career navy men.

After fitting out and passing her shakedown trials, the 709 was ordered to report to the Naval Operating Base at Argentia, Newfoundland, to be part of the Greenland Patrol. Proceeding to Norfolk, thence to Portsmouth, Virginia, to patch some seams split during depth-charge practice, she went on to Portland, Maine, where she had new radar installed.

On the afternoon of 18 January 1943 she began her voyage to Argentia in company with USS *Storis,* a Coast Guard cutter. The skies were overcast and a stiff northeast breeze was blowing as the two ships made their way across Casco Bay, rounded the Portland light buoy, then headed east-northeast at ten knots. According to plan, the senior officer of the two-ship convoy on the *Storis* signaled the 709 to begin zigzagging, a normal procedure in waters where U-boats might be lurking. Condition II watches were set, the men alternating four hours on with four hours off duty.

Shortly before sunset it began raining, and as darkness settled the wind increased and visibility became increasingly poor. Captain French signaled the *Storis* and requested permission to stop zigzagging to make it easier on the vessel and crew, and this was granted. He stayed three thousand yards astern of the *Storis,* maintaining contact by using the new radar. The convoy continued through the night in this fashion until daylight, at which time the 709 took position seven hundred yards astern of the *Storis.* They tried zigzagging but had to stop because of poor visibility due to driving rain. The weather steadily worsened. Twenty-five-foot waves were slapping the ship from the port quarter, with winds gusting at fifty knots or more, causing the little vessel to roll, pitch, and toss unmercifully. The brand new radar suddenly refused to work and no one could fix it. At 1800 the captain radioed this information to the *Storis.*

The gale steadily increased, and with darkness the little ship was wrapped in a violent, nightmarish murk. Nasty rollers slapped the ship, one striking the pilothouse with a cannonlike bang, tearing away a section of rail and lifelines on the port side, startling the men on watch and waking everyone below. The lookout lost the *Storis,* swallowed up in the blackness. No one slept. When the long night finally gave way to the first signs of daylight, the *Storis* was nowhere to be seen. They attempted to raise her by radio, but ice had begun to build up on the antennae, causing them to short out. They never saw nor heard from the *Storis* again. Half of the crew were seasick. The compartments—fore and aft crew's quarters and wardroom—were in shambles. Cooking was out of the question; in any event, few had any desire to eat.

A new and more sinister problem arose. The combination of sea spray and the frigid temperature was causing ice to form. It had already fouled the antennae and now was building up on vents, depth charges, pilothouse windows, ladders, hatches, and everything else exposed, especially on the port side. Footing had become treacherous. Four men were assigned to chipping ice with hatchets and cleavers.

At 1500 Captain French figured from his dead reckoning that they were about twenty miles east of Halifax. He knew they closed the harbor entrance at sunset with submarine nets. Changing course for Halifax would mean heading into the wind and sea, which would slow them down considerably. They would not make Halifax in time. He decided to stay on course with a following sea which, though rough, was helping to sweep them in the right direction.

The men chipping ice seemed to be keeping it under control, and things began looking good enough during the early hours of that evening to lift the captain's spirits. He was confident the voyage could be completed without further incident. He had no way of knowing what lay ahead.

The ship steamed along fairly well during the early hours of the evening, but shortly after midnight the rain had turned into a driving snow, blowing horizontally, driven by a howling arctic wind. The thermometer plummeted from 25 degrees Fahrenheit to zero. By 0300 it read minus 18 degrees. The storm had changed from an old-fashioned northeaster into a dangerous, full-blown blizzard. Ice was building up with such speed that all hands were ordered to chip, even those who had just come off watch.

Saltwater ice is a sailor's nightmare. When fresh water ices, the ice is rock hard and chips easily, breaking off in big chunks. But saltwater ice is mushy and impossible to chip off in chunks. It takes twice the energy and time to remove, and no sooner is it removed from one place than it builds up in another, so it's like shoveling sand against the tide. The pilothouse windows kept icing over, and someone had to chip them clear every few minutes. The direction and force of the wind caused the port side to build up with ice a foot thick in some places, causing the ship to begin listing to port.

The captain tried various speeds and courses in an attempt to make more favorable conditions for chipping ice. He tried reversing course, hoping it would ease the stern sea and give the men a better chance to chip ice off the depth charges. Getting rid of the charges would lighten the ship. None of the measures worked. He returned to the 065 (T) heading as before.

The crew was tiring, but they doggedly continued chipping, bracing themselves against freezing cold, stinging salt spray, slippery footing, and the violent heaving of the ship. The ice kept gaining on them. By the time one area was cleared, the previously chipped area was filled with ice again. They formed teams of three men each, one team chipping a few minutes at a time while the other team went below to change clothes and "rest"—a euphemism for holding on with what strength one had left to keep from being thrown about the deck, because actual rest was impossible. The only food anyone had eaten since leaving Portland was cold meat and cheese between slabs of soggy bread.

On the afterdeck Ensign Jordan and a gunner's mate chipped steadily at the port K-gun and cleared it for firing. Encouraged, the captain grabbed an ax, and he and Steffen, the gunner's mate, chipped away furiously at the starboard K-gun, finally clearing it. Spent, they set the charge on "Safe" and launched it; then they went below to the after crew's quarters for a breather. No sooner had they stepped off the ladder when there was a loud explosion underneath their feet, lifting the hull and knocking them down. The depth charge had exploded, despite their precautions to set the safety. It was not a good sign, although the charge had done no perceptible damage to the ship.

Topside there was little respite. The ship pitched and rolled unmercifully, the men chipped away stubbornly, and the ice, insidious and evil, kept building up. Snow and salt spume blew parallel to the sea at blurring, stinging speed. The wind chill factor was 28 degrees below zero. At 0432 the captain increased speed to eleven knots in order to increase their chances for reaching some kind of haven by dawn. He was fully aware that the higher speed would be more uncomfortable for everyone, but it was no time to think about comfort.

George Gagnon, chief boatswain's mate, a resolute, experienced career navy man respected by his officers and men alike, had been chipping without letup for several hours, exhorting and encouraging the men by word and by example. Working his way aft along the starboard side to chip ice in the vicinity of the ship's wherry, he was thus engaged when a wave suddenly slapped him, knocking him back. Before he knew it, he had lost his footing and fallen overboard. Just as he was slipping over the side, one hand felt a line, which he grabbed with all his strength and held fast, dangling in water so cold it numbed him.

Adrenaline pumping, he hung between life and death for an eternity; then, with a strength he never knew he had, he pulled himself back aboard. By the time the men, including the captain, got to him, Gagnon had grabbed up his ax and was doggedly chipping away as though nothing had happened. The captain had to force him to quit, ordering him below to the engine room, the warmest compartment on the ship. He told the ship's cook to go with him. In civilian life the cook had been a Red Cross instructor and filled the role of ship's doctor when needed.

By now the men were reaching the limit of their endurance. The captain knew better than anyone how serious things had become, but he set a good example, encouraging individual men when necessary and chipping ice shoulder to shoulder with them. He broke out a bottle of brandy, rationing it out to anyone who requested it.

The ship was now listing 25 degrees to port through the sheer weight of the ice. In an attempt to stabilize the ship, the captain ordered Steffen and several men to shift ammunition from port to starboard. It was hard, dangerous work with the slippery deck heaving under them, but the physical exertion was warming, and after two hours of it they succeeded in easing the list back to 10 degrees.

At dawn on 20 January the storm hadn't abated; indeed, it was worse than ever. The same fifty-knot wind and seas with thirty-foot-high waves were crashing over the ship with deadly force. Relentlessly, the ice kept building up. Again the ship was listing badly, groaning under tons of ice and now barely responding to the helm. Visibility was less than two hundred yards. The men chipped solely to keep warm, knowing they were fighting a losing battle with the ice.

The captain stood at the entrance to the pilothouse pondering his situation and looking at the men. He had not heard one single word of complaint, nor had he seen a single sign of the anxiety he himself was feeling inside. He must have felt a great sense of pride in his men, but there was no time to think about that, for he had the responsibility of making sure everyone got through this alive. He and his exec, Al Jordan,[1] huddled over the charts, trying to estimate their position by dead reckoning. Concluding that they were in the vicinity of Louisbourg, Nova Scotia, the captain ordered a change of course to head for it. The new northerly course caused the sea, previously at their stern, to buoy up the port side, the side that was listing. The vessel had no fathometer or radio direction finder, the lead lines were iced in beyond recovery, and both sonar and radar gear were useless, so everything depended upon the accuracy of their dead-reckoning position. If the plot was correct, they could make landfall at Louisbourg by 1100.

Jordan and the radioman tried rigging an auxiliary antenna onto the port stay in an attempt to send out International Code distress signals. They were not certain the signals were being transmitted but hoped that, no matter how weak they were, someone would pick them up.

By now the ship was listing so badly that the threat of capsizing was real. French agonized for his men and his ship, racking his mind for measures to take for their safety. He ordered all available weather gear for protection from the elements and had all classified documents placed in a weighted mail sack and brought up from below to the pilothouse. By 0900 the ice had won the battle and was in control. All chipping stopped. The axes and cleavers set aside during rest periods were themselves frozen and icebound. Steering by the helm was lost, the rudder frozen solid in its pintles. A twin-screwed vessel can, in normal conditions, be steered by its engines, but with the 30-degree list to port the starboard screw was almost out of the water, making steering by engine virtually impossible. The men of USS SC 609 huddled in the pilothouse, their gray faces peering silently into the wall of mist, straining for some sign of land.

At 1114 someone sighted what he thought looked like offshore swells. A minute later they spotted seagulls. The mist suddenly cleared. Five hundred yards dead ahead was a harbor.[2] Suddenly they saw ships at anchor, a picturesque setting, a church steeple surrounded by a cluster of neat white houses. The little fishing village of Louisbourg, Nova Scotia, never looked as lovely to anyone as it did to those spent and haggard men of the 709. They shouted, they hugged each other, they high-fived, and some even sobbed in their relief.

But Lady Luck wasn't quite ready yet. The ship was in an awkward approach position for safe passage into Louisbourg Harbor. Too far west of the entrance, they were inside a dangerous shallow-water area near Rochefort Point. Between the Point and Battery Island the narrow passage is bracketed by treacherous shoals, navigable only by shallow-draft boats steered by experienced seamen and only when the tides were right. Drifting slowly towards this dangerous area, the men on the 709 could see white water and huge flumes of spray with every wave lashing at the reefs. With no helm, the ship was moving slowly toward these reefs.

Desperately, the captain and the quartermaster tried to steer by engine, but the sodden iceberg that had been a ship would not respond. A sudden gust lifted the ship like a giant, unseen hand, thrusting it hard forward. Yawing, she heaved dangerously to port, while both men frantically gripped the helm. "Port engine ahead full!" the captain shouted, thinking he could swing right. The icy ship-mass hung sluggishly, lurched 45 degrees sideways, then began careening toward the rocks. "Hold fast! Stop all engines!" With a dreadful grinding noise the 709 slammed hard onto the reef on its port side, starboard screw racing wildly, its propeller beating the empty air.[3]

It was 1131, 21 January 1943. Twenty-six frozen, exhausted men stared across the calm waters of Louisbourg Harbor. They could see the church and the neat little houses, but the warmth, the hot food, and the voices of other human beings they promised were as remote as if they had been a thousand miles at sea. They had been too busy fighting the ice and sea to know that the Maritime Provinces had been assaulted by one of the worst blizzards in history, and Louisbourg was right in the path of it. Winds gusting to ninety miles per hour at times had slammed the tiny village, and everything there had come to a standstill.

Captain French ordered the whistle blown and told the signalman to fire rocket flares. He tried backing the port engine at full speed, but the ship was stranded hard and fast. The hull appeared sound except for a few seams split when it scraped the bottom. The ship was taking on water, but slowly.

In Louisbourg someone spotted the 709 and notified the Canadian naval officer in charge. A small harbor craft signaled, asking the subchaser to identify itself. In his reply Captain French reported the seriousness of their situation and requested immediate medical attention for two crew members. They watched as the harbor boat went to the dock, picked up a pilot, and headed out toward the 709. She got within 100 yards of the 709 but could reach no further on account of the shoals. She signaled that she would go back to get help.

The captain went below to the wardroom, sloshing in foot-deep icy water to make sure all classified papers and codebooks had been removed from the ship's safe. He ordered everyone to go topside and to don their lifejackets. They huddled on the starboard (high) side, bracing themselves from the pounding waves that kept smashing into the side of the ship. The relentless wind still howled and snow was still blowing horizontally. There was nothing anyone could do but hold on.

After an hour or so, a Canadian navy launch approached. Pulling up just outside the shoals, she fired several line rockets in an attempt to get a line to the stricken vessel, never once getting close. The 709's men attempted to float a line out, hoping it would come close enough to be picked up by the launch, but this also failed. It was getting colder as the afternoon waned. With darkness approaching, the launch abandoned attempts to fire lines and sent a message that they were returning to anchorage. Their last message, as they turned away from the 709, was "Have courage."

The men of the 709 were alone, without power, heat, food, or light. No one had slept for the past forty-eight hours. Their clothing was stiff, half frozen. Totally spent from fighting the icy storm, now they faced another bitter cold night with nothing but their flickering body heat to keep warm. Some were already so weak they showed signs of resignation, as though they didn't care—a common precursor of hypothermia. There was a real danger that they all could slowly freeze to death.

The incoming tide caused the ship to list even more, in turn causing the level of flooding in the compartments to rise. The captain knew they were in danger of capsizing. Reluctantly, but for their own safety, he ordered the crew out of the pilothouse, where they had been huddling together for body warmth. All available blankets, mattresses, and pillows, most of them wet, were brought topside for protection.

Since no one had eaten for two days, Tom Harvey James, mess attendant and the sole black member of the crew, offered to go below to find some food. He labored aft across the icy deck with its 30-degree slope, groping his way to the hatch leading to the after crew quarters. Descending the ladder he stepped into frigid, knee-deep water. Stumbling, sloshing, grabbing at anything he could, he reached the galley. He found a large can of applesauce. Grabbing it under one arm, he stumbled and sloshed back to the ladder, raised himself, and managed to get back to the pilothouse. The men gave him a rousing cheer, then gulped down the applesauce.

During the night a few signals were exchanged between the 709 and shore. Captain French was frustrated with the messages people on shore kept sending, like "Help being delayed. Have courage. Save your light." When he got a message asking for suggestions for rescue, he lost his patience and replied sharply: "Send a shallow draft whaleboat immediately. We cannot last much longer." She was less than a mile offshore, hard aground where she had struck the reef, looking more like a lump of ice than a ship.

SC 709 loses her battle with ice, 21 January 1943, near Louisbourg, Nova Scotia. *Courtesy of Jean Kyte*

In the village of Louisbourg, two different groups of seafaring men were making plans for rescuing the men from the beleaguered vessel, neither aware of the other. One consisted of fishermen, natives of the village, who knew the waters thoroughly—the tides, the currents, and how to work them to best advantage, and where and when to get through certain openings and between certain reefs when conditions were just so. They knew these things just as their fathers and grandfathers had known them, from a lifetime of fishing. All they knew about SC 709 was that it was a U.S. Navy ship and there were men trapped inside who would freeze to death if something wasn't done quickly. They knew the surf would batter it to pieces unless they did something soon. They phoned Ottawa to report the accident. Ottawa told them the navy had assured them "salvage operations were progressing favorably." The fishermen knew better. The men on that subchaser were freezing to death and no one seemed to care.

While they were thus engaged, a second group of men had been following the plight of the 709. Lying at anchor in the harbor and tied together were the barkentine *Angelus* and the schooner *Eliza Gorham.* Captain Jensen, master of the *Angelus,* an experienced seafarer and whaler, had observed the unsuccessful efforts of the navy launch and was gravely concerned with the delays and failures. Jensen had been told where there were two Novi shallow-draft dories that he could borrow. He conferred with Captain Borgen, master of the Eliza Gorham, also an experienced whaler, and the two of them drew up a rescue plan. At evening mess a call was issued for volunteers from both sailing ships to assist in the operation, and to no one's surprise every man from both ships eagerly stepped forward. Night had fallen, so they decided to make the rescue early the next morning.

With the first light of dawn on the morning of 22 January the frigid air in Louisbourg Harbor stabbed the nostrils like two ice picks. With the thermometer at 17 degrees below zero, the wind chill factor was 50 below. The half-frozen men of SC 709 could be seen from shore, still clinging to the rail in various attitudes, unmoving and seemingly lifeless. Hypothermia had begun its slow, relentless progression, and several men were already sinking into that illusion of peace that it can bring, lulled by numbness and exhaustion.

The two groups of rescuers, each oblivious of the other, began their respective rescue missions. The group of troubled fishermen gathered early over hot coffee, and by 0800 Ed Levy [4] and four other fishermen boarded the *W.G.,* a boat owned by Wilbert Goyetche that he used around the harbor as a pilot boat. It had a shallow draft, offering the best chance to get across the reef. Wilbert and Ed, with three brothers, Nelson, Charles, and Joseph Bagnell, made ready to go out and take those men off the 709. However, since the harbor was now frozen over, they needed a bigger vessel to break a path. They phoned the Dominion Coal Company for a tug. It would delay things, but there was no other way.

Meanwhile the group from the two sailing ships was moving ahead with its plan. Captains Jensen and Borgen had already noted the ice floating in the harbor and figured out a different approach. Taking the crews of both ships ashore, Captain Jensen borrowed a truck, picked up the two Novi dories, and, driving south, turned sharply east onto Rochefort Point, the end of which was only a few hundred yards from the 709. They pushed the dories across a snow-covered pebble beach to reach the water. The men jostled each other for seats, all wanting to go, but in the end two men for each dory were selected. In the lead boat were Walter Boudreau and Clarence Mullins of the *Angelus,* and in the second boat, Ivan Chiasson and John Hillier of the *Eliza Gorham.*[5]

The two boats shoved off, and the oarsmen immediately found themselves fighting hard as they rowed through choppy, treacherous, ice-cold waters. Boudreau said, "It was one of those situations where you'd have a sea breaking here and one breaking there and if you happened to get under one of them, well, that was it." By skillful oarsmanship the dories danced around and avoided each breaking wave. The men would row this way and one of them would look and say, "There's one there," and they'd go hard right. Seconds later the same thing would happen and they'd go hard left. "Those dories were so maneuverable, they were like bicycles," said Boudreau. But they still had to know how to row them. These men were Newfoundlanders and experienced boatmen. They knew how.

It took twenty minutes of strenuous maneuvering to reach the beleaguered subchaser. Boudreau guided his dory close to the starboard (high) side of the 709 near the stern. The men at the rail were practically motionless, half-frozen, unable to move. Boudreau yelled at them, extending an oar. They were moving too slowly for the men in the dory, who were in no position to fool around because of the heavy swell. The breaking waves were causing the dory to crash dangerously against the subchaser.

Slowly they came to life as the dory banged hard against the icebound hulk. One man finally roused himself enough to holler in a broad Southern accent, "Ooh, man, is I ever glad to see you!" One man, then another, struggled over the rail and slid into the arms of the men in the dory.

There was no time for talk or gentleness. No sooner were the two men in the dory than Boudreau and Mullins quickly shoved away and headed for the Canadian navy launch which, with Captain Borgen aboard, had heaved to, ready to take aboard as many survivors as possible. Once the first two were transferred to the launch, Boudreau and Mullins swung their dory around for a second rescue trip. By now the second dory, with Chiasson and Hillier, had retrieved two more men and was heading for the launch. Each of the dories took off three men on their second trip. It was hard, exhausting work that took over two hours. Then the launch, with ten survivors, headed for the Louisbourg pier, where ambulances and women of the Navy League were waiting.[6]

Meanwhile, from the opposite direction, the harbor tug, closely followed by the *W.G.* with Ed Levy, Goyetche, and the Bagnell brothers, approached the 709. The tug turned away from the breaking water and the *W.G.* approached through the treacherous mass of white foam across the reef—a feat impossible with a boat other than one like the *W.G.* with its shoal draft and men who knew how to do it.

The first attempt was unsuccessful and they had to circle a second time. The remaining men on the 709 were so cold they couldn't straighten their hands to catch lines. A line was finally gaffed, and the men rolled and slid over the side of the ship into the waiting boat, some barefoot, some with only socks on their feet. There was no time for niceties. The fishermen simply grabbed them—sixteen in all—and pulled them into the boat.

Later, Ed Levy told how the good ones helped the bad ones, and how they let the ones who could stand up continue standing in the back part of the boat. Several of them had frostbite. Some were so frozen they couldn't walk.

It took less than an hour from the time the *W.G.* left until they were back at the wharf. Surprisingly, neither rescue party was aware of the other until both operations were successfully completed and everyone was on dry land. By now the 709 was being pounded to pieces.

The ten men rescued by the men of the *Angelus* and *Eliza Gorham* were taken to a Navy League hut, where women of the village had set up an emergency hospital ward. Shortly after that, the fishermen arrived with the remainder of the men. Nurses and women volunteers gently removed the iced clothes from the frozen men, bathed them in warm water, patted circulation back into frozen limbs, wrapped them in blankets, and fed them soup and coffee—the first hot food they had eaten since leaving Portland four days before.

In a letter to his command in Halifax, the Canadian officer in charge reported the details of the rescue:

> Throughout this rescue everyone was filled with admiration for the United States personnel, whose extraordinary courage, cheerfulness, appreciation and gratitude for anything that was done for them was commented on by all. Their loyalty to the service and their devotion to duty are perhaps exemplified by the action of one—the second in command [Al Jordan], who was badly frostbitten but was later reported as doing well—who was found sound asleep but with his hand hanging out of the bed on a bag of confidential books which he had been told not to leave.[7]

When the men had revived enough, they were taken to the military hospital twenty miles away in Sydney for full medical treatment.[8] Some of the men recovered very quickly, while others remained in Sydney for several weeks. No one lost his life. George Gagnon, CBM, USN, the only serious casualty of the experience, lost two toes.

As is customary in such cases, the U.S. Navy held an official inquiry and concluded that, under the severest of conditions, everything possible had been done to assure the safety of the crew and prevent loss of the ship. Several men, including both officers, received commendations. In his testimony, Peter Federspiel, Yeoman 1c, stated: "During my 14 years in the navy, mostly in China waters, I can say that if it were not for the commanding officer's skill, courage and excellent judgment in emergencies, I and the rest of the crew would not be here to make any statements." Chief Boatswain's Mate Gagnon echoed Federspiel, giving credit to the CO's training as an officer and his good judgment in applying it for "the saving of our lives."[9]

In the weeks following the grounding, equipment was removed from the ship under the supervision of Harry Luessen, the 709's quartermaster. As preparations were being made to salvage the ship, yet another storm slammed into the coast, breaking her up beyond repair. The wreck could be seen for several years afterwards, until finally the sea claimed her completely.

SC 709 was only sixty-seven days old when, fresh from her festive commissioning in sunny North Carolina, she succumbed to nature's frozen fury in remote Louisbourg, Nova Scotia. Her only reward for this ordeal was the dubious distinction of living the shortest life of all the wooden subchasers of World War II.

6

The Mediterranean

It was a year after Pearl Harbor before there were enough patrol vessels, landing craft, and auxiliary ships to send overseas in quantity. By the spring of 1943 several large task forces began to cross the Atlantic. The third one to go comprised eighty-nine ships, including thirty-one LSTs (landing ships, tank), thirty-seven LCIs (landing craft, infantry), a tanker, a net tender, and a fleet tug, with an escort screen of five destroyers, five SCs, three PCs, and two YMS minesweepers.

SC 692 was one of the five SCs that left Bermuda on 13 April in a formation of ships so large it spread out from horizon to horizon—fourteen miles across and twelve miles from the lead ship to the last ship.[1]

Because the SCs could not carry enough fuel and water for transoceanic voyages, they had to pull up close abreast of the tanker every three days to refuel while under way. It was no easy task. Refueling at sea sounds fairly simple but actually requires expert shiphandling—particularly when the seas are running heavy. The little ship first had to stay well out on the tanker's port quarter to avoid the turbulence of her wake, then angle in toward her port side amidships, slowing to match the big ship's speed of eight knots.

Lines for water and provisions also had to be brought over, making three different supply lines strung between the two ships in addition to the hawser. The eight-knot stream of sea water being pushed outward from the tanker's huge bow impinged on the SC's bow, tending to drive the smaller ship toward or away from that menacing steel cliff. Too much toward and the SC could crash into the cliff. Too much away threatened to break the connections between the two ships. Every officer who ever commanded a small ship that required fueling at sea remembers the tricky, constant attention to maneuvering it took to keep his ship at the proper speed and the proper distance.

The supply ship would forge relentlessly through the long Atlantic ground swell at nearly ten miles an hour and the SC would have to pay close attention to get close enough to pass lines, then settle on a parallel course about ten yards abeam. It then had to work its helm and engines carefully to stay in place alongside the tanker.

Edward P. Stafford, then commanding the SC 692, describes in one word how his hundred-ton SC approached the ten-thousand-ton tanker: "Gingerly."[2] His explanation: "Because you were approaching a vertical gray steel cliff the top of which was even with your radar housing at the highest point of your mast."

Gibraltar was a big thrill for the youthful sailors, passing the famous rock as they entered the Mediterranean. The SCs were deployed to strange-sounding places like Nemours, Oran, Arzew, Bizerte, Beni Saf, and Mers el-Kabir, where strange languages and customs gave them enough to talk about and remember for a lifetime. The duty was primarily that of escort and patrol interspersed with dirtier jobs, such as when SC 503 was called upon to take aboard ninety dead and wounded men from LST 333, which had been torpedoed by a submarine the night before. By the time she arrived in port the 503's deck was a mass of bloody bodies, some lifeless and the remainder badly wounded—a gruesome cargo which, once delivered, necessitated breaking out hoses and brushes for a complete scrub-down.

SCs were always in danger of being mistaken for submarines. Just before 0400 on the morning of 14 July 1943, while on patrol duty near Scogliotti off the southwest coast of Sicily, the men on watch on SC 1030 were startled to see PC 591 bearing down upon their starboard beam only 400 or 500 yards away. The PC had been patrolling another sector. She was sending a series of short flashes with her Aldis lamp. Just minutes before, Lt. Charles F. Highfield, commanding the 1030, had relieved his third officer, Lt. Burton L. Youngman, who was still on the flying bridge. Youngman grabbed an Aldis lamp and sent back the prescribed code to the PC's challenge. The challenge was unanswered, and the PC continued on its collision course.

Captain Highfield immediately ordered the ship to general quarters and all engines reversed—but too late. The PC rammed them on the starboard side amidships, its bow cutting a neat "V" into the engine room and ending four feet from the ship's keel.

The 1030's starboard engine was destroyed, and the engine room rapidly filled with water up to six feet. No one was hurt, but boatswain's mate Joe Lojko, who had been descending the ladder from the flying bridge just as the ship was struck, was thrown off the ladder onto the PC's bow, landing on the mousetrap rails. Shaken up but not seriously hurt, he was able to assist with lines to make the SC fast to the port side of the PC in case she started sinking. Fortunately the steel bulkheads at either end of the engine room held fast, preventing water from entering other compartments. It became obvious the 1030 was not going to sink, and a tug subsequently arrived to haul her into Bizerte.

Like many such incidents in the war, the ramming of the 1030 by PC 591 has never been fully explained, and no official report from the patrol craft was ever found. One member, James D. McLelland, of the 591's crew claims the 1030 had been off course for most of their watch and that the two ships kept meeting at the turn-around location, a spot near where the ramming took place. He adds that both ships had been at sea for an extended period, with many hours of general quarters. Crews may have been tired and in need of rest. After dry-docking and repair in Algiers, the 1030 served admirably in the Mediterranean, participating in the invasion of southern France.

Operations in the Mediterranean were constantly fraught with tension because the enemy was close enough to be a threat. On the night of 6 August 1943, SC 503 was slowly steaming through the Adriatic at four knots, escorting a water barge from Palermo to Ustica, an island thirty miles north. Sometime after midnight, two large warships were spotted approaching at high speed. "Rich" Crolius,[3] the skipper, ordered his signalman to challenge the lead ship in order to establish his own identity and avoid being assaulted by friendly fire. To his surprise, however, the confirmation came with a flash of light followed by a loud boom and the hiss of red-hot six-inch projectiles over their heads. The lead ship had fired a salvo at them, fortunately too high because of the close range.

Shocked, Lt. Crolius checked his secret publications for accuracy and ordered the signalman to repeat their friendly status. The second reply was prompt and menacing, and this time the salvo landed even closer. The SC turned on its coded recognition lights. This time both ships opened fire. In desperation Crolius turned on his twelve-inch signal light to illuminate first his own ship and then the warships, hoping they would recognize his friendly status. While he was doing this, his radioman was on an emergency circuit with the battleship *Philadelphia.* After frantically reporting to an admiral that their little ship was being fired on by friendly ships, a quietly authoritative voice came through: "I'm sorry, son, there are no friendly ships in your area."

Suddenly the two unidentified warships ceased fire, changed course and sped away in the darkness. The 503 hastily collected two of their men who had been on the water barge and proceeded for cover at flank speed. When they arrived alongside the *Philadelphia,* the anxious skipper reported to the Command Center. Only until then did he learn the two warships had been identified as enemy cruisers of the Italian navy.

The *Philadelphia* dispatched air patrols, but by then one cruiser had fled to Taranto, the other to Naples. Months later, in Naples, Crolius ran into an Italian gunnery lieutenant who had been on the lead cruiser. The lieutenant remembered the incident and said they had thought the 503 was a torpedo boat rendezvousing with a submarine. When the 503 illuminated, they assumed it had pinpointed the firing bearing and, thinking they had been discovered, they ran from the "torpedoes."

The fury of war came directly to two subchasers early in the morning of 23 August 1943, laying to rest the notion of some SC sailors that their small size rendered them impervious to attack by bombing. They were the first SCs in World War II to be sunk by enemy planes, but they wouldn't be the last.

Three subchasers lay at the mole known as berth three in the harbor at Palermo, Sicily. Inboard was SC 694, centered was SC 696, and outboard was SC 771. The night was calm, the moon was in the last quarter, and visibility was good. Palermo had been taken by American forces a month earlier, but German dive-bombers kept flying over, and attacks were frequent both night and day.

At 0410 a Red Alert was sounded, and all hands went to their battle stations. The 771 got under way at once, backing away and moving out. At 0420 the sound of aircraft was heard approaching in what appeared to be a steep glide. Lt. Roger Robinson, commanding the 694, gave the order to commence firing, but before the order could be executed a loud explosion was heard on the 696. A 500-pound bomb had penetrated the flying bridge and her main deck and exploded in the forward fuel compartment. Burning oil was thrown in all directions, starting fires on the 694 and on a British merchantman, the SS *Speedfast,* which was moored two hundred feet away.

The explosion caused extensive damage to both subchasers. The entire midship section of the 696 broke out in flames and the heat was so intense that everyone expected the magazine to explode. The fire spread to the 694 and the two ships began burning furiously in their midship sections. Twenty men on the 696 and four on the 694 were killed instantly. Everyone else, including twenty-three wounded, got safely ashore before the two ships, welded together by the tangle of wreckage between them, began drifting away from the dock, the mooring lines of the 696 having been severed by the initial explosion. An hour later the fire reached the magazines. Two giant explosions and both ships sank at once.[4]

With the amphibious assault at Anzio on the mainland of Italy, a sizeable group of subchasers found out what their job in the war really was. Fourteen SCs were used in "Shingle," the code name for the assault, which took place on 22 January 1944. For twenty-seven days the chasers were busy at almost everything but chasing submarines.

A typical example was SC 522.[5] Leaving the dock at Bagnali at 1200 on 20 January she proceeded to Castellamare Bay where at 0415 she sortied with her assigned assault group and proceeded to designated point William shortly before midnight on 21 January. After the arrival of three British cruisers who were supporting the landing assault, the convoy proceeded, with the SC 522 and SC 978 taking up their positions as guide boats for four columns of LCAs (British landing craft) and LCSs (landing craft, support) loaded with American Rangers.

At 0045 on 22 January the first group of assault craft got under way and headed on the attack course directly for a casino on the assigned (Yellow) beach. The two subchasers reached their designated point two thousand yards off the beach at 0140 and signaled the assault boats to go; all of them hit the beach at the center point at 0203. Some twenty minutes later the assault craft returned and the SCs guided them to their transport ships.

After repeating this operation two more times, with the coming of daylight the 522 was assigned to sink mines that were floating in the area, using gunfire. Then she was ordered to lay smoke.

On Sunday, 23 January, she went alongside USS *Woolsey* to remove three wounded British soldiers and transport them to a hospital ship. Four days later she performed a similar operation, transporting twenty-two survivors from USS *AM 104* to a hospital ship. At dusk on Saturday, 29 January, the British cruiser HMS *Spartan* was hit by enemy air attack, and the 522 went alongside to assist, although the *Spartan* was burning badly. She was able to remove four wounded sailors and a newsreel photographer and his camera before the captain of the *Spartan* ordered her away.

After delivering the wounded to HMS *Delhi,* the 522 returned to the *Spartan* to render further assistance, only to see her sink before their eyes. They remained in the area in hope of picking up more survivors, but they did not recover any. The next day they assisted the newsreel photographer in taking close-up pictures of what remained of the *Spartan.*

On Wednesday, 2 February, the 522 sighted an American pilot bailing out of his crashing A-36, picked him up, gave him first aid and dry clothes, and took him into Port d'Anzio. Then on 3 February in company with SC 649 the 522 rendezvoused with two RAF Spitfires who guided them about 20 miles seaward, where three American airmen were floating in a raft, survivors of a B-26 that had been shot down. After picking up the three men and taking them in to Port d'Anzio, at 2215 they went back on assigned patrol duty outside Anzio Harbor. The 522 then spent three days on smoke patrol, until relieved 7 February to proceed to Naples.

During her 27 days at Anzio, the 522 had expended over 2200 rounds of antiaircraft ammunition and logged 112 Red Alerts for which general quarters was sounded.

SC 497 was control vessel for the second wave of assault craft in the Anzio landing, and for the remainder of its ten-day stay off the beach she worked extensively and often, laying smoke screens. The 497 acted as secondary control, with PC 626 the primary control for the landing waves. The assignment was to lead LCVP landing craft (for vehicles and personnel) from LST 379 to within hail of the primary reference vessel, there joining PC 626 with the LCVPs from LST 358. She was to wait off the primary vessel with both groups of LCVPs circling until dispatched by the wave control officer. PC 626 led the wave in, with the 497 keeping the LCVPs closed up. They were to proceed in this fashion to fifteen hundred yards from Red Beach, but when they got to within twenty-eight hundred yards the wave found itself in the midst of a group of floating mines.

By this time the scout boat was clearly visible to the LCVPs, so for the 497 to proceed any further would have incurred needless danger in view of the mines. The LCVPs therefore were sent in, and the 497 was ordered to stand by for smoke patrol in the southwest corner of the anchorage. At 1005 the 497 proceeded to assist in rescue of men from a minesweeper that had struck a mine, and at 1130 it sank five floating mines with fire from the 40-mm guns, undergoing three attacks by enemy fighter-bombers during the day.

On 23 January the 497 stood by the entire day prepared to lay smoke and at 1745 after dark, there was a heavy air raid on the ships and the 497 laid smoke for 45 minutes. The next evening another heavy bomber attack to seaward spread to the anchorage and to the beach. The planes dropped numerous star shells, lighting up the harbor brighter than daylight. The 497 laid smoke for an hour and twenty minutes before running out of oil.

At 0200 on the 25th another raid took place, lasting 45 minutes, with many flares and bombs, and the 497 laid smoke during the entire attack. At 0530 another attack came and they laid smoke for 25 minutes.

On the 26th three different fighter-bomber attacks came and the 497 expended 26 rounds of ammunition at the attacking planes. The men saw near misses with glider bombs when the planes attacked two merchantmen and a destroyer, and the 497 expended sixty rounds of ammunition at the glider bombs, with no visible results. While this was going on, they attempted to lay smoke, but the generator was faulty. At 1825 they picked up a number of soldiers who had leaped into the water from a transport ship that had encountered a near miss.

Another heavy raid accompanied by starshells occurred at 1855. At 0520 on 27 January a heavy raid began over the anchorage and the 497 laid smoke for an hour. Three more attacks took place during the day, with the expenditure of fifteen more rounds from the 40-mm. At dusk a red alert was sounded and smoke was laid around the Biscayne until 1745.

On 28 January from 0045 to 0143 the 497 laid smoke around the Biscayne during yet another air attack. With the arrival of daylight the attacks continued, with more shooting at the attacking planes.

On the 29th two attacks took place, with more AA return fire and smoke-laying. At 1755 an extremely heavy glider bomb and torpedo attack began, with HMS *Spartan* and a Liberty ship both hit. The 497 continued laying smoke through this attack. The *Spartan* sank and the 497 recovered five survivors from the water, all in a bad state of shock but without wounds. The men were delivered to a British cruiser standing by.

During the rescue operation Philip R. Monoghan, Seaman 1c, dove into the water and swam to an unconscious survivor forty feet off the bow despite the litter of wreckage, the confusion of ships under way and nearby, and the

Spartan sinking. He went over without a line, and his carbon dioxide life preserver slipped off when he struck the water, yet he did not hesitate. When the unconscious man was retrieved and brought aboard, he showed no signs of breathing, but the men on the 497 revived him by artificial respiration.

On the 30th more smoke-laying went on during three red alerts. The 31st was their first day of respite, there being no air raids and no smoke-laying. The first and second days of February brought more attacks, and the 497 laid smoke off Anzio Harbor.

Just after midnight on 2 February the 497, suffering from a slipping clutch and worn controls, collided with a British LCT (landing craft, tank), damaging her bow. She was sent to Naples for repairs, a timely blessing for her men, who had been under constant attack for ten days with only a few hours' sleep. During the ten days she was at Anzio, the 497 had expended 170 rounds of 40-mm and 70 rounds of 20-mm ammunition and had made enough smoke to blanket the State of Rhode Island.[6]

Early in the morning of 17 September 1943, while operating in the Gulf of Salerno, SC 508 was directed to lay a smoke cover for other vessels in anticipation of an imminent air attack. The sea was calm, the moon was bright. The attack soon came. The enemy dropped several starshells and the 508 had little or no time to maneuver before a plane, making a low run from port directly overhead, dropped three bombs, each estimated to be 500-pounders. The first bomb struck the water close aboard the after port side of the 508 and exploded, sending up a column of water right next to the ship and lifting the stern three feet out of the water and twisting the ship to starboard. Several depth charges broke loose and were thrown over the side by the explosion. The charges had been set on "safe" and did not explode.

The hatch to the lazarette was flung open and the burning smoke pot fell into it. Someone quickly prevented fire by flooding the lazarette with carbon dioxide from extinguishers. The binnacle was torn loose and its compass light extinguished. The port shaft was bent, the toilet in the after crew's quarters was torn from its foundations, and the refrigerator compressor pipes were broken. Both peloruses were thrown out of alignment, and there was derangement of sonar and radar circuits. Fortunately, there were no injuries; in his Damage Report (21 September 1943), Lt. Roger U. Wellington, commanding officer, stated "the fighting efficiency of the ship was impaired but not critically . . . this command is highly pleased with the manner in which the ship and her equipment came through. It is a fine tribute to the designers and builders of the hull that she was able to withstand almost completely such a serious blow."

From 21 January to 7 February 1944 SCs 522 and 978 were two of fourteen SCs up to their thwarts in the Anzio invasion operation. The 522 and 978 sortied with three British troop transports just prior to H Hour at 0030 on the morning of the 22nd and acted as guide boats for four columns of LCA and LCS landing craft loaded with American Rangers from the transports. A British lieutenant commander boarded the 522 as squadron control officer, and the two chasers proceeded toward the designated point two thousand yards off the beach. The first flight of assault craft were released, headed straight in, and landed right on target at the center of Yellow Beach. The two SCs stood by and waited for their return, then, guided them back to the transports. The round trip operation was repeated two more times, with second and third flights of Rangers. After the safe return of the third wave, the 522 stood by as directed, to be ready to lay smoke, detonate floating mines, and participate in rescue.

Most of the next two days were spent picking up and transferring wounded British and American soldiers to hospital ships. The 522 rescued a fighter plane pilot who had been shot down into the sea and brought him to Port d'Anzio, and on 3 February the same SC recovered three American airmen in a life raft, survivors of a B26 bomber that had been shot down. The 522 was then assigned to making smoke for three days.

During the 27 days of activity the ship's log recorded 112 red alerts for which general quarters was sounded, due to the incessant presence of enemy aircraft and their attacks.

SC 638, under the command of Lt. James A. C. Doran Jr., USNR, was another of the plucky little SCs at Anzio, first as guide and control at Peter Beach on D-Day and then engaging in a wide variety of tasks similar to those of the 522. Dodging mines and warning others about them they anchored a thousand yards off the beach under enemy artillery fire and saw several mines explode under DUKWs (amphibious trucks) on their way in. They then laid smoke and searched the waters for survivors of a British destroyer hit by bombs, finding only one dead body. The next day they laid smoke again and fought off two air attacks. That night the weather turned nasty, with twenty-foot waves and winds gusting at thirty-five knots.

At dawn they went to the assistance of LST 422, which had struck a mine, resulting in numerous chemical explosions aboard. In the 638's log, Doran's laconic report of this incident reads: "Picked up six survivors," but Lt. Col. Bill Hutchinson, who commanded the 83rd Chemical Battalion on board the LST, later cited them for "acting without fear for the loss of their vessel or their lives by bringing their craft into mined waters, and without fear for their own personal safety gallantly risked their lives to save the lives of our men by leaving their craft and going into the water."

The 638 returned to anchorage only to encounter another air attack while laying smoke. It then observed a Liberty ship being pounded by bombs and went to her rescue, picking up ninety survivors from the water and from life rafts. The next day was quieter and more routine, with smoke-laying and only two enemy air attacks, and the day after that seemed almost like "respite care" to the men when they were ordered to escort a group of LCIs back to Naples.

The respite was short-lived. After taking on water, fuel, and provisions in Naples, the 638 returned to Anzio to continue laying smoke and patrolling. Later that day a bomb suddenly exploded so close to her port beam that the ship and everything aboard was badly shaken up. Depth-charge racks were torn off, deck plates in the engine room were lifted, and several seams were sprung. Fortunately no one was injured, and with both engines and the hull badly in need of repair, the 638 managed to keep going.

Two more days were spent with smoke-laying and disposition of mines, only to have this activity interrupted by going to the assistance of another Liberty ship hit by bombs. The ship had a cargo of ammunition that caused several bad explosions, and it was impossible to get too close, yet the 638 was able to pick up a survivor clinging to the anchor chain of the stricken vessel.

The day after this incident, the 638 lost radio communication when a sister ship alongside accidentally severed her antenna with its 20-mm gunfire while shooting at enemy planes. Two days later, in a heavy gale, a navy tug hit a mine off the Anzio breakwater. The 638 managed to remove five severely injured survivors from the sinking tug and take them to safety aboard a hospital ship—despite the twenty-foot waves.[7]

During the twenty-seven days the 638 was at Anzio, the log recorded a total of 457 red alerts, of which 115 were actual bombing attacks. The fuzzy-cheeked youngsters and green reserve officers were now not just good sailors and seasoned warriors. Overnight they had become men.

Fifty-five years later W. C. Thompson, a crew member who lived through the Anzio experience, says,

> We spent the war on the edge. We did it all and then some. In retrospect we lived charmed lives. We returned from each expendable assignment with everyone still aboard. Nobody knew we existed nor did anyone care except when they had a nasty little job that had to be done. Most war stories require a hero or heroic events. We didn't get any credit for going in harm's way. The big ships were the heroes. We were the working stiffs.

SC 525, also at Anzio, had the good fortune to assist in knocking out "Anzio Annie," a giant cannon the Germans had rolled up on railroad tracks, thus saving the lives of countless troops ashore. Ship's cook Robert Clarkson vividly remembers his Mediterranean experience on the 525, not so much for the fighting but as "one rough place to sail. I was the most seasick s.o.b. in the fleet."[8] His queasiness is understandable because of a phenomenon peculiar to that area known as the mistral, in which gale-force north winds sweep down from the Alps and out across the sea. The mistral has plagued Mediterranean sailors since the days of Homer.

SC 651, a veteran of the Sicily and Salerno campaigns, was assigned to antisubmarine patrol in the vicinity of Anzio Harbor during the weeks following the Allied takeover in January. Anzio was quiet now, with little enemy activity other than an occasional scout plane flying over too high for their guns. Early on the morning of 21 April 1944, having refueled and taken on water and provisions, the ship was lying to, awaiting orders.

The radioman came up to the bridge and handed the captain a message from Commander Escort Sweep Group ordering the 651 to proceed immediately to the assistance of PC 558, which reportedly had just sunk a midget submarine five miles northwest of the Cape D'Anzio lighthouse.

Joseph Walker Barr, Lieutenant (jg), USNR, commanding, from Vincennes, Indiana, with a bachelor's degree from DePauw University and a master's degree from Harvard, had never been to sea before enlisting in the navy but had been recommended for command after completing his training at SCTC. The few months he had been aboard SC 651 had seasoned him for whatever lay ahead. The ship had seen plenty of antiaircraft action.

Ten minutes after receiving the message, the 651 was heading out toward the lighthouse. As they passed it, the lookout reported a floating object off the starboard bow about four thousand yards distant. Sounding general quarters, Barr ordered the engines ahead full and the helm brought around to bear on the object. Closing to two thousand yards, he could see a small wake trailing behind a dome-shaped object and, fifteen feet back of that, a rudder sticking above the surface. It was heading toward a cluster of ships, including a hospital ship, in Anzio harbor. It was a midget submarine, all right, and Barr estimated its speed at about five knots. He changed course to bring it onto his port bow so as to clear any stern torpedo tubes, just in case there were any.

They were still close to Anzio Harbor, and the object was heading directly for the ships at anchor. Barr, recalling Commander McDaniel's blistering tirade about the Germans and Rule No. 1 for what to do in this situation, decided he had no choice but to ram. Calling for flank speed, he ordered the depth charges armed and ready and began closing on the object, changing helm orders repeatedly to stay on a collision course. The target, ignoring the 651, continued on its course and speed, heading straight toward the big ships in the harbor.

On the 651 the men were ready, the ship leaping ahead full speed, engines throbbing and plenty of bone in her teeth. Barr, on the flying bridge, crouched at the voice tube, eyes on the target, giving orders to the helmsman, "Come right slowly . . . ease the rudder . . . steady . . . steady as you go . . . right slowly . . . ease. . . ." At five hundred yards Barr straightened up, thinking. He had read a U.N.I. bulletin recently about a one-man "human torpedo" developed by the Italians. This object he was about to ram fit the description—a human torpedo. He thought, why would anyone in his right mind blow up his ship by ramming a torpedo? Seized with doubt, by now less than three hundred yards from the object, he ordered, "Hard right rudder!" The helmsman responded and the subchaser veered sharply to the right, heeling over dangerously to port, its gunwales only inches from the water and everyone hanging on tightly. "Ease the rudder," called the captain, then, "Steady as you go," and "All engines one-third," as the little ship came around on a course parallel to the object. The waters swirled all around the ship as the wake caught up with them. They were now fifty yards from the "torpedo" and running parallel to it.

"Ready fire," he ordered, then, "Commence firing!" The 40-mm and 20-mm guns opened up point blank and scored direct hits almost immediately. The dome and its rudder kept going for a hundred yards or more, then dove beneath the surface. Ordering left full rudder, Barr had hardly begun a sonar search when they saw something dead ahead. They began firing at it, when it suddenly began waving its arms. It was a man, obviously the operator.

The 651 approached him cautiously, making sure he had no weapon in either hand. Someone extended a boat hook, he grabbed it, and they pulled him aboard. He was in a bad state of shock. He couldn't speak English. He pulled a wallet out of his pocket, opened it, and held it out, pointing at a picture of a young woman holding a baby. Barr felt a twinge. His own wife had given birth to a baby girl only a few weeks before. The man was Guenter Kuschke, a first class seaman in the German navy. He wore the uniform of a Nazi petty officer and a device around his neck similar to a Monson lung. They stripped off his clothing, wrapped him in a blanket, and gave him cigarettes and coffee. Ens. Harry C. Tee, the executive officer, dressed a wound in his shoulder.

After he had recovered somewhat from his initial shock and fear, the captain and the executive officer began questioning him in German. Was it a small submarine? A torpedo? Did it run by diesel or electricity? How many more were there? Where was his home port? He answered all questions with, "Ich wünsche nicht zu sprechen, ich bin ein deutscher Soldat." (I don't want to talk, I am a German soldier.) He told them he was twenty-three years old, lived in the Ruhr near Alsace-Lorraine, and was married. They gave up the questioning and transferred him to the nearest senior ship, DE-136.

The 651 was ordered to proceed back to Anzio Harbor, and later that day Joe Barr wrote up a report of the incident in which he commended his crew and officers for acting coolly and efficiently at all times. "[T]hough we were proceeding at flank speed in mined waters and engaging a totally unknown weapon . . . they realized the urgency of the attack and knew that if we did not get the enemy in about five minutes he would be in a perfect position to strike at our shipping in the anchorage. Their conduct was in the best traditions of the naval service." Then he spent the remainder of the afternoon and evening relaxing with his officers and some of his men. The report was distributed through the various channels of command.

Two weeks went by, and the incident was almost forgotten, until one morning Barr received an order to report to the admiral in command in Anzio. Dressed in freshly cleaned navy blues, he arrived at the appointed time and was ushered into the admiral's office, where the admiral told him to sit down.

The admiral said, "Son, I have here two sets of papers, both of which I have read, and both of which have two different recommendations. The first one is from the Office of Naval Intelligence, and it states that on the morning of April 21st you captured one Guenther Kuschke, a German petty officer, took him aboard your ship, and proceeded to question him about details of his vessel, where he was going, where were his orders, and other questions of a nature pertaining to his mission. Is this true?"

"Yes sir," replied Barr.

"Son, were you aware that such questions were not within your jurisdiction, and by the Rules of War the extent of your questioning was limited solely to his name, rank, and serial number?"

"Yes, sir."

"Were you aware that the questions you asked of the prisoner were the type that, in time of war, could have led to a compromise of our position or our situation with relation to the enemy, and therefore should have been left to the Office of Naval Intelligence?"

"Yes, sir, although I may not have been certain of it at the time."

"Are you certain of it now, son?"

"Yes, sir."

The admiral paused. He took the second sheaf of papers in his hand. "The Office of Naval Intelligence recommends remanding this case to a general court-martial." There was another moment of silence. Then he continued.

"Son, I have here another statement, one from Commander of Escort Sweeper Group, which says that on April 21 you correctly identified a floating object as an enemy human torpedo and proceeded to direct your guns at it and successfully sank it and recovered its sole pilot, one Guenther Kuschke. Is this true?"

"Yes, sir."

"And his statement goes on to say that your quick and effective actions prevented an attempt to damage allied shipping in the Anzio anchorage, and he recommends that you be awarded the Bronze Star Medal for skill and devotion to duty in keeping with the highest traditions of the United States Naval Service."

Silence.

"Son, if you were in my position right now, how do you think you would choose between these two recommendations?"

Barr looked helplessly at the admiral, not knowing what to say. The corners of the admiral's mouth curved ever so faintly into a hint of a smile. Rising, he came around his desk and placed a hand on Barr's shoulder.

"Son, I'm sure you understand courts-martial are necessary and proper for maintaining proper order and discipline in the navy. But I happen to believe there are times when other methods can accomplish the same objectives, and I think this is one of those times. I'm not going to have you court-martialed, because I don't think you're the type to repeat a mistake. Moreover, aside from that, I believe your actions were most commendable and worthy and I'm going to recommend you for the Bronze Star." The admiral held out his hand and the greatly relieved Barr shook it, thanked him, and left.

A few weeks later the medal was presented to Barr, with the entire ship's company present. The citation read: "For meritorious service as Commanding Officer of the U.S.S. SC-651 during a war patrol of Anzio, Italy, on April 21, 1944. After assisting in the identification of a floating object in the water as an enemy human torpedo, Lieutenant Barr directed the delivery of accurate and concentrated gunfire against the target to sink the enemy torpedo and to effect the capture of the operator, thereby frustrating probable attempts to damage allied shipping in the Anzio anchorage. His professional skill and devotion to duty were in keeping with the highest traditions of the United States Naval Service."[9]

After the war Lieutenant Barr had a long and distinguished career, serving in Congress as a representative from Indiana and then as assistant secretary of the treasury. For the last 28 days of Lyndon Johnson's administration, he was secretary of the treasury. Joseph W. Barr died in February 1996.

After laying smoke close inshore in waters too shallow for ordinary minesweepers the SC 525 was returning to a yard tug for repairs to one screw. Robert Clarkson ("the most seasick s.o.b.") was in the galley washing pots. All of a sudden there was a loud bang and his range exploded. All the dishes and the meat from the refrigerator came tumbling down on top of him. He yelled "MINE!" thinking they had hit one, and ran for the ladder. The executive officer was at the hatchway and without thinking Clarkson shoved him aside and went up the ladder in two steps. Once topside he saw a British tanker coming in to hit them again. In his panic he reached out and pushed at her bow, thinking he could fend it off. He and the ship were lucky. Damage was slight and no one was hurt.[10]

The SC 532 was at Anzio a total of 61 days. Art Malecki, Radioman 1c, learned to envy the men who served on destroyers.

> Destroyers were always supposed to be the most rugged duty in the navy, but they were actually good living ships. We guys on the SCs felt like we

> were on liberty whenever we went aboard destroyers. They had movies, comfortable bunks, cake and pie in their mess hall, a ship's store that sold candy, a laundry, and a nice big radio room. We had none of these things. On the 532 I lived with fifteen other men in a compartment no bigger than a large bathroom and sometimes it smelled worse.

Warming up, he adds,

> A night snack in the galley began by turning on the overhead light to watch and hear thousands of cockroaches rustling for cover across the galley floor. (Yes, you could actually hear them.) Then, taking a piece of bread out of the warm refrigerator, we would hold it up to a light and pick out the maggots before eating it. Most of the ports were filthy and when we tied up rats would inevitably get aboard. Later at sea we would often confront a rat and shoot at it with small arms. It's a wonder we didn't kill each other.[11]

There were times when the little subchasers encountered natural hazards almost more dangerous than the enemy. One such incident happened when SC 676 was steaming alone on a routine trip from Bizerte to Palermo.[12] They were pinging away with sonar, minding their business with everything routine until, without any warning, the ship suddenly lifted on its port side and heeled dangerously 60 degrees to starboard. The port engine and screw stopped and all systems on the ship were disrupted. The 676 had been attacked by a rogue whale. The creature, apparently resenting the echo ranging pings created by the sound gear, had simultaneously attacked and surfaced under the ship, almost causing it to broach. As the ship passed over it, the port propeller cut the whale badly, causing the water to turn red in an ever-widening area. An RAF bomber passing overhead saw the blood and managed to fly low over the beast and machine-gun it out of its misery. The collision caused some leaking, and the 676 wound up in dry dock in Tunis for a screw replacement. The damaged screw appeared as though a giant had picked it up and crushed it with his bare hands.

The Germans were in the habit of planting antipersonnel mines off beachheads that they considered possible future allied landing sites. SC 978 and SC 1029 were converted to shallow-water minesweepers, utilizing German gear that the navy had somehow captured. On the morning of D-Day, prior to the landing, they swept with three-hundred-foot cables running through cleats on the fantail, dragging buoys that were set to plane three feet under the surface. Henry Serra, Ship's Cook 1c on the 978, remembers sweeping at the Bizerte beachhead when the Allies found themselves fighting the French to go in. One of the enemy's tactics was to send out their equivalent of Navy Seals to attach mines to the undersides of Allied ships. Small anti-personnel depth charges were employed to counter such tactics, and Serra witnessed enemy personnel being killed under water by this method.

When asked if he had ever experienced true fear during his SC experience, Mr. Serra replied:

> The first time we saw action was when we were passing through Gibraltar and an enemy sub hit a couple of our ships. The ships were not very close and the only feeling I remember was one of anxiety, not fear. But when the Germans began dropping bombs and we were shooting at them with our 20-mm guns I had a fear that was so powerful I've never forgotten it. I was a loader on one of the 20-mm guns and I was winding the magazines while the gunner was shooting at an enemy plane. He swung the barrel over my head to track a plane, something we had never done before in training or in drill. With every shell fired the heavy compression emitted from the barrel felt like an air hammer hitting me on the head. I felt a fear like nothing I had ever felt before or after. If we hadn't been 3,000 miles away I would have jumped ship and walked home right then and there. After that first wave of terror we went through dozens—maybe a hundred—such shootings and I never had the same feeling. In fact, I never felt fear again.[13]

7

Normandy, the Channel, and Southern France

Much has been written about the Normandy invasion on 6 June 1944. That date is permanently stamped in the minds of those who were there. Operation Neptune-Overlord was so huge, so complex, so overwhelming, that individual ships and participants alike were mere microcosms in a grand plan—like ants in a vast army of ants—swarming across a narrow body of water, each with his own special duty to perform, his own microscopic plan to execute. Nineteen subchasers participated in this huge and complex operation, either as escort vessels, control vessels, or both.[1]

SC 1354's assignment was to escort a group of LCTs (landing craft, tank) across the Channel and then, at Omaha Beach, to act as secondary control vessel at Dog Red Beach. Henry R. Stern, Lieutenant (USNR), commanding, was also to be landing control officer for the LCTs. A graduate of Yale and Columbia law school and SCTC, and by now an experienced navy man and a fine officer, Lieutenant Stern was well prepared, and so was his ship. His executive officer was Lt. (jg) Dale F. Galles of Billings, Montana, and his gunnery officer was Ens. Thomas H. MacElwee, now living in Denver.

The 1354 was part of Task Force 124, Assault Force "O" under the command of Rear Adm. John L. Hall. She left Portland early 4 June at approximately 0300, escorting a group of LCTs, but at 0700 received notification to return to Portland, General Eisenhower having decided that the seas were

SCs 978 and 655 taking supplies and provisions from USS *Brooklyn* during the invasion of southern France *National Archives*

too high to make a safe landing. It was Sunday, so after they reached Portland the crew requested that a church service be held aboard ship, to which Captain Stern agreed, and he himself conducted it.

The following morning they again started out, purposely making only two knots speed and taking all day. The sea was moderately heavy, and the LCTs bounced around a lot, making it difficult to keep station. Hundreds of ships spread out on both sides to the horizon, in the largest amphibious invasion in history. The weather was cold, gray, and windy. It took several hours of wallowing across the choppy sea before the bleak coast of Normandy could be seen stretched out before them. A firsthand narrative emerges from the recollections of three who were there:[2]

> The ships slowly, steadily, approach their designated beaches, rising the crests and pitching into the hollows of the gray-black water. A group of

LCVPs joins the LCTs behind the 1354 as it draws closer to Omaha Beach. There is no perceptible enemy fire. Lieutenant Stern on the flying bridge, with clipboard in hand, personally directs the departure of the landing craft. He orders his signalman to hoist the flag Baker, indicating to the landing craft that the 1354 is secondary control for Dog Red Beach. The sounds of messages crackle up from the radio shack as ships keep talking to each other. Lieutenant Stern waves the LCTs and LCVPs in. Everyone is bouncing around in the choppy water.

The battleship *Texas* is pounding the beach from a great distance with 16-inch shells. The waves hit the beach, taking some enemy fire laterally along the beach. Landing craft stay on the beach, don't back off and return. An LCVP comes alongside. An army lieutenant says he has half of an artillery piece, can 1354 locate the other craft with the missing half? They try on their radio but not successful. The army lieutenant goes on in.

They're at general quarters all day until dark, remaining on station. At one point they fire their 40-mm at gun flashes on the beach. An LCVP comes out with wounded. They get on the radio and locate a hospital ship and give them directions. The weather moderates in the afternoon, then clears up and warms up. One LCVP comes out with prisoners. On the radio they find where it should go. Some prisoners are Asian, they probably were forced labor.

In the afternoon the beaches still look very bad. They see a cluttered array of shot-up LCTs and LCVPs. Occasional enemy fire drops in the water in their area. No enemy planes have been spotted. Destroyers come in very close to beach and fire at a church, cutting it down to the ground. Probably a fire control point for the enemy. British LCTs are very long compared to U.S. craft, have rocket launchers covering tank deck. They fire all the rockets at the beach in one long blast. Many craft of all types everywhere, all U.S.

Our assigned section of Omaha Beach turns out to be a disaster. We're close to shore with sunken debris and equipment and carnage floating around, landing craft coming and going. We're keeping mobile. We stay on station. During the day we are asked to report conditions by radio. As it gets dark activity slows and we secure from general quarters, set condition II. At 2200 enemy air attack, return to general quarters. Enormous barrage of antiaircraft fire from the fleet. Shrapnel falling sounds like rain hitting the sea. A near miss explodes and I fall on my knees, embarrassed. After two or three of these attacks, we no longer go to general quarters nor do we fire at unseen targets. Our crew needs sleep.

D plus one and no enemy fire. We patrol seaward, staying in Omaha beach area—patrol, act as messenger, etc. We anchor at night or tie up alongside Rhinos (steel boxes with large outboard motors, used as lighters). We get our food, water, and supplies from U.S. merchant ships by signing chits. They are very cooperative. We're pretty much on our own except when we get radio orders to go somewhere or do some particular errand. June 19—gale winds, we stay under way keeping out of harm's way. Storm wrecks the "Mulberry," a manmade port on the open beach—changes entire logistics pattern for supplying army. We stay until sometime in July.

It is impossible to fully describe the confusion and disarray of ships and landing craft when the Omaha Beach landing took place. Capt. W. D. Wright, USN, deputy commander of Assault Group O-2 in LCH-86, found the landing craft waves in such chaos and so inextricably confused he had to order them back to their line of departure to reform. Communications between army and navy as to order of unloading ships broke down, and at times conditions were horribly entangled. Through it all, SC 1354 performed her part so well that Captain Wright later commended her performance in a memo:

> The SC-1354 was directed to locate all ships carrying infantry and get them into the beach. This was carried out with extraordinary skill and speed. In

SC 1332 is one of several Allied ships driven onto the Normandy coast during a seventy-five knot gale, 18 June 1944. *Courtesy of John K. Carl*

the follow-up phase of the operation, SC 1354 rendered valuable service in the control of incoming convoys. This ship was the most outstandingly efficient control ship in the Omaha area.

For his valor at Omaha Beach Lt. Henry R. Stern received the Bronze Star; his "extraordinary forethought in directing ships and small boats into the beach . . . his determination to remain at his post in spite of enemy fire and without injury to his vessel . . . were in keeping with the best traditions of the offensive spirit of the United States naval service."[3]

Two months after the Normandy landings, on 15–17 August 1944, the Allies made one last major amphibious assault in Europe, with the invasion of Southern France. Code-named Operation Dragoon, it turned out to be the smoothest and best executed landing operation of the European war. Four different landing beaches were selected in the vicinities of Nice and St. Tropez, with the city of Marseilles westward as the principal military objective. A dozen or more subchasers participated as control vessels, including SC 535, SC 639, SC 978, and SC 1030. The Germans had heavily mined the shallow waters along the beaches.[4] The 978 received a unit citation for her performance during the dangerous pre-invasion minesweeping operations.

The subchasers' war in Europe provided ample proof of the versatility and usefulness of these vessels, from landing control to smoke screening, minelaying, rescue, and ferrying to antiaircraft defense, to say nothing of their escort and patrol work. Meanwhile their original purpose, to hunt for submarines and to protect other ships from being torpedoed by submarines, was still an important, ongoing activity.

Although many submarine contacts and depth-charge runs may have seemed lethal to the subchaser that made them, it was difficult to prove a "kill" to higher authorities without hard evidence. An oil slick was not regarded as proof. Accompanying the slick there had to be flotsam of a type that proved beyond doubt that an enemy sub had been sunk. A lifejacket had to be made of enemy kapok, not just any kapok. Paper scraps had to have some text or markings of an enemy nature. Pieces of wood or plastic had to be traceable to the enemy for usage and origin. Throughout the war, SCs reported submarine contact runs, half of them reported as sure kills by their commanding officers. The "true kill" story of SC 1290, for which no credit was ever given, shows how close the call can be.

On 20 April 1945, in the English Channel, SC 1290 was returning independently to her home base in Weymouth from Southampton under the command of Lt. (jg) Moses M. Falk when a message came from SC 1321 saying she had a sub contact. The 1290 came to general quarters and closed the 1321 rapidly to assist, then stood clear to allow the 1321 to make an unhindered attack. The 1321 made her run and dropped five depth charges. The 1290, receiving information and data from the 1321 during the attack, estimated the location and directional movement of the target and signaled the 1321 that she would follow up with an attack of her own. The 1321 agreed and stood by while the 1290 made a run. Falk had estimated the sub's course as being to his portside, SSE, speed seven knots. He plotted his run and made an attack, using mousetraps to obtain greater covering area. Less than two seconds after the launch, four of the mousetraps exploded in a cluster at approximately 120 feet depth, tossing up large sprays of water. Mousetraps were designed to explode only on contact, so whenever they exploded it was a good sign that they had hit something hard, like a sub's hull. Immediately thereafter some men on the 1290, including the third officer on the flying bridge, stated they saw an "oval-shaped dark hue" in the water at the point of contact. But none of them could be absolutely sure of this. Closing, the 1290 dropped two depth charges over the spot, set for detonation at seventy-five feet.

Coming about with left full rudder, the 1290 picked up its first good sound contact, with echoes sharp and clear and good recorder traces. The target appeared to be moving right, heading northeast. The contact continued strong, and Falk made a careful, deliberate attack with a pattern of five depth charges, two of them with K-guns to give a perfect diamond pattern. Immediately after the fourth depth charge exploded, seven men on the 1290 saw a black hull rise from the sea, roll over somewhat, then submerge. The column of water that arose from the explosion of the fifth depth charge prevented further observation. The water darkened over the area and an oil slick appeared from which samples were taken. Sound contact was lost momentarily.

Captain Falk sent a radio message to shore authorities reporting the location of the attack and continued searching to regain contact. At 1300, after SC 1321 had left the area to rejoin her convoy, the 1290 was joined by SC 1330 and SC 1358, sent from Portland Harbor to assist in the search. Believing that the sub had been heading in the general direction of No. 1 buoy when he last had contact, Falk, as senior officer present, assigned the 1358 to a position two miles east of the buoy with instructions to circle the buoy at that distance in a counterclockwise direction, gradually confining her search circles. The 1330 was assigned a position three miles due west of the buoy to proceed clockwise to circle the buoy, gradually confining her circles. The 1290 did the same four miles from the buoy. Such disposition of the three subchasers gave good coverage for an area of over fifty square miles, using the buoy as a pivot. Since their circles would all be getting smaller and smaller, he knew it would be difficult for any U-boat to get through the screen.

At 1358 the subchasers were joined by a British destroyer, HMS *Tamby*, who started south at the buoy and zigzagged on a search that took her gradually southward and out of sight. The 1330, after completing her search, followed the *Tamby* out toward the Channel.

Falk decided a careful investigation of the waters very close to the buoy was in order, on the possibility that the sub might be lying on the bottom under the buoy—a favorite tactic. The 1358 was still searching nearby when the 1290 moved close to the buoy, circling it twice while slowly closing the range and carefully pinging. At 1555, with the buoy aft of the 1290's starboard beam, a strong contact was made on a target heading south-southeast. In his report Falk later wrote: "This contact was excellent; strong asdic returns, fine traces, sharp clear echo pitch, down Doppler and strong screw noises."

Steadying up for the attack, the 1290 made a deliberate mousetrap run in which three projectiles exploded two seconds after hitting the water. Circling about, the 1290 again picked up the target still heading south-southeast. Falk then made another depth charge attack using the diamond pattern. SC 1358, standing by, signaled that heavy oil was coming up from the area of explosions. The oil came up in large bubbly masses and spread out over an extensive area. Mingled with it were blobs of heavy black oil like lumps of black lard. The 1358 dropped a dye-marker over the spot. The 1290 circled, resumed contact, and made another mousetrap run resulting in three explosions in three seconds. By this time the sub was moving much slower and was doing less maneuvering. Maintaining contact, they followed the sub as it slowly moved to the left to evade, then made another attack with four remaining K-gun charges as the sub took a northerly direction.

Falk radioed the 1330 to rejoin him immediately. He received a message ordering him to return to Portland, which he disregarded, firmly convinced that he and his ship were ready for a "kill." The target had become very slow and sluggish, and there was no difficulty maintaining contact. The screw noises could be heard turning very slowly and clearly. The SC kept him dead ahead, going in a gradual circle to the right at between two and three knots. Falk made his last attack with three mousetraps, two of them exploding two seconds after hitting the water. He was now completely out of depth charges and mousetrap projectiles.

Three minutes after this attack, five muffled explosions were heard under water close at hand, the first three in rapid succession, the fourth after a short interval, and the fifth after a longer period. Although out of ammunition, the 1290 held clear contact and ordered the 1358 to make further runs, which she did. The third oil slick of the day made its appearance, spreading out in a large area. Falk stood by while the 1358 continued making runs, scoring hits with her mousetraps. After a final depth-charge attack, the 1358 reported that she felt she had hit something. After that, all contact was lost by both subchasers, and when another hour of search proved futile, they proceeded into Portland Harbor.

During that day the weather conditions were ideal with a smooth sea, very light wind, good visibility, and mild temperature. Careful checks were made of the charts to rule out non-sub contacts. Ship's personnel were highly experienced. The 1290 had a first class sonarman with over three years' experience and above-average ability. Falk concluded his official report with the observation that "in his opinion a definite sub contact was had and the severest of damage inflicted . . . the attacks were fatal, the sub was either completely broken up or left in such condition that return to base was highly unlikely."

SCs operating out of Portsmouth were under the control of the British Admiralty, and Falk's report, complete with the range recorder paper, was forwarded to the Admiralty for evaluation. No official credit for a sub kill resulted. In Paul Kemp's compilation of German U-boat losses in World War II the U1169 is listed as having been lost at an undetermined date in April 1945 in the English Channel, "exact location unknown." Neither the cause nor the number of casualties is known, the only notation being "U1169 had been ordered into the English Channel and later disappeared. It may have been that she was the victim of a mine, but the possibility that she was lost as a result of an accident arising from mechanical or drill failure cannot be discounted."[5]

A few pages later U235 is also listed as a loss on an undetermined date in April 1945 with the notation, "U235 had been ordered into the English

Channel and then disappeared. There is no Allied claim to account for her loss, and she may have been the victim of a mine, accident arising from mechanical or drill failure, or a battery explosion resulting from inadequate battery ventilation while snorkeling."[6]

Could SC 1290 have sunk U1169? Or U235? No one will ever know for sure. One thing we do know, however. The plucky little subchaser and her tenacious skipper did everything right.

8

The Shetlands Bus

The door of the Quonset hut opened and the light from inside flooded the wooden ramp leading down to the dock. Three men emerged, carrying heavy cases of radio gear down the ramp to the waiting ship. The low reverberations of the ship's generators were the only sounds in the silence of the cold night air. Dark figures in pea jackets and watch caps helped them load the cases aboard, and in a few minutes all was secured. One of the men stayed on the dock to cast off the lines while the subchaser backed off, wheeled around and disappeared into the black night. By the time the man had returned to the warmth of the Quonset hut, the ship was already pitching and rolling in the cold waters of the North Sea.

The *Hitra* had just left her secret base in Scalloway, a remote fishing village in the Shetland Isles, and was on her way eastward to occupied Norway. She carried two men and two tons of equipment and food supplies for operating a radio station on Stavenes, a remote island outermost in the Strong fjord. The men would spend the next few months secretly reporting German shipping activity to the Allied Command in Britain.

Hitra was a "Shetlands Bus," one of three American-built SC subchasers that had become the only means of access to—and escape from—Norway and the claws of the German Gestapo. The subchasers were vital to Norway and to the Allied Supreme Command.

War had come to Norway on 9 April 1940 when the Germans surprised the little country with a swift, powerful invasion. Norway's King Haakon VII and his retinue barely escaped to England aboard the Royal Navy cruiser HMS *Devonshire.* Remnants of the Norwegian army vanished into the hills or fled to the Shetlands using boats of all sizes, even rowboats. It took only two months for the Germans to gain complete control of Norway, which gave Germany greatly widened access to the North Sea and the Atlantic beyond.

Once in London, King Haakon wasted no time setting up a government-in-exile, a body that existed for the remainder of the war. The secret collaboration between British and Norwegian forces began almost immediately. Less than two weeks after the takeover, radio transmitters were sending information about German naval movements to British Intelligence.

At its narrowest point, only 190 miles of North Sea separate Norway from Britain's Shetland Isles. Small fishing vessels called smacks were quickly pressed into service to cross this natural corridor, which was an invitation for escape, counter-resistance, and sabotage. By September 1940 the first secret agents had been ferried over to establish contact between the government-in-exile and resistance groups forming in Norway. Soon more than thirty smacks were making crossings, and by Christmas over two hundred refugees and more than a hundred British soldiers had been transported. A secret base for the operations was established in Scalloway in the Shetlands and the frequency of the crossings gave rise to the name "The Shetlands Bus."

The crews working the Shetlands Bus were civilian irregulars—young Norwegians, many of them fishermen—with a strong sense of patriotism and a zest for adventure. "The Shetlands Gang," as they called themselves, was dedicated to the task of transporting military personnel, saboteurs, radio equipment, and arms to Norway, returning with condemned refugees or Norwegians wishing to join the Allied forces fighting the Germans. One of the leaders was Leif Andreas Larsen, a man of great courage, initiative, and imagination, who had been going to sea since before he was sixteen. For Larsen, no mission was too risky or impossible, and word of his deeds spread until he was known to everyone as "Shetlands Larsen." The British Admiralty called him simply "The Larsen." His wartime exploits were so notable that he became Norway's most decorated hero, and a statue in his honor stands today on the waterfront in Bergen.

The Shetlands Gang was clever and resourceful at avoiding detection, and for many months the little smacks carried on their clandestine tasks without incident. With thousands of fishing boats moving daily through the many leads and fjords, the Germans found it difficult to adequately patrol the coastline.

But after two years of successful smuggling, the Norwegians began feeling the effects of increased German vigilance. During the harsh winter months of 1942–43, enemy patrols combined with the savage weather to sink ten Norwegian fishing boats, resulting in the loss of forty-four crew members and sixty passengers. The slow-moving smacks, with the characteristic "tonkety-tonk" of their single-cycle engines, could be heard for miles across the water. No match for enemy planes and patrol ships, they had to be replaced with vessels that were quieter and faster, with better armament and longer cruising capabilities.

By August 1943 the right buttons had been pushed at Allied Headquarters in London, and Admiral Harold R. "Betty" Stark, commander of U.S. Naval Forces in Europe, had come to the rescue by ordering three American-built SC-class subchasers to be transferred to Britain. Consequently, in August 1943 subchasers SC 718, SC 683, and SC 1061, stationed in Miami, received secret orders to detach from their command and report to Brooklyn Navy Yard to await further orders. SC 718 was destined to become a living symbol for all the *Shetlandsbussen,* as we shall see.

When the three subchasers arrived at Brooklyn Navy Yard, the commanding officers were given strict orders to warn their crews to button their lips about their movements and the movements of the vessels. They were told only that the ships had been selected for a special purpose, which would be made known in due time.

Naturally much speculation and rumor circulated among crew members. Some of them believed they had been selected for a highly dangerous mission. Their suspicions were reinforced a few days later when giant cranes hoisted the SCs onto three Liberty ships and preparations began for transporting the crews and ships to an undisclosed destination. When the day of departure arrived, a pall of uncertainty weighed heavily in the minds of the sailors and loved ones who had come to bid them farewell. The scene, always wrenching during wartime, was more poignant than usual.

After the ships were under way, the men were told that they were going to Belfast in British Northern Ireland. The crossing took six days and was uneventful. In Belfast the SCs were hoisted back into the water, and on 14 October 1943 the three vessels steamed up the Firth of Clyde to an American base at Roseneath, Scotland.

SC 718 was delivered to Belfast aboard a Liberty ship in 1943. *National Archives*

The men on the subchasers were not aware that a few days earlier a group of Norwegian sailors had been sent to Roseneath and was eagerly awaiting their arrival. On the designated day the Norwegians gathered on the dock, watching intently as the vessels rounded the headland in column formation and steamed into the Gareloch. When they saw the subchasers the Norwegians could hardly contain themselves. They cheered and punched and slapped each other, excited as schoolboys. To them the SCs looked like small destroyers.

Not until the ships tied up and the skippers reported to their command did the Americans learn the purpose of their journey, which was to train the Norwegians in the operation of the subchasers, guns, propulsion equipment, and all other mechanisms aboard. Upon completion of the training they would hand the ships over to the Norwegians. On learning this, the Americans were dumbfounded, disappointed, and even indignant, but there was no choice except to follow orders. In the end the transition went smoothly, and, despite the language barrier, the men quickly bonded in a spirit of cooperation. The training period took only a week, the transfer of command was completed, and the Americans were sent back to the States full of whopping stories about their "suicide mission."

To the Norwegians, accustomed as they were to the bare-bones rigor of their fishing boats, the SCs were an extraordinary windfall. Not in their fondest dreams did they expect to take over such "luxury ships." They marveled at the central heating, oil-fired galley, refrigerators, water fountains, hot showers, typewriters, and toasters. The electric generators, one of them declared, "would light the village of Scalloway."[1]

After taking command at Roseneath the Norwegians moved their newly acquired "young destroyers" to Londonderry, thence to Scalloway, for fitting out. They removed all depth-charge racks, mousetrap projectors, and K-guns and installed an extra set of davits so that, instead of one dinghy, each ship carried two. The dinghy motors were equipped with special mufflers for quiet operation. They removed one of the Oerlikon 20-mm guns amidships and installed a 2-pounder aft and two .50-caliber machine guns on the flying bridge.[2]

The newly acquired vessels were christened *Hitra* (SC 718), with Ingvald Eidsheim commanding; *Hessa* (SC 683), Peter Salen commanding; and *Vigra* (SC 1061), Leif "Shetlands" Larsen commanding. It would take volumes to describe all of their exploits during the two years that followed, but a few stories convey the flavor of the times.

Once, approaching the coast of Norway, the *Vigra* passed a nest of German vessels moored a thousand yards away. A heavy snowstorm provided cover, but while they waited at the rendezvous point for agents who were supposed to meet them, the sky suddenly cleared and the glow of a full moon appeared. To avoid being seen, the *Vigra* quickly retired behind an island. Sending a dinghy ashore with a search party to look for the agents, the crew spent the rest of the night playing cat and mouse with the enemy. The agents never appeared. Just before dawn the search party returned, and *Vigra* wasted no time standing out to sea and returning to the Shetlands. For "The Larsen" it was just another routine trip.

On a similar mission *Hitra* was approaching Sunnfjord in the dark of night to pick up an agent on shore. The lookout spotted a German patrol boat inspecting each creek and cove with powerful searchlights. Eidsheim had orders to avoid confrontations if at all possible. With only a moment to consider whether the agent might already have been arrested and they were heading into a trap, he decided to get out. It was a wise move. He later learned that a coastal steamer had been torpedoed with eleven lives lost, and the Germans were making a widespread search for subs. Had he been discovered, a force of German minesweepers would have swept in and *Hitra* would never have survived the unequal battle.[3]

Another time the *Hitra* and *Hessa* sailed across to Gangsoy on the middle of Norway's west coast and put ashore four agents and a ton of equipment. Part of the equipment consisted of two kayaks with battery-operated motors dubbed "Sleeping Beauties" by the British. The four men also brought along a dozen magnetic mines and five radio transmitters. Their mission was to attack ships at anchor south of Stad, using the Sleeping Beauties somewhat as mini subs, but traveling shorter distances and with smaller explosive charges. However, four days later the Germans discovered the men, forcing them to drop the equipment and run for their lives. They managed to get over to the south side of Bremanger, where they were picked up by the *Hessa* after a week of great suspense. Following this the Germans were more vigilant than ever in their pursuit of the Shetlands Bus and their daring men.

Later in the war an observer from Admiral Stark's office wrote: "It would be difficult to sum up the value of these three craft in their contribution to the [Allies]. Hundreds of tons of stores and supplies have been delivered to Resistance groups. An enemy plane has been shot down. Countless agents have been taken in and out and great numbers of marooned allied airmen, including Americans, have been helped to evade the Gestapo. Despite very heavy weather the ships have required minimum repairs."[4]

Hitra made 43 of the 116 trips across the North Sea that the three subchasers logged. The SCs landed 192 agents, delivered 383 tons of stores and equipment, and saved 373 refugees. The numbers might seem small compared with other war statistics, but the achievements were hugely critical to Norway and the Allies during the Occupation. Their interception of German communications and the prompt reporting of German ship movements helped lead to major successes, including the sinking of the battleships *Scharnhorst* and *Tirpitz.* Without the Shetlands Bus to maintain the steady stream of agents and supplies to keep the lines of communication open, such stunning victories would not have been possible.

In the winter months, the seas between the Shetlands and Norway are among the stormiest in the world. The subchasers went to hundreds of different locations along the Norwegian coast, with some journeys two thousand miles and three weeks long. Norwegians have been daring sailors for a long time, but these journeys differed considerably from Viking voyages, always made—sensibly—in summer when, in latitudes that far north, there is continual daylight. All the subchaser voyages required sailing alone in the depth of the subarctic winter. Each landing was secret and had to be made in darkness. It is quite possible that in all the history of man's seafaring, no other series of journeys has been undertaken deliberately in such bad weather and in such small ships.[5]

The story of what happened to these three gallant subchasers after the war is almost as compelling as their adventures during the war. Two of the SCs are lost forever, but the third, the American-made USS SC 718, which became Norway's *Hitra,* is afloat and operating today—in mint condition—at the Norwegian Naval Base near Bergen, a living symbol of the *Shetlands-bussen.* She was discovered by accident in 1983, half sunk and rotting away. After years of effort and appeals for funding, she was lovingly restored to her wartime condition by interested and patriotic Norwegians. (See appendix B.)

9

"Greek's" War

Bill "Greek" Pappas served briefly on the carrier USS *Franklin,* but he was scared to death of planes and claims to have been kicked off because he refused to fly in one. (To this day, Pappas has never flown.) In a letter, "Greek" writes about life on SC 986 in terms for which the word "colorful" seems an inadequate description. His style reminded me of a poem I received from an ex-subchaser sailor[1] exalting the lowly cockroach:

Hi'ya Cockroach!
T'rou' da bilges went da cockroach, t'rou' da bilges, t'rou' da galley.
Found day food and found day feasting, t'rou' da galley, t'rou' da lockers,
'Til we catchem wid da Flit gun, den day take da Flit gun from us,
Move us over at da table, holler "Guts!" and pound da table,
Claim day cannot eat dat moose dung! So went sailors t'rou' da bilges,
T'rou' da bilges, t'rou' da galley. Locked demselves inside da lockers,
Barricade demselves wid broomsticks,
Lived on scraps da bugs would t'row dem,
While da cockroach, unmolested,
Took command and gave da orders, and da Navy was no wiser.
So at night we roam da bilges. T'rou' da bilges, t'rou' da galley,
And at night you hear us scratching, t'rou' da bilges, t'rou' da galley.

Here, in his own words, is Bill Pappas's story:[2]

Before going into the navy I was one mean rotten son-of-a-bitch. Of course the navy made me believe otherwise, once I discovered something called Love of Other Shipmates. But I had my problems. One day the cook told me I was to be next week's mess cook. I told him, "Not me, pal, that's a sissy job." He reported me to the skipper who, incidentally, was one helluva guy.[3] He buttonholed me on the main deck and sat me down on the steps. He sat beside me, not mad, but straight from the shoulder man-to-man and explained the duties of each man aboard ship. When he finished he got up, patted me on the shoulder and said "OK, Greek?" "Yes, sir, captain," and I was mess cook the next week, no problem.

When I first went aboard the 986 I knew it was love at first sight. I was striking for gunners mate, so I started right off working with mousetraps and depth charges. There were two Texans who were the lead gunner's mates and they didn't like Yankees, especially hunky Yankees, and I was both. After a while I got pretty good with the mousetraps and depth charges. There was this time I was working on them, and these two guys were on my back chewing me out as usual, so without looking up or nothing I tossed a detonator over my shoulder and yelled "Catch it!" It was the only way to shut them up.

On convoy duty we went out, picked up our tankers or freighters or whatever, and took them where they wanted to go. We hit a lot of storms and rough weather at sea. Sometimes the crew from the ships we escorted would come over to check out the SC and they all asked the same question: "How do you guys do it?" They'd say, "We thought sure as hell you sank. You guys are real sailors." We felt real good after those compliments coming from other sailors.

We had a skipper named Richard King Johnson. What a guy! But we had two southern officers that were like the two Texas gunner's mates. They didn't like Yankees, especially hunky Yankees. Me, being Greek, I had it twofold. There was a boatswain's from Georgia who didn't speak to me for three or four months until after an incident in Jamaica when I was coming back off liberty and saw a gang of natives beating on a sailor. I ran up and jumped in. I really didn't see who it was till after we beat hell out of them. He put his arms around me and said, "Greek, we're shipmates forever!"

Then there was Mindo and Masserelli, two of my closest shipmates. Oh, the trouble we got into when we were on liberty! Mindo was from Brooklyn and used to go around singing, "When it's apple blossom time in Orange, New Jersey, we'll make a peach of a pear." This he did when he got seasick, and that was all the time, when on patrol. Masserelli, he was something else. After each liberty he would be sitting on his bunk picking and saying "Goddammit, I got the crabs again." Christian was our ship's cook. When he went on liberty we knew what was for chow the next morning: Shit on a shingle.

One time we had a Mexican kid on board. I don't recall any other name but Poncho. I came topside after chow one day while on convoy and saw him sitting on the deck near the fantail not looking too good. I said "Hey, Poncho, what's up?" He looked up and said, "Señor, are we doing what that sheep is doing?" and he pointed to another subchaser off to starboard pitching and rolling out of sight and doing all the other things that happen in a storm. When I told him yes, he said, "Chees, no wonder I am seek!"

Once when on lookout with Poncho I learned how to sing a Mexican song that I still remember to this day. Another time he got a package from home and it had a bush or vine full of little green somethings and he was eating them like popcorn. I asked to try them and he said, "Señor, I don't think you should eat these, they are hot." I said, "What the hell, I'll try them." Bad move. I popped a couple into my mouth and thought my head would explode. They were so hot I ran topside and jumped overboard, rinsing my mouth with seawater. I remember it was a while before the heat left.

I already mentioned the two officers and the two gunner's mates who didn't like hunky Yankees. One night on the midwatch, this one officer from Georgia was on controls and I was at the helm. He started running down the Yankees and hunkies—meaning me. He was on it for a while and said that any self-respecting Southern girl would never go out with a Yankee, especially a hunky Yankee. I finally said, "Sir, one of these nights you're going to turn up missing at sea with bullshit talk like that." Of course he put me on report, but it all ended after I was called before the skipper and told him the story. But this officer kept on my back from then on.

We all had nicknames. Mine was Greek and his was Cowboy. I was in the wheelhouse one day when Cowboy yelled from below, "Hey, Greek, go tell the cook to make some cherry pies." I went down to the galley and told Christian what Cowboy wanted and he said he had no shortening to bake pies. I went back to the wheelhouse and yelled down to Officers' Quarters, "Hey Cowboy, Christian don't have any shortening to make the pies." Then I went back to the galley. I no sooner started talking to the cook when Cowboy came sliding down the ladder. He said to Christian, "When I give an order for pies, if you're out of shortening I don't give a damn if you have to use axle grease. I want pies. Do you understand?" Christian said, "Yes, sir." Then Cowboy turned to me and said "As for you, Greek, I am an officer in the United States Navy and I am to be addressed as 'Sir.' Understand?" He turned to leave. I said, "Sir, I am Pappas, gunner's mate. From now on you do not call me 'Greek.' That name is only for my shipmates."

So we had our orders to make cherry pies. I really hated to do this to the skipper, but there was no other way. In the medical locker were fifteen or twenty brown bottles of medical supplies, a "pill for every ill." One of them was a full bottle of laxatives. We took about one-third of the bottle, crushing the pills into powder and cooking them in with the cherries for the pie. We used cooking oil for the crust—not too bad, a little hard. We used two big baking pans, one for the officers and one for the crew. Of course the crew didn't get the laxative pie.

I didn't see the officers for a couple of days; then I got to the skipper and was talking to him about nothing in general. He mentioned the pie and how good it was, but he said the cooking oil we used gave all three officers the runs. Day and night they took turns running to the head. I was sorry the skipper had to suffer along with the two rebel officers.

Our ports were every island in the Caribbean and some in South America. Name a port and we were there picking up or dropping off freighters or tankers. I got to know all about standing watches—bridge, helm, sonar, radio and radar watches. I was six feet three inches tall and the skipper made me helmsman because I was pretty good at it and could lay the ship right into its berth like putting a baby in its crib. We had two possible sub sinkings, one off Cuba and one off Devil's Island, but you know "possible" ain't fact. Remember how the fish came up after a depth-charge run? I had made a beautiful harpoon and I used to get tuna five or six feet long. We cut off filets and tried cooking them. They looked just like a big hunk of beef, but they didn't taste right. When I got home I found out from my dad how to prepare tuna. He said you have to soak them in salt water to draw out the blood.

A few times we went through the Canal into the Pacific to train destroyers for antisubmarine tactics. On one occasion a destroyer sent us a message, "Heading back to port at twenty-six knots. Can you keep up?" We said, "Let's go." Guess what. The destroyer crapped out and we had to tow it back into Panama City.

Once we were at an island where there were some rocks offshore and some of the crew off a sub we were operating with were tossing lines out in an attempt to fish. I was swimming nearby. I liked to swim under water. These guys started catching sharks. I kept on swimming until I saw a fish about two or three feet long with a big grin and a mouth full of teeth. When I got back aboard ship the skipper chewed me out for swimming with the sharks. I told him I wasn't afraid until I saw that fish with all the teeth. He really went bonko. He said, "You crazy Greek son-of-bitch, that was a barracuda!" At the time I didn't know—never heard of a barracuda.

After maybe a year we got orders to head up to Seattle. Went through the Canal and went to San Diego, San Francisco, then to Seattle. That's when we hit a hurricane, or rather the hurricane hit us. Talk about rough. Our radio, radar, and sonar were gone, as well as the crew and the officers, especially the two rebel officers. They were as good as dead from being seasick. A motor machinist' mate and I had almost complete run of the ship. We took turns at watch, he at the helm, me on the flying bridge. All we had for chow was eggs and more eggs. We cooked them in an electric coffee urn we had installed while in San Diego. We had no communication for two days. We switched watches, taking turns at the helm.

The captain gave me the helm and went below for a minute. I was looking out through the ports and dead ahead I saw a dark object getting closer. I figured it out and swung the ship about in a hurry. It was the coast of Washington the hard way. At about that time we started to pick up a woman's voice over our radio. It was a heavy overcast and no way in the world to get a fix. The woman's voice kept repeating over and over, "Ship on radar, we have you at such and such location. Take a heading west to [whatever]." Then after a while she told us to head north on course so and so. I was still at the helm. Then we were told to get on a course heading east for the Straits of Juan de Fuca. After what seemed forever it became calm and we were told to take out charts for Juan de Fuca.

The captain relieved me from the helm, the rest of the crew and officers seemed to come back to life and I went up on the flying bridge with the skipper to act as lookout. He said, "Greek, I'm putting you in for something, I don't know what, maybe the Medal of Honor for saving the ship." I don't know whether he was kidding or not, I was still seventeen years old, so I said, "What's a medal of honor?" He started to tell me, but I cut him short and said, "I ain't no hero. How about giving me my Third Class Gunner's Mate rating?" That's how I got to be Gunner's Mate 3c.

In Seattle we got new engines, then got orders to go to Alaska and the Aleutians, to train Russian officers. After training the Russians, we were to turn the ship over to them. We headed north through the inside passage. What a beautiful piece of country we passed! We saw a number of smoking volcanoes, and it was beautiful. I said it already, but believe me, it was something to behold. We stopped off at two ports—Ketchikan and I can't remember the other place—then went into Kodiak.

While in Kodiak some high brass had never seen a subchaser in action, so it was set up to take them on a little shakedown. The skipper put me on as helmsman that day. So we went out into the Bay of Alaska with a load of brass topside. The skipper ordered flank speed and right 10 degrees rudder. I went right the 10 degrees, then, forgetting, went the other 20 degrees, making it full right. Then it came. "What the hell! Greek, are you on right full rudder? LEFT full, not right!" So I swung left—left—left. The ship dipped so hard I could have sworn the radar dome touched the water. It was a thrill, believe me. The brass we had aboard went crazy. They were so thrilled at our ship's performance I wouldn't doubt they are still tossing that in on some of their war stories. We went through the whole general quarters drill for them, rockets, depth charges, the works.

From Alaska we went to the Aleutians—Unimak, Unalaska, Adak, Amchitka, Tanaga, Attu, Dutch Harbor—to train the Russian officers who were to take over our SC for the Russian navy. Each day we would go out in the North Pacific or the Bering Sea, and almost every two hours we would hold general quarters. In between I taught ordnance, along with seamanship. We were working with two Russian icebreakers, and they were monsters, really big ships.

There were hundreds of islands up there. I didn't know where we were most of the time. We were in the Bering Straits, the Chukchi Sea, and the East Siberian Sea at times. We didn't have to worry about ice, since we had both Russian ice breakers beside us at all times. We anchored every night in a different location. I made the Russians wind in the anchor each morning, since it was a tough-ass job. I don't remember the water being rough but it was always cold, really cold—and misty. It's the kind of cold that penetrates and you never felt warm. The only shower, when you felt like one, was with cold salt water, using saltwater soap. Funky, dirty, filthy, 99 percent of the men had beards. You could never feel clean right after a shower.

The two Russian ships had a lot of women aboard. They were all big, fat, and ugly but very nice people. I was aboard both of the icebreakers many times to have chow. Something like the British, it was tea, tea, tea all the time. The Russians also had chow aboard our ship. You remember how our jellies were in gallon tins? Almost every day I would break out a tin and the Russians would dig into it with their hands, grabbing a fistful and jamming it into their mouths. They had jam or jelly all over their faces and smeared it on whatever piece of ordnance we were working on at the time.

The day came that I'd been dreading, when I was to be transferred from my ship back to the States. A longboat came by and picked me up. I made my goodbyes to my shipmates, which really didn't affect me too much until about a hundred yards out, when I looked back and then I broke down and cried because I had lost my ship. I know for a fact that there is not a sailor in all of history who did not love his ship and feel as I did when he had to leave her. Ain't it something? All ships have male names but a seaman always refers to his ship as "she" or "her."

There were a lot more things that happened and I can still remember most all of them, but they are about liberties and brawls, drunks, and destruction.

10

Adventures in the South Pacific

The trickle of new warships didn't begin arriving in the South Pacific until early in 1943, because the navy first had to concentrate what little power it had to fight the Battle of the Atlantic and meet the demands of the war in Europe and the Mediterranean. A group of nine subchasers arrived in Nouméa, New Caledonia, in January 1943, making the crossing in twenty-one days under their own power. Sailing in the company of several other ships, they provided the convoy with antisubmarine protection. The navy oiler USS *Tallahassee* acted as their mother ship, supplying them every three days while under way with food, fuel, and water.

The young crews got plenty of training in seamanship during the refueling exercises, particularly when the seas ran heavy. One night SC 504 went alongside the *Tallahassee* for the purpose of refueling and replenishing water. A motor machinist's mate accidentally reversed the lines, allowing one fuel tank to be filled with water and one water tank to be filled with diesel oil. Later that evening, when switching tanks, the engines suddenly sputtered and died. The convoy steamed along, unaware of the 504's plight, now dead and adrift in the vast Pacific. The quartermaster hurriedly aimed his signal lamp in the direction where he thought the *Tallahassee* would be and signaled for help. Fortunately, they saw his signal. After they learned of the 504's plight, they signaled "Rig for towing," then, making a wide circle, the tanker came back, and without stopping, shot a monkey fist and line over to the helpless 504 and took it in tow. The crew spent several hours cleaning up the mess, cursing the man who had caused it in the first place. From that time on until the end of the war, they never got the taste of diesel out of their drinking water. The unlucky motor machinist's mate bore the brunt of his shipmates' derision for the remainder of his duty aboard the 504.[1]

Pacific convoys in those days took the southern route in order to avoid contact with the enemy as much as possible. It was a route that brought the young farm hands and grocery clerks who had never been away from home to islands of storybook beauty—islands with romantic names like Tahiti, Bora Bora, Pago Pago, and the Fijis. At each of these they made brief, but memorable layovers that occasionally resulted in an over-rambunctious crew member or two being placed on report for being AWOL or worse. Still waiting for them ahead lay islands with strange names that would become etched in their minds, names like Kolombangara, Espíritu Santo, Tulagi, Munda, Efate, Rendova, Vella Lavella, and Guadalcanal. Street-tough city kids and downy-cheeked farm boys on the ocean for the first time in their lives gazed in awe at sunsets that flooded the entire sky in brilliance, bathing the ocean orange-red as the burning ball sank below the horizon. And then when night closed in the stars—millions of stars—stretched across the sky. Fifty-seven years later, old SC graybeards still remember honing their skills as young navigators, taking sights on the limpid diamonds of the Southern Cross, a galactic jewel of a constellation seen only in the Southern Hemisphere.

When the ships reached the equator, there were ceremonies in store for the "pollywogs"—those who were crossing zero latitude for the first time. On most of the SCs hardly anyone, including the officers, had ever been below the equator. Ceremonies were at the discretion of the commanding officers, with mild hazing, haircutting, running a gauntlet of paddles, hosing, walking a greased plank etc., after which the polliwogs were declared by King Neptune to be "Shellbacks"—veterans of the sea.

Christmas came during that first voyage and Lt. Dudley P. Towne, the twenty-one-year-old CO of SC 504, held worship for members of his crew down in the radio shack, an experience he recalls today with a shake of his head and a remark to the effect he wouldn't care to see a recording of that effort.[2]

So it was that early in February, SC 504, SC 505, SC 521, SC 531, and SC 668 arrived in the Solomon Islands—an area which, only a few weeks before, had been the scene of several great naval battles in the straits between Florida Island and Guadalcanal. The first SCs to arrive on the scene, their officers and crews, were looking forward to their assignments, whatever they might be.

Their reception at Guadalcanal/Tulagi was less than auspicious. The admiral in command was deeply preoccupied with grave matters resulting from the sinking, only a few nights before, of the cruiser USS *Chicago* in the Battle of Rennel Island. The base was being harassed daily by Japanese Betty bombers. The admiral had been expecting reinforcements in the form of heavy cruisers and carriers. When the only vessels to show up were a handful of pint-sized wooden subchasers, he was furious.

Unaware of these things, Lt. William E. Reid, commanding officer of SC 505, in accordance with navy protocol, innocently sent a message to the admiral announcing their arrival. When he received the admiral's reply, he was shocked to read, "We're fighting a war here. We don't need you. We don't want you. If we want you later we'll let you know." Thoroughly chastened, Reid conferred with his fellow officers about what to do next. He decided to ask the admiral for an audience. He was similarly rebuffed. The admiral would neither acknowledge the 505's presence nor agree to see anyone from the ship. The frustrated Reid was only able to console himself with the knowledge that his sister subchasers had received similar rejections. They were like a group of ugly ducklings spurned by their mother duck.[3]

For a month they lay idle and unemployed, feeling as useless as flotsam. The crews spent the time reading, writing letters, playing Acey Ducey,[4] and envying the bigger ships as they went about the business of fighting a war that did not include them. On the 505 the crew amused themselves by practicing underwater diving, equipped with a stolen diving helmet and a hand-operated pump. At night they tracked a lone Japanese observation plane that routinely came over and which they nicknamed "Washing Machine Charlie" for its rattling engine noise. They were eager to shoot him down, but the captain vetoed the idea because part of Charlie's plan was to draw fire to help him locate antiaircraft guns. From their anchorage in Tulagi they had a perfect view of the nightly air raids at Guadalcanal, watching the bigger ships and shore batteries sending up fire, like little kids watching their big brothers on a playing field. Their only shipboard excitement during this period was to light off the engines every few days and cruise around to beg food and water from whatever ship or shore facility felt generous enough to give it to them.

There being no liberty port in the jungle-infested islands, the morale of the subchaser crews and officers dropped to near-zero. Diversions were scarce. Some crew members adopted ship's pets—monkeys, grungy dogs, cats, and cockatoos—but the beleaguered animals lived precarious lives, not only due to their surroundings but because every subchaser had a sailor or two aboard who loathed animals. Thus would ensue a battle of wills between the animal lovers and haters, a battle invariably lost by the animals themselves when they were cruelly and clandestinely tossed overboard during a midwatch at sea. The instances of "petricide" would have filled a court-martial docket for years.

Finally, after four weeks of idleness, the SCs were grudgingly accepted by the Guadalcanal/Tulagi command, presumably as necessary evils more than as useful weapons of war. Their very presence was their only trump card, since it was obvious that they might as well be used for something other than continuing as the beggars they had become. They began to take on rudimentary assignments like patrolling harbor entrances, escorting ships to and from various islands, and ferrying personnel.[5]

SC 504 was assigned the lowly task of ferrying passengers and mail between Tulagi and Guadalcanal, a job that had to be done by someone, even a proud little warship like a subchaser. Once, while 504 was ferrying several very senior army officers, the harbor was attacked by Japanese dive-bombers. The captain instructed them to go below to the forward crews quarters to be out of the way. The gasoline tanker AOG *Kanawah* was hit during the attack and the 505, standing close by, assisted in beaching the sinking ship on the side of the main channel to keep the harbor open. When the raid was over the VIP passengers returned topside, their faces ashen, saying little, and disembarking as quickly as possible. No volunteers for the navy would ever be found from that group.

The 504 took a marine surveying crew aboard for several days to take a survey of the waters around the Russell Islands, about fifty miles northwest of the protected areas in Guadalcanal/Tulagi. The work was conducted during daylight hours, and when night fell the ship worked its way into a small, shallow inlet, where the men covered it with palm fronds to hide from the enemy still occupying the islands. The survey was successful, but it was never used, since the Russell Islands were bypassed in the U.S. offensive.

Another time the 504 rendezvoused with a U.S. submarine to relieve it of a group of coast watchers who had been compromised and were in immediate danger of capture. The group included two Catholic nuns.

By March of 1943 production of ships in the United States had improved to the point where greater attention could be given to the Pacific war. More and more ships were arriving daily to bolster the small fleet, which had been scattered so thinly throughout New Caledonia, the Solomons, and the eastern Australian coastal areas. Several convoys of ships made the long voyage across the Pacific with large numbers of infantry- and tank-landing craft and an increasing number of SCs, minesweepers, and other patrol craft. One of these convoys was escorted by SC 730, SC 518, SC 641, SC 648 (my ship), SC 698, SC 701, SC 739, SC 751, SC 760, SC 761, and SC 982, all arriving at Nouméa or other points by the end of March.[6] Of these, the 730, 641, 761, and 982 were sent to the Guadalcanal/Tulagi area and the others were dispatched to Brisbane and to the west coast of Australia.

The time was quickly approaching for the United States to take the offensive. Vella Lavella, a mountainous, jungle-covered island with no good harbor, largely ignored by the Americans and used only as a barge stop by the Japanese, was settled upon as a worthy target. Admiral Halsey and his staff believed it could be made into a good fighter-plane base. A landing took place at Barakoma Beach on 15 August. Twelve LCIs (Landing Craft, Infantry) carrying 4600 officers and men from the army, marine corps, and Seabees, and several high-speed APD transports, were used for carrying troops, while twelve destroyers and two SC subchasers provided escort and screening services. The SCs picked for this, one of the earliest amphibious landings in the Pacific, were SC 760 and SC 761,[7] though their duties did not include that of control vessels at the beachheads. Instead, they were assigned to furnish antisubmarine patrol at the two ends of Gizo Strait.

While on this assignment they were attacked by Japanese torpedo bombers—the only immediate enemy response to the surprise landing. The two subchasers had their first taste of exchanging fire with the enemy and maneuvering wildly to avoid bombs. Fortunately the bombs splashed nearby, with no direct hits or damage. The destroyers *Conway* and *Eaton,* partners in the same screen, had their hands full laying down smoke and dodging torpedoes. It was a hot little attack, full of escapes and near misses, but not a single American ship was damaged. Samuel E. Morison, naval historian, wrote of this fracas: "Besides luck there was a sound plan, fine shooting, well-laid smoke screens, smart shiphandling, and plenty of plain courage."[8]

In the days following, the destroyers withdrew, leaving a skeleton group of patrol craft for screening the unloading of supplies and equipment at the beach. SC 505 was conducting an antisubmarine patrol outside the roads into Barakoma Beach, where three LSTs were unloading, when it was attacked by five Japanese dive-bombers. Coming in fast on the port quarter, the planes strafed the little ship and dropped five bombs. Zigzagging at flank speed, the

505 returned fire with its 20-mm and 40-mm guns. No bombs hit the ship but near misses damaged the sound gear and the ship's electrical system. The last bomb dropped landed twenty feet off the port bow, causing the ship to heel over at a 65-degree angle and inundating the deck with two feet of water. One man was hit by shrapnel, while several others suffered minor injuries as a result of being tossed about the ship. Smoke was streaming from one plane as it disappeared behind the hills and crew members were certain they had hit it. Adm. T. S. Wilkinson, commander of the invading task force, took notice of this in a letter to Admiral Halsey: "The spirited defense of this small vessel alone against a heavy dive-bombing attack was highly commendable."[9]

Subchaser Sinks Sub

SC 669 was the only subchaser in the entire war to receive official credit and recognition for sinking an enemy submarine. It happened not far from the harbor entrance to the island of Espíritu Santo in the Solomons when, at 1045 on the morning of 29 May 1943, SC 669 picked up a positive, clear, submarine contact with her echo-ranging gear. Lt. Frederic Gibbs, commanding, immediately called the ship's company to general quarters and prepared to attack with mousetraps and depth charges. After fifteen minutes of tracking and maneuvering, the 669 dropped five depth charges, but no indications of a hit came to the surface, not even an oil slick. They radioed authorities at the navy base with an account of the attack.

Continuing the search, at 1130 the 669 regained contact three miles from the channel entrance. Swinging about, and carefully maneuvering into firing position, Gibbs gave the order to fire at a range of eight hundred yards. Seconds later, eight mousetrap projectiles arced from her deck and splashed into the water three hundred feet ahead. Eighteen seconds later, two out of the eight mousetraps exploded, indicating a direct underwater hit on a hard object. Circling, the 669 returned to the site of the explosions and straddled it with three depth charges.

Seconds passed as they circled the area, searching for some sign of a hit in the roiling water. Suddenly a giant air bubble broke the surface, followed by another. Then the water darkened and an extensive oil slick spread out from where the bubbles were seen. Several small pieces of wood and a part of a life jacket floated to the surface. Samples of the oil were taken and the piece of life jacket was recovered and examined. It consisted of a sack of coarse cotton material, about eighteen inches square, containing a stuffing resembling kapok. A further sonar search failed to regain contact.

At 1220 PC 477 took charge, instructing the 669 to stand by and continue searching. At 1348 PC 477 dropped several depth charges, but no evidence of a hit came to the surface. At 1420 DD 449, the *Nicholas,* arrived on the scene and took over the search but also failed to pick up any contact. After an hour or so the *Nicholas* left the scene while ordering the 669 to continue patrolling, which she did until 0800 the next morning without further contacts. A search of the area was made by fathometer soundings from the destroyer USS *Sumner* without result.

The written opinion of analysts delegated to assess whether or not it was a kill stated: "Charts do not show any wrecks in the vicinity. From the time the first contact was made until the wreckage was observed, the target was reported to have moved some three and one-half miles. The air bubbles, oil slick, small pieces of wood and part of a life jacket might well be the only wreckage coming to the surface through the comparatively small hole a mousetrap explosion would produce. It is believed that the target was in fact a submarine and was probably sunk."

That a Japanese submarine was sunk in that area has been confirmed by historians. In their book, *The Japanese Submarine Force and World War II,* Carl Boyd and Akihiko Yoshida list the Japanese submarine RO-107 as having been "lost to a U.S. destroyer off Kolombangara Island, Central Solomons at 0450 on 12 July 1943."[10] The identity of the attacking vessel, the location, the time, and the date of the attack are incorrectly listed but are close enough to the confirmation found in *Jane's Fighting Ships 1947–48*: "R.O. 107, 525 tons, sunk by U.S. Subchaser SC 669 May 28, 1943 05.35S 167.17E. New Hebrides, 30 miles W. of Cape Lisburn, Espíritu Santo Is."[11]

The final endorsement and proof is to be found in OpNav-P33-100 New 5-46 from the Chief of Naval Operations, Navy Department, which states: "28 May 1943 RO-107. Cause of sinking: U.S.S. SC 669. Position 15 35'S, 167 17' E." This stamp of authority laid to rest any further doubts, and historians can rest in the knowledge that SC 669 did indeed sink a Japanese submarine.

An Easter Sunday

According to Lt. Carroll F. Sweet, commanding officer of SC 738, any skeptic who may have been aboard his subchaser on Easter Sunday, 25 April 1943, was about to have an experience that would give him food for thought.

The 738 was one of the SCs early on the scene in 1943 in the southwest Pacific. She was assigned to the then tiny Seventh Fleet being organized under the command of Rear Adm. Daniel E. Barbey, who took his orders

SC 669, the only SC subchaser in World War II credited with sinking an enemy submarine *National Archives*

from Gen. Douglas MacArthur, Supreme Commander of Southwest Pacific Forces. The 738 and several other subchasers operated out of Brisbane, Australia, doing mostly escort and patrol work up and down the coast.

On this particular date, SC 738 and another SC were escorting a convoy along the east coast of Australia. Moving at a slow five knots, they were proceeding northeast from Moreton Bay (Brisbane) with plans to go inside the Great Barrier Reef and terminate at Townsville, some 250 miles north of Brisbane. The 738 was screening for submarines on the starboard bow, the other SC on the port bow of the convoy.

The lead ship of the convoy was HMAS *Kurumba,* an Australian fleet tanker. She was flanked by two smaller cargo ships loaded with ammunition. Behind this tier were the *Van Vlissenberg,* a coal-burning interisland transport from the Netherlands East Indies loaded with Australian troops, and a Norwegian tanker, *Nord.* The captain of the *Kurumba* was the convoy commodore and Sweet's ship, the SC 738, was screen commander since he was senior escort officer. The CO of the other subchaser was a young but experienced officer who had taken over command only a few days before.

Enemy submarines were active along the Australian coast at that time and a number of ships had been torpedoed and sunk, particularly ships that had been traveling alone without escort, then in very short supply. At the pre-sailing conference it was made clear that the *Nord,* capable of somewhat higher speed than the other ships, was destined for Rockhampton and would, when the convoy was east of that city, be detached and proceed to port independently.

Following standard procedure, battle stations on the escorts were manned an hour before sunrise, a time when the waters are still too dark for lookouts to spot low-lying submarines, but surface ships, with superstructures outlined against a clearing sky, are increasingly visible to submarines. When dawn broke the *Van Vlissenberg* was nearly a mile behind its station. At this slow speed, an aggressive submarine could easily maneuver undetected into a position to attack. The convoy commodore quickly recognized this problem and, when daylight permitted use of flashing light signals, he and the escorts tried, without success, to get her back on station. The *Van Vlissenberg*'s captain claimed his Malay stokers either could not or would not shovel coal any faster.

Meanwhile, since they were off Rockhampton, the *Nord* was detached and proceeded to head west independently as agreed.

Lieutenant Sweet decided to take drastic action with respect to the *Van Vlissenberg.* He signaled to the other SC: "Round up straggler and return." The subchaser immediately increased speed and changed course to the west. Sweet expected her to go to the rear of the formation and circle the convoy flank. But when he saw her heading west he realized that she was mistakenly heading for the *Nord.* He began signaling her with flashing light. For some time there was no response to his signal and the SC continued westward at high speed. Finally she signaled back saying she was ready to receive messages. But at that very moment the bulb in the 738's signal light blew out and they were unable to send.

Frantically, they looked about the bridge for a replacement bulb but couldn't find one. Someone went aft in great haste to get one from the lazarette. By the time they finally got the signal light working the SC was so far away that Sweet had time to blink only two words: "Come back." Fortunately she must have understood, because she came about. Sweet then directed her to proceed to the *Van Vlissenberg,* which was now farther behind than ever. The SC took a course that would intercept her, crossing the port quarter of the convoy, an area through which the ships had already passed. As they watched her they saw her suddenly stop and come about. Then came her signal, "Am picking up survivors. Request permission to search for more."

Survivors? Survivors from what? Sweet suddenly realized this probably meant a ship had been sunk from torpedoing. And the submarine responsible for the torpedo could still be in the vicinity, perhaps watching them this very moment, and even maneuvering to fire at one of the ships. The 738 was now the lone escort leading the four-ship convoy, the only defense against real danger lurking nearby. The convoy's safety became Sweet's primary mission. Yet to deny the SC's request might doom some men who could already see their prayers being answered. After one of those lonely moments known only too well by ships' captains when a decision has to be made quickly, Sweet signaled, "How long?"

The word came back, "Thirty minutes."

Sweet responded, "Permission granted."

He ordered the ship to general quarters and increased speed to broaden the patrol area. They listened carefully for an echo on their sound gear and scanned the sea all around for a periscope "feather." The thirty minutes seemed like three hours. Finally the last second ticked away and the little SC headed at top speed for the *Van Vlissenberg*. She was alongside the straggler for only a few moments, then returned to her station on the port bow of the convoy. She reported that she had picked up eleven survivors of a southbound ship[12] that had been steaming without escort when torpedoed the night before. Men were still missing but the SC found no sign of them after a reasonable search. It was concluded that they had either been lost in the sinking of the ship or had fallen prey to sharks during the night.

The survivors said they had seen the convoy outlined against the backdrop of the breaking dawn and had done their best to attract its attention, but lost all hope of rescue when it passed by without seeing them.

This could have happened on any day of the year. But this wasn't just "any day." This was 25 April 1943—Easter morning—a day that took on a very special meaning for those survivors of the torpedoed ship. Through a set of improbable circumstances and blunders, the SC was suddenly in exactly the right spot to find them. When ordered to round up the straggler the skipper, who should have known better, pursued the wrong ship. This act alone took him off course. Then when he was so slow in responding to the 738's first signal, he kept going farther off course. When he finally responded, what caused their signal lamp to blow out at exactly the same moment, making it impossible to order him back? And why didn't the 738 have a bulb replacement on the bridge (as was usual), causing several more minutes to pass while the SC continued at high speed on the wrong course? When the SC finally headed for the *Van Vlissenberg,* her course crossed the exact spot where the exhausted survivors were still floating. Without these accumulative blunders, the eleven men would certainly have been passed by and would have perished.

On that Easter morning could everyone involved have been "brushed by the hand of God," as Lieutenant Sweet so firmly believes?

Oh, yes—the SC was hardly back on station when black smoke began pouring from the stack of the straggling *Van Vlissenberg.* Soon she began moving up. When she was back on station, Sweet breathed a sigh of relief. But she didn't slow down. She kept on coming at high speed. Soon she was in the front of the convoy and abreast of the escorts. She surged even further ahead before, finally, she slowed down and gradually dropped back into her proper position. This she dutifully maintained for the rest of the voyage. It seems that when the captain told his recalcitrant stokers that a ship had been torpedoed and only a few survivors had been recovered, they suddenly found new life and shoveled coal so fast that for some time he was unable to control the vessel's speed.

The Captain's Disappearance

How would you like to be second in command of a subchaser at sea off Papua New Guinea, and learn that your captain is missing? Lt. (jg) Albert L. McNomee, USNR, [13] executive officer of SC 741, faced this problem one morning in October 1944 when the quartermaster informed him that the captain, Lt. (jg) Bertram W. Meershaw,[14] USNR, was nowhere on the ship and had not been seen by anyone for four hours.

Lieutenant McNomee's worst fears had turned into stark reality. For the past several weeks the captain had been acting strangely, and McNomee had been pondering what, if anything, should or could be done about it.

There was the time, for instance, when they were ordered to escort a Dutch freighter from Langemak Bay, Finschhafen, back down to Milne Bay. The trip turned out to be a farce because one engine was down and the 741 could only make eight knots, whereas the Dutchman took off at eleven knots and after an hour they never saw her again. When they arrived at Milne Bay the captain stormed in to the port director and said the next time a freighter disobeyed his orders he would fire a shot across her bow! The port director merely shrugged and asked him if he had noticed the five-inch gun on the freighter's stern.

Then there was the time the captain submitted a stack of job orders to base repair as big as a double deck of playing cards. A few were essential, but many were trivial or even comical, like the order to elevate the stanchions along the after deck to permit slinging a tarpaulin as a sunshade (making it impossible to train the guns). The base lieutenant stopped that one in a hurry. He altered the forward blowers to permit more air in the crew's quarters, but they leaked badly. He built a huge air intake along the starboard side of the pilothouse to bring more air into the wardroom and cut a vent over his bunk for personal comfort. It leaked. Then he rigged the dinghy for sail, when they badly needed an outboard to expedite supply.

One of the strangest things Meershaw did was while they were in dry dock. The base lieutenant discovered him systematically boring holes on either side of the keel under the ship's compartments, an old wooden boat sailor's trick for draining and cleaning the bilges. But in the navy no captain can change the watertight integrity of his ship without the permission of BuShips (Bureau of Ships). This time the base lieutenant gave Meershaw an ultimatum: Be out of dry dock and ready for sea by 0800 the following day! The holes were plugged, the bottom painted, and they were launched and out of there pronto.

Captain Meershaw did not fit the mold of the usual subchaser skipper. He was thirty-nine years old, whereas most SC skippers were in their early or mid twenties. He was independently wealthy, had owned a sixty-five–foot schooner before the war, and was a member of the Cruising Club of America. He was a sailor at heart but, in McNomee's view, not much of a navy man.

For six months SC 741 had been operating in various patrol and escort work along the coast of New Guinea, New Britain, and the Admiralties. At noon on 30 September the ship cleared the harbor at Milne Bay, having received secret orders to proceed independently to Hollandia and stage for the Philippine invasion. The 741 had never been in combat. That afternoon they held their first antiaircraft target practice during Meershaw's tenure as captain. They expended forty-five hundred rounds of ammunition without once hitting the target being towed by a target plane.

At 2000 that evening Meershaw called Lieutenant McNomee down to the wardroom. He was very upset about the dismal target practice. He appeared very unnerved, flushed and trembling. He told McNomee he had lost confidence in the crew and more importantly, in himself. He felt that if he went on he would surely put the ship on a reef, but if he turned back he would face a court-martial for failing to carry out orders. He wanted McNomee's advice.

McNomee told him he believed he was suffering from operational fatigue. He pointed out that their orders stipulated a stop in Langemak Bay to pick up a ship's cook. McNomee suggested they continue on to Langemak where he could have a physical exam. If the doctor felt Meershaw had a bad case of fatigue, the worst that would happen would be a trip back to the States. Meershaw thought this was good advice, and McNomee left him in the wardroom. But he got hold of the pharmacist's mate and told him to give the captain a sedative. The pharmacist's mate gave him a double dose of phenobarbital. The sedative calmed the captain down and he slept for six hours, giving McNomee time to navigate a tricky cluster of reefs called Tufi Leeds and set a straight course for Langemak Bay.

Meershaw returned to the bridge at 0200 and for the next twenty-two hours never left it. Taking over the watch, he thought the compass was wrong. He ran a range near Buna that proved otherwise. That evening at 2000 he backtracked for two hours so he could arrive at Langemak in daylight. At midnight McNomee urged him to get some sleep. "Captain," he said, "You are so groggy and tired you are finding it difficult to function. You must get some sleep and John[15] can easily handle his normal watch." Meershaw had eaten nothing except a ham sandwich brought to him by the cook, and part of that lay on a plate on the flag bag. Unsteadily he left the bridge, returned to the wardroom, and fell on his bunk. Stoltz took the watch and McNomee waited until Meershaw appeared to be asleep. Then he turned in.

McNomee's wakeup call came at 0345 and he took over the watch from Stoltz, who returned to the wardroom to hit the sack. The sea was calm, the night was clear, and the course was straight for Langemak. McNomee estimated they would be there by 0700.

At 0615 he made landfall, but he did not call the captain because he wanted him to get as much sleep as possible. By now McNomee was convinced that something was seriously wrong and that if Meershaw would not go to sick bay he would ask the doctors to examine him on board.

At 0730 he put the ship right in the center of Langemak Bay and told the quartermaster to call the captain. The quartermaster returned to the bridge and reported that the captain was not in his bunk. McNomee ordered a search of all topside areas where a man might crawl or fall. The quartermaster reported that the captain was not aboard.

McNomee called the entire crew to quarters and asked who was the last man to see the captain. John Stoltz said that, when McNomee had relieved him, he had gone to the wardroom and the captain was in his bunk. After John went to the head, however, he noticed that the captain had left the wardroom. John thought he had gone up to the bridge.

At this juncture McNomee was convinced that Meershaw had jumped overboard in a suicide attempt. He had no idea how long he had contemplated the move after leaving the wardroom, but concluded that the best estimate was 0400.

McNomee sent an urgent priority message to the airstrip at Finschhafen, saying his captain was lost at sea and giving their latitude and longitude position at 0400. He requested a plane take off immediately to search the area. With a terrible feeling of loneliness and not knowing what else to do, he docked the ship and went ashore to find an admiral. The senior officer present was a Captain Bumpus, to whom he told the story at great length, concluding with his opinion that it was a suicide. Bumpus, a sympathetic listener, called in some legal officers. There was a lengthy discussion in which the legal counsel brought up the matter of criminal intent. Had someone pushed the captain overboard? McNomee quickly pointed out that Meershaw engendered pity rather than hatred, since there had been a large turnover of crew members and the new men had little experience with him.

At 1130 they were still discussing the problem in Captain Bumpus's office when a messenger handed the captain a wire that Meershaw had been found. He had been rescued alive by an Army picket boat convoying a group of LCVPs. A C47 plane had spotted him, dropped a green dye marker, circled the area, and then signaled to the picket boat.

McNomee left Captain Bumpus shortly after noon and returned to the ship to find Meershaw lying in his bunk, badly sunburned and suffering from exposure. The pharmacist's mate was attending him.

The captain, upon seeing McNomee said, "Mac, I've got my confidence back. We've wasted a lot of time, so let's get out of here!"

"Captain," McNomee said, "how do you explain that you have just spent more than seven hours in the water?"

"Oh, I slipped on some oil and fell over the side."

"Captain," said McNomee, "we are in deep trouble, and I have always found it best, when in trouble, to tell the truth. I just can't believe you slipped and fell overboard because I had the watch and I would have seen you or heard you call."

Meershaw paused for a moment, then said, "You're right, Mac, I didn't slip." He hesitated, then said, "I jumped." But before he could elaborate, two corpsmen from the base came down the ladder with a stretcher. They removed him to the base hospital.

At the hospital Meershaw confessed to the doctors that he had jumped over the side with the intent to commit suicide. He tried swallowing lots of salt water but that only made him sick. Then he changed his mind about suicide and decided to stay afloat as long as possible. He kicked off his shoes and trousers and tied knots in his shirtsleeves and used the shirt as a flotation device by trapping air in it. He remained afloat for seven hours with nothing but his shirt and a will that turned from despondency to strong resolve. He was fortunate that the sea was calm; otherwise he would have perished.

Meershaw stayed four weeks in the hospital and then was sent home to the States, where he received medical care. Lieutenant McNomee assumed command under Article 181 of Navy Regulations, taking the ship to the Philippines and serving as skipper until relieved in April 1945.

11

Arawe

The Harbor Nobody Wanted

"Unspoiled . . . a breathtaking country . . . land of amazing variety . . . lush tropical rain forests . . . pure white sandy beaches . . . balmy desert islands . . . stunning reefs . . . brilliantly colored coral . . . unrivaled hospitality . . . friendly smiles." Such images, from a travel folder that today advertises South Pacific tourist resorts, would not have been apparent to the men of Task Force 76 early on the morning of 15 December 1943, as they stealthily approached the fetid, steamy shores of Arawe on the west coast of New Britain. Their minds were concentrated on the tough little job at hand, which was to land troops of the 112th Cavalry Regiment[1] as quickly and silently as possible without the Japanese knowing about it.

Arawe was a last-minute substitute for a larger attack planned for Gasmata, farther east, that had been abandoned when the Japanese moved in additional troops to thwart such a move. The objective at Arawe was supposedly to establish a PT base, although Cdr. Morton C. Mumma, in charge of PT boats in the Southwest Pacific, argued forcefully that he wanted no part of Arawe, since he had all the bases he could use. An airstrip five miles east of Arawe was neither strategic nor was it an objective. The Japanese had been using Arawe for little more than a small staging area for barge traffic along the coast. General MacArthur himself might have been hard pressed to state a reason for taking Arawe unless it appealed to him, as to the proverbial mountain climber, "because it's there." Historian S. E. Morison summed it up best when he wrote that Arawe was "the harbor that nobody wanted."[2] Like the subchasers that would participate, the operation itself was small, hastily conceived, and unpopular.

The harbor at Arawe is a fairly large body of shallow, coral-infested water between an island and the mainland, with an inner harbor where most of the enemy were encamped. This inner harbor could only be reached by shallow-draft vessels winding their way through a tortuous, reef-bound channel. Numerous small islands dotted the area outside the harbor.

As amphibious landings go, Task Force 76 was minuscule compared to most, totaling only 36 ships altogether. Three subchasers and two APc coastal transports, APc 4 and APc 21, would be used on D-Day for guide boats, inner patrol, and rocket support. The subchasers picked for this ill-conceived assault were SC 699 for control vessel and SC 981 and SC 742 for rocket support. As to how specific ships were picked for various assignments, no one ever knew, nor did anyone ever question. Ships, like men, took their orders and carried them out.

The Arawe landing, small as it was, provided a number of firsts. One of these was the use of inflatable rubber boats to carry the assault troops for two subsidiary smaller landings an hour prior to the main landing. The inner harbor of Arawe was too shallow for LCIs and LSTs, the larger old standbys for carrying troops and tanks. Instead, LCR inflatable rubber rafts, each holding ten men, would paddle into the beach and make the assault. Ironically, the use of rubber boats seemed all too appropriate for an operation supported by ships of the Donald Duck Navy.

Still another first at Arawe was the use of a new type of amphibious craft for transporting and launching the weapons and troops for the main landing, which would follow the two rubber-raft landings an hour later. The USS *Carter Hall* (LSD-3) had joined the Seventh Amphibious Force only a few weeks previously. She looked like an ordinary cargo ship but was actually a "floating dry dock" that could carry all the amphibious vehicles in her hold. When in position and ready, she would let the hold be flooded, open the gates in her stern, and, like a mother turtle laying eggs, allow the "Alligators" (tractors) and "Buffaloes" (tanks) with their crews to crawl out under their own power. With their steel tracks they could climb over the many coral reefs in the path of approach and make their way to the beach.

Yet another first was the 112th Cavalry Regiment itself. This group of intrepid fighting men, later dubbed "The Little Giant of the Pacific," had turned in their horses in Nouméa and become an infantry unit assigned to MacArthur's Sixth Army. Their prior experience in amphibious landing was negligible—an unopposed assault on Woodlark Island in July and a practice landing on Goodenough Island only ten days before. They had never been in combat, but they were to prove themselves more than worthy of the task.

Finally, Arawe was to be the first assault in the Pacific that would support the ground troops with high-angle fire from rockets launched from subchasers.[3] The 981 and 742 had been equipped with rocket launchers to rake any spontaneous enemy fire from the beach minutes before the arrival of the first landing boats. Two amphibious "ducks" (DUKWs) were also armed with launchers.

A week before the landing a reconnaissance group had landed on a small beach a few miles east of Arawe, and after a few hours of reconnoitering returned and reported there were only a few Japanese in the vicinity and no real defenses. Their observations concurred with information gathered earlier by scouting planes. The group stated that they didn't think they had been observed by the enemy during their visit to the beach.[4] They were mistaken.

On 14 December, the day before the landing, the Fifth Army Air Force pasted Arawe with 433 tons of bombs. Then early in the morning on 15 December the ships of Task Force 76 approached, reaching the transport area at 0330. It was a bright, clear night, the moon had just passed full, the sea was calm, the visibility excellent.

Two APD attack transports stood by with the raiders who were to land first. At 0505 APD *Humphreys* and APD *Sands* launched fifteen rubber boats apiece, each laden with ten troopers. The boats from the *Humphreys* were equipped with small outboard motors that were to propel them to Pilelo Island for the purpose of capturing a Japanese radio station. The boats from the *Sands* had no motors and instead were propelled by the troops themselves, equipped with paddles. Their objective was a small beach a few miles east of Arawe designated Blue Beach. The beach was at the head of a cove dominated by steep cliffs. The planners believed a stealthy landing would take the enemy completely by surprise.

After the APDs launched the rubber rafts, the ones from *Humphreys* motored into Pilelo, met no resistance, and easily captured the radio station, using flame-throwers to eliminate a few of the enemy hiding in caves. The fifteen rubber boats from *Sands* began quietly paddling toward Blue Beach, guided by SC 699, which took them to a thousand yards from the beach and then stood by while the boats kept going in. No one knew or even suspected that the enemy had seen the reconnaissance scouts and had expected a landing to take place there. They had placed several heavy machine guns in sites that would enfilade the approaches.

The rubber boats were a hundred yards from the beach when the Japanese guns opened up. The staccato barrage of heavy machine gun fire and rifles swept among the boats with devastating results. Men thrown into the water with full packs drowned within seconds. Others were killed outright and many were wounded. Twelve boats were punctured immediately and sank. Survivors in the water struck out seaward to avoid being hit. APD *Sands* could hear the crackling of guns and see tracers of crossfire but, not knowing the exact location of the enemy emplacements, was forced to hold fire for fear of hitting the troops.

The 699, commanded by Lt. James E. Foristel, a lawyer from St. Louis, made her way toward the stricken boats. Under heavy fire from the shore emplacements, her men began pulling troops from the water. When it was over they had taken sixty-nine survivors aboard, fifteen of them wounded. Two dead men were also recovered.[5]

By this time the *Carter Hall* had disgorged her cargo of Alligators and Buffaloes, which then sloshed and clanked their way through the reefs to the beachhead in Arawe Harbor. SC 981 and two DUKWs fitted with four-and-a-half-inch rockets effectively silenced a machine gun that had been harassing this group.

The 699 headed for the Arawe beach,[6] but when she reached a point about fifteen hundred yards south of Pilelo on her way to discharge the survivors, fourteen Japanese Val type planes swooped in and began bombing the harbor and everything in it. All ships opened up in a furious barrage of antiaircraft fire. No bombs hit, but there were several near misses. One plane fell among the ships.

After a few minutes of eerie quiet, the low-flying Vals came in again at high speed, five of them aimed directly at the 699 and strafing. The 699, crowded with survivors huddled all about the ship, kept blazing away. One Val crashed on the beach, but, since other ships were also shooting at the same planes, no one could tell for certain which ship scored the kill. The planes disappeared over the hills as fast as they came in, and this time the 699 was able to transfer the survivors of the rubber-boat disaster to LCTs and LCMs (landing craft, mechanized), who took them ashore.

The beachhead was secured fairly easily with a total of 1,904 troops landed on D-Day.[7] However, the action was only just beginning to warm up. On 16 December a second echelon of LCTs was assigned to bring renewed supplies across from Finschhafen. SC 743, under the command of W. W. "Bill" Robinson,[8] led this group to provide navigation and additional firepower, such as it was. Also in the group were two APcs and the YMS 50, a minesweeper. Army engineers met the group at the entrance to Arawe harbor and, after instructing the LCTs which beaches to head for, told Robinson to report to the beach master to arrange for the return schedule after the LCTs had unloaded. The APcs also came in to unload, while YMS 50 remained on patrol outside the harbor entrance.

Just then Lieutenant Robinson, who was leaning over the side windscreen of the flying bridge talking to the beach master, saw a row of splashes zipping towards them across the water, aimed just forward of the pilothouse. At first there was no sound, but suddenly enemy planes had swooped in upon them, strafing and dropping bombs as they flashed by. All ships let loose, smoke filled the air, and the hills reverberated with noise. When it was over, Robinson looked down from the flying bridge and saw a large pool of blood on the deck amidships. Two men of the 743 were down on the foredeck, Kilgore[9] with no apparent mark on him and Gentry[10] face down with the middle of his back completely ripped away. Both men were loaders on the 40-mm gun. When they were knocked down, Worthington "Worthy" Adams, the executive officer, stepped in to load. Kittelsen,[11] on one of the 20-mm guns, had been hit on both inner thighs with a large piece of shrapnel. There were several bullet and shrapnel holes on the ship but no structural damage. The acrid odor of gunsmoke hung in the air.

Kilgore had been killed instantly, the only sign a tiny bullet hole in his chest, while Gentry had been hit mortally by shrapnel from an antipersonnel bomb. Kittelsen, seriously wounded and in shock from the loss of blood, was removed from the ship by stretcher. (He recovered and was able to rejoin the ship later.) Two other members of the crew received minor wounds, which were treated by the ship's pharmacist's mate.

The effect on the crew after this furious little battle was noticeable in the subdued quiet that followed. The deaths of two close shipmates—buddies—made them keenly aware of the stark reality of war, a war in which "even you" could possibly get killed or wounded. It was a time for sober reflection. After the first few days the shock gradually wore off, and there was a noticeable air of renewed pride and confidence about the ship and determination to see this through, come what may. Innocence was gone. The fuzzy-cheeked boys had grown up.[12]

The battle for Arawe was not over yet. The 743 continued its patrol of Pilelo and Arawe Islands, waiting for the LCTs, which seemed to be taking an inordinate amount of time to unload. At 2030 the 743 hove to a mile or so off Arawe, remaining dead in the water to keep phosphorescent wake from revealing her position to enemy aircraft. At midnight the ship again came to general quarters when enemy aircraft began bombing Pilelo Island by the light of a three-quarter moon. The ships held fire, since they were not under attack, but the pyrotechnic display was pretty frightening. One plane flew directly across the moon and dove, dropping a bomb in a wide burst of white light; then others, flying lower, dropped more bombs that gave off an orange glow. Heavy concussions were felt as each one exploded.

At 0145 a bright green flare descended east of Marklo Island and fizzled out with lots of smoke. The 743 got under way, slowly moving away, heaving to about two miles south of Pilelo Island. Five minutes later they spotted a single plane approaching from over Marklo Island. All ships opened fire

From her flying bridge, SC 743 displays four battle trophies.

as the plane kept coming in. It dropped a bomb between the 743 and YMS 50 and streaked down the 743's starboard side, two hundred feet above the water. They scored hits, but the plane kept on. Someone said he saw a splash. They cruised to the area and smelled lots of gasoline but saw nothing.

Shifting position to be nearer Kaprimati Island and less conspicuous if attacked again, the 743 moved very slowly to reduce its wake. At 0223 the Zeros returned. One came streaking in low, down their port side. They opened up with a furious barrage, hitting the plane, but it kept going until out of sight. It dropped a bomb that landed in the water 150 yards away, with no damage. They again shifted position, moving very slowly, and had proceeded only a half mile when another plane came flying across Arawe Island, her engine exhausts flaring bright orange. All ships opened fire, but the plane kept going until out of range. Minutes later a "Rufe" flew directly overhead, two thousand feet up. Their firing came close and the plane went immediately into a dive, leveled off and disappeared behind Marklo Island.

The attack was over. Robinson secured the men from general quarters and set Condition II with the starboard watch, all guns cocked, loaded, and manned. The port watch lay down at their battle stations. The night passed with no more attacks. At 0630 they began patrolling off Arawe, waiting for the LCTs to unload. At 0800, when the LCTs still had not appeared, APc 21 steamed in to find out what was causing the delay. Just then they were furiously attacked by several Val dive-bombers, protected by fighter planes. They came swooping in at a steep glide from the east, over Pilelo Island. While the ship opened fire on a fighter plane, a Val dive-bomber hurtled down and dropped a bomb that just missed them. But another Val made a direct hit on APc 21, blowing it up with a terrific explosion. By now the 743 was firing at a second fighter plane coming in low on the starboard quarter. Two Vals whizzed by from aft, banking and swooping to confuse the ship's fire. The sky was filled with American and Japanese planes in a furious dogfight. Planes came low around the end of Pilelo Island and headed for the 743 from astern. The men kept firing point blank as they came, then wavered, banked steeply to the right, and veered off. One, smoking badly, splashed off the end of Pilelo.

Circling back to the vicinity of where APc 21 had exploded (she sank in four minutes), the 743 began searching for survivors but discovered that they had already been picked up by army LCMs. Shortly after that, the LCTs finally emerged and the convoy for the trip back to Finschhafen got under way. In seventeen hours of continuous red alerts and air attacks at Arawe, the 743 expended 2,915 rounds of ammunition.

It still wasn't over. At noon on 21 December, six days after the initial landing, SC 738, having escorted another echelon of supplies to Arawe, was patrolling three miles south of Umtingalu, the village at Blue Beach. Because the enemy had daily continued its surprise air attacks, the ship was at general quarters and steaming at twelve knots. The CO, Lt. (jg) R. B. Woodcock, was on the flying bridge when one of his lookouts spotted a group of more than forty planes dead ahead. At first mistaken for friendly P-47s, they were actually Val dive-bombers, moving in a westerly direction at about eight thousand feet. They passed into the sun momentarily and suddenly several peeled off and commenced diving directly at the ship. The 738 was ready.

Woodcock ordered hard right rudder to make as small a target as possible. At 700 feet the two lead planes released their bombs. All guns on the ship opened fire, and one of the planes was hit. It turned west, smoke pouring out of it, losing altitude fast, and finally crashed west of Arawe. Another Val began smoking after pulling out of her dive but circled the ship two hundred feet above the water while they concentrated all their fire on her. She finally flew off, smoking badly. In the attack the enemy had dropped between fifteen and twenty high-explosive bombs, none of which hit the ship but which burst all about them. One bomb emitted yellowish fumes that no one could ever explain. Several smaller bombs were seen dropping, one type resembling an indoor baseball and another about three inches in diameter and fourteen inches long. No one on the ship was injured.

While this attack was going on, the 743, some distance away, saw black smoke pouring out of the 738 and believed she had been hit and was afire. The smoke was caused when the engines stalled while the ship was turning hard right. The Japanese thought they had set the ship on fire and released news—later retracted—about sinking a heavy cruiser in their next press report.

This attack over, Captain Woodcock and his men assessed the situation, all agreeing that another attack would follow. Repairs were made to the twin-mounted .50-caliber gun on the flying bridge that had jammed in the noon attack, and the men remained at general quarters. The ship's engines had performed so badly that it was likely they would fail completely in another attack, making her a sitting duck for enemy bombers. From previous tactics used by the enemy, they knew the attack would come from the west, from out of the sun. Woodcock decided to conduct antisubmarine patrol about a mile offshore between Umtingalu and Cape Ainto, with the idea in mind that, if an attack developed, the ship might escape notice by hiding north of Cape Ainto.

At 1700 the radio crackled with a report that sixteen unidentified planes were approaching Arawe from the northwest. Seconds later, spotters on the ship saw several groups of five planes each at twelve thousand feet. These were intercepted by Army P-47s and never got near the harbor. But only seconds after that a group of Zeros and Val dive-bombers screamed low over Cape Ainto, passing the 738's portside only five hundred yards away. Woodcock's forethought about hiding behind the cape proved wise. Only one of the planes spotted them, a Zero, which peeled off as it went around Cape Ainto and came in strafing. All guns on the 738 opened up at the Zero, which immediately began smoking and finally crashed in flames into the woods west of the ship. Immediately after that, seven planes turned and came in ragged formation to strafe the entire port side of the ship while being chased by two P-47s. The 738 was firing every gun point blank at the planes, two of which commenced smoking while the propeller of a third was blown off.

Like angry bees the planes continued to swarm around the cape and the ship. A Zero circled and came in strafing on their port bow. The 3-inch .50-mm jammed and gunner's mate Lloyd W. Ross jumped from his seat on the cannon and ran to the forward .50-caliber machine gun and began firing. A signalman, F. E. Brown, on the other .50-caliber, was also shooting. They could see the wing guns smoking as the plane continued strafing. One of its bullets hit Brown's gun cradle, nicked the left grip, and lodged in his neck. The gunners scored hits that killed the pilot, causing him to crash into the water by the mouth of the river. Brown kept insisting on remaining at his gun. They got the 3-inch/50 working again and scored a direct hit on a Val dive bomber, knocking its tail off and causing it to drop headfirst into the sea half a mile away. Two Zeros came in from the stern, both forced to turn away by the gunners on the 20-mm and 50-caliber guns on the afterdeck. The lead plane began smoking and hits were scored on both planes but they kept flying. More planes passed by with everyone blazing away, but they continued on course and there was no smoke.

Just how long this action lasted is hard to estimate, but it took a lot less time than it does to tell about it— perhaps only a few seconds! Scattered attacks continued. No one will ever know exactly how many planes rounded the cape that afternoon. Bill Robinson, observing from the 743, said there were so many planes flying around the 738 that they never expected to see anyone on board alive again. Miraculously, Brown was the only one wounded. He insisted in staying at his post, and they almost had to use force to get him away from his station long enough to be treated by the ship's pharmacist's mate.

In his official report of the attack, Lieutenant Woodcock, a fine officer, conservatively estimated that the ship had surely destroyed three planes, probably had destroyed three more, and damaged a minimum of five. He described the planes as "like ducks in a shooting gallery but considerably more vicious."[13]

The fight for the harbor nobody wanted was an empty victory in terms of the global war. Arawe was of little value to either combatant. Once secured, the harbor was never used by MacArthur's forces. Few people today ever heard of Arawe, since most historians have ignored it, but Samuel Eliot Morison had this to say about Arawe: "The heroes of the Arawe operation were the little fellows of the spitkits and the splinter fleet, faithfully landing their cargoes despite vicious air attacks and lack of protection from their own air force."[14] The brave sailors who lived through Arawe never forgot the harbor nobody wanted.

12

Dead End for Dead Reckoning

Standing on the barren shores of the North West Cape, Australia, you look across a roiling sea with angry surf pounding jagged rocks and spray-lashed coral reefs. Below the surface, tidal currents and undertows constantly ebb and flow, their force and direction changing with the moon, the time of day, and the seasons, influenced by ocean currents that begin as far away as Antarctica. Riptides, undertows, and cross currents on that desolate shore of western Australia are as unpredictable as the weather itself.

It was in this lonely spot on a wild, stormy night, 22 June 1943, that SC 751 met her fate, and it was here that Ens. Thomas K. Parkison, USNR, lost his life. Circumstances surrounding the disaster are obfuscated by missing log entries, unwritten night orders, and conflicting eyewitness statements. Nevertheless, the facts available point to a profound error in determining the ship's actual position. The captain's fix, based on his dead reckoning, placed the ship fifteen miles north of where it really was. This might be expected from an inexperienced navigator, but the captain of the 751 was an excellent navigator with years of experience and plenty of above-average intelligence.

When thirty-four-year-old Bobbie C. Davis, USNR, received his ensign's commission, he had twenty years' experience in yachting, ocean racing, and outside cruising under his belt. He was a true yachtsman, thoroughly grounded in small ship piloting and celestial navigation, well known in Tampa for his boating ability. Yet such are the ways of the sea, the winds, and thc ocean currents that no one, no matter how experienced, can ever leave anything to chance. The unfortunate demise of SC 751 originated with overconfidence in the captain's dead reckoning position, and was then compounded by a series of blunders at the time of changing the watch. Since the safety of a ship and its crew rests solely in the hands of the commanding officer, he has to bear responsibility for the result, whether good or bad.

Commissioned in June 1942, Davis zipped through sound school in San Diego and SCTC in Miami, and, because of his outstanding qualifications, was sent to Quincy, Massachusetts, to assume command of SC 751, still under construction. After the ship's commissioning on 27 November 1942, he took her on her shakedown cruise down to Florida, thence to Panama where, some time in January, he was joined by Ensign Parkison, who reported aboard to assume the duties of executive officer, with Ens. William D. Goldfarb, USNR, as third officer.

At Balboa the 751 and ten sister subchasers joined a large convoy of ships headed for the South Pacific, departing on 18 February 1943. Upon their arrival in Nouméa, the ships were sent to different places, some to the Solomons, some to Australia. The 751, in company with SC 739, proceeded to Brisbane and down the Australian coast, across the Australian Bight to the Indian Ocean, then up to Fremantle, from where she was assigned to patrol the harbor and escort convoys up and down the western Australian coast.

On 16 June 1943 the 751 received orders to escort SS *Ondina* from Fremantle to Exmouth Gulf in company with PY 10, the USS *Isabel.* Lt. Franklin D. Buckley, commanding the *Isabel,* was appointed SOPA (senior officer present afloat) for the two escorting ships. Departure, scheduled for 0730 on 17 June, was delayed for eight hours by a tropical storm that made visibility poor. The storm was actually a small hurricane, with high winds, lots of rain, and turbulent seas. It was still raging when they departed Fremantle at 1530 that afternoon.

During daylight hours the steaming formation consisted of the two escorting vessels in the lead, thirty degrees and fifteen hundred yards off the *Ondina.* At night the ships formed a column, with the *Isabel* leading, *Ondina* next, and SC 751 astern, the ships maintaining station fifteen hundred yards apart. Speed of the convoy was nine knots. They were buffeted by unceasing winds of Force 6 and 7 and very heavy seas; when it wasn't raining, the skies were gray and overcast.

On the 751 Captain Davis, unable to obtain sextant readings because of the overcast, constantly moved from chartroom to bridge and back, to plot and re-plot his estimated position. Steering was difficult, and the little ship struggled to maintain its station in the convoy. It pitched and rolled as only a subchaser could, pounding into every wave and sending great splashes of white flume across the deck as high as the bridge. The four-hour watches routinely changed, Goldfarb and Parkison taking their turns as officer of the deck (OD), and most of the time the captain stayed with them, either on the bridge or in the chartroom, occasionally going below for an hour or two for rest. This went on for three days, until, by the morning of 21 June, Lieutenant Davis had had only nine hours of actual sleep since departing from Fremantle.[1]

At 0930 on 21 June, Davis took what he believed was a good running fix by sighting bearings on a point known as Red Bluff. At that time the convoy was headed northerly on course 012 degrees (T) and was getting closer to the point at which they would turn east to proceed into Exmouth Gulf. The wind was coming across their starboard beam at eighteen knots and seas were still high. At 1525 he got another fix, this one doubtful, from the north point of a reef near what he believed might be Maud Landing. At 1610 the convoy changed course to 000 degrees (T) and at 1635 the course was changed to 340 degrees (T).

Exmouth Gulf is a body of water lying between the mainland and a projection of land called the North West Cape. Picture the mainland as the back of your right hand and the Cape as your thumb. The ships are slowly coming along outside your thumb towards a point on a line drawn at right angle from the thumb's tip. The space between the thumb and the hand is Exmouth Gulf. To make the turn and enter the Gulf, the ships would have to be north of, and well clear of, the tip of the thumb (North West Cape).

At 1739 Lieutenant Buckley, captain of the *Isabel,* sent the following message to the other two ships: "Will not enter tonight. At 1800 change course to north and begin zigzag plan 39. At 0200 change course to 104 degrees using same zig-zag plan." The words "Will not enter tonight" signified that, although the convoy would reach a point beyond the tip when it could safely turn east and enter the approach to Exmouth Gulf, the SOPA had decided to wait until daylight to ensure a safer passage. The course changes he directed meant they would continue north until 0200 and then turn to go east towards the coast (and eventually turn again to the south as they proceeded into the gulf).

With night approaching, the 751 took its position fifteen hundred yards astern of the *Ondina* and commenced zigzagging according to Plan 39. The winds had picked up to twenty-five knots, and the sea was getting even rougher. The speed of the convoy was estimated at 8.3 knots. Both the *Isabel* and the *Ondina* were displaying wake lights. A half hour before midnight, Captain Davis realized that they were gaining on the *Ondina,* so he ordered the 751's speed reduced to 7.5 knots.

Shortly before midnight, Ensign Goldfarb relieved Ensign Parkison of the watch. At midnight both lead ships extinguished their wake lights. Almost immediately, no one on the 521 could see the *Isabel.* Captain Davis, who remained around the bridge and pilothouse constantly, decided to increase speed in an attempt to catch up with the ships ahead. After an hour vainly trying to sight the *Isabel,* he increased the speed to 9.3 knots, hoping to regain station. But at 0145, with poor visibility, they realized that they had lost sight of SS *Ondina* also. SC 751 was now on her own.

At 0200 Lieutenant Davis ordered the course changed to 084 degrees (T) in accordance with Captain Buckley's instructions. They now found themselves running into a squall, with a gale wind blowing at thirty knots. The seas got heavier than ever, and waves began breaking over the pilothouse. Davis estimated his speed over the ground at eight knots. After half an hour steaming on 084 degrees, he changed course (as Buckley had previously ordered) to 104 degrees (T). At 0236 he eased back 4 degrees to 100 degrees (T). It was a wild night for the little ship on an ocean like that. Visibility was only five hundred yards.

At 0320, leaving Ensign Goldfarb in charge of the watch, Lieutenant Davis, very tired, went below to get some sleep. In the narrative report he wrote a week after the grounding, he stated that he orally instructed Goldfarb to awaken him at 0500.[2] But no such instructions appeared in his night order book, and Goldfarb denied having any recollection of such an order. The course the ship was maintaining (100 degrees (T)) headed them eastward, directly for the coast, but according to Davis's calculations their position was such that he would have plenty of sea room at the time of the wakeup call at 0500.[3]

For reasons that are not wholly clear, the captain was not awakened at 0500. At some time between 0530 and 0545, Ensign Parkison appeared, to relieve Ensign Goldfarb as officer of the deck. At 0550 Goldfarb had been relieved, Parkison had the watch, and the captain ostensibly was still below. At 0555 the ship struck and grounded fast on a reef. At the moment it happened the two officers were inside the pilothouse. Ryan, the quartermaster, who had been up in the crow's nest on lookout duty, was coming down the ladder to be relieved. In the officers quarters the captain, hearing and feeling the grind of the ship's bottom scraping the reef, sprang out of his berth and ran up the ladder to the bridge. Up to the moment of impact, no one had seen any white water breaking over any reefs.

Thus far we have related the facts as they seemingly existed, although they would be clouded by contradictions in later testimony and written statements. We shall return to the contradictions, but first let's see what happened to the 521 and her men after the ship struck the reef.

Reaching the deck while the ship was still bouncing, Captain Davis immediately stopped the starboard engine. The port engine had stopped on grounding. He tried throwing both engines in reverse, but the ship was listing to port. The starboard propeller was beating mostly at air and the port propeller, in contact with the reef, wouldn't budge. The ship was pounding on her bilge and taking water in the engine room and sound room. The transmitter generator was immersed in salt water, preventing use of the radio for sending messages. The main generators were secured because of the danger of short-circuiting.

Davis ordered all secret, confidential, and coded publications to be placed in weighted bags but refrained from throwing them overboard because they were in shoal water. He ordered both life rafts to be launched and secured alongside the ship by a painter.

It was morning and the seas had subsided somewhat. To the east, across the water about three and a half miles away, they could see a long low rise of land. By 0815 conditions looked good enough to attempt reaching land in the twelve-foot wherry. Selecting one officer and three enlisted men—Ensign Parkison, Del Fattore, Aceto, and Cifone[4]—Davis placed Parkison in charge and instructed him to make land as quickly as they could and find someone who could assist them. The wherry, with the four men, cast off at 0845. Parkison took with him the service records and the muster roll of the crew. By now the wind had abated to about twelve knots, and the sea within the reef was a short chop about eighteen inches high.

Moments after the wherry had departed, someone on the ship sighted the USS *Isabel* heading north, about a mile to westward. They broke out the Very pistol and fired three red shells as a distress signal to get the *Isabel*'s attention. But she kept steaming north, finally disappearing into a rain squall. They fired forty rounds from the 20-mm guns to attract attention. No sign of the *Isabel*. It began raining harder and visibility dropped to zero.

In the wherry, the men discovered they could make fairly good progress. They were about half the distance to shore, however, when a heavy squall struck. The rain closed in on them, and the wherry just bobbed around. The swells turned into high, slapping waves that broke over the wherry, dousing everyone and filling the boat with water. It took only two of these for the wherry to swamp and begin sinking. They got in the water, which was about chest high at that point, and clung to the boat. They tried to turn it over to empty it, but it bounced around, knocking them all about. It hit Aceto on his leg and then a can of emergency rations hit him hard in the head, stunning him. A big wave broke up the group. Aceto went under. When he came up he was alongside Del Fattore, who could see he was hurt and held on to him hard. The four men managed to get back to the wherry.

Because the rain had let up enough that they could see the ship, they decided to try to swim back. Del Fattore, holding Aceto, struggled, half swimming, half walking, rising and falling with each swell. Cifone, a strong swimmer, yelled to Ensign Parkison, who was still hanging onto the wherry, to try to make the ship. Twice he struggled over to Parkison to assist him, but Parkison would not let go of the wherry. Cifone decided he'd better go for the ship. The three enlisted men struggled through the heavy surf towards the 521.

From the ship the men had first seen the wherry about half of the distance to the mainland. It was then lost from sight in the rain squall. That was about 1030, and the wind was gusting at thirty knots. At 1100 they again sighted the wherry, a little closer to the mainland. But from that time on the wherry kept drifting to the south and losing distance from the mainland. At 1200 they could see the men in the water about one mile south of the ship. They were in the breakers and on the reef, making their way back to the ship by swimming and wading on the reef. As they got closer they could see that Ensign Parkison was outside of the breakers to seaward and that Del Fattore was supporting, carrying, and swimming with Aceto, and Cifone was swimming by himself. They were to landward of the breakers and on the reef. They saw Parkison swimming. He seemed to be making headway, although he was outside the breakers.

At about 1300 the three enlisted got back and were hauled aboard, severely chilled and bruised. At 1330 they could still see Ensign Parkison, outside of the breakers and swimming. A heavy rain squall closed in, blanketing everything. When it cleared they saw nothing. Ens. Thomas K. Parkison, USNR, a fine young officer, had disappeared and was never seen again.

Captain Davis ordered two more magazines of 20-mm to be fired as a distress signal. At 1800 he set a special lookout watch to change hourly. The tide came in and surf began breaking over the fantail, causing the ship to roll badly to port. Davis feared the ship might roll over on its side. He ordered the Very pistol to be fired, first at six-minute intervals, then every ten and fifteen minutes. The wind continued to increase and by midnight was blowing in the neighborhood of forty knots.

Shortly after midnight, Australian Army Forces, who had earlier been alarmed by the sound of 20-mm guns firing somewhere at sea, sighted the Very signals. They had armed themselves to the hilt when they heard the guns, thinking there might be some sort of invasion. But when they saw the Very signals they knew someone was in distress.

On the 751, after a restless night during which no one got any sleep, Captain Davis decided they had better abandon ship. The surf was pounding the ship so badly that he was afraid it could start breaking up. He ordered both life rafts to be lashed together, along with some bulkhead shoring materials, and ordered every man to don his life jacket. At 0830 they all went over the side and walked the rafts across the reef to deeper water. They then began, half swimming and half paddling, toward the mainland. For a while they seemed to make progress, but at about 1100 the wind and tidal set were too strong. The rafts began moving southward and back toward the reef. Bruised and battered by the heavy surf, they could only hang on. They were in a treacherous, precarious, exhausting situation, with riptides and cross currents keeping them from moving anywhere.

From out of nowhere a PBY patrol plane appeared, sent by Australian authorities to find the source of the previous night's distress signals. The men on the rafts yelled and waved, and the plane waggled its wings but then flew off. (Later they learned the pilot had returned to base to unload excess fuel to make his landing easier and to take the men aboard.) At 1430 the plane returned, and after making several approaches finally landed in the choppy water. All the men were taken aboard, most of them completely exhausted, badly cramped, and chilled. The plane landed in the Bay of Rest, and all the survivors were boated to the AVD seaplane tender USS *Childs,* where they were given dry clothing and hot food. Cifone went to sick bay with severe chills and shock, and Del Fattore was treated for lacerations of the right foot. M. M. Petek, Boatswain's Mate 1c, fractured a finger. He had been a strong figure when they were all on the rafts, encouraging, cajoling, and making them hold fast.

On 24 June, the day after their rescue, Bobbie Davis and William Goldfarb were transferred to the USS *Chanticleer,* an ASR submarine rescue vessel. Standing out of the bay and clear of the reef, they launched a surf boat. In the boat Davis and Goldfarb, accompanied by two officers and some crew members of the *Chanticleer,* approached the SC 751 inside the reef. They went aboard and salvaged all publications, radio transmitter, sound recorder, and other gear of a vital nature. Then they inspected the wreck to determine the possibility of salvage. They found the ship was resting solidly on the reef, which was flat. There was no sign that the keel had been broken, and the entire starboard side was intact. The engine room had been holed on the port side, allowing the hull to fill with water whenever the tide rose and fell. At low tide the reef was practically bare.

The consensus of the boarding party was that practically all equipment could be salvaged from the 751 intact and in good condition, leaving the hull bare and possibly lightened to such an extent that it could be pulled from the reef, patched, then towed to a point where it could be repaired and kept in commission.

As is customary with collisions, sinkings, or groundings, a board of investigation was subsequently convened, and for three weeks hundreds of pages of testimony from the surviving officers and men were duly recorded. Opinions of the board were formally rendered and filed in the navy's Office of the Judge Advocate General (JAG). Some of these files have been withheld from public view on grounds of personal privacy, reasonably enough for material that becomes part of an officer's personal service record; there is no argument here. But the public records of the board of investigation still leave many questions unanswered.[5] Lost files, missing log entries, and contradictions of eyewitness accounts lead one to the conclusion that questions concerning the fate of SC 751 on that terrible night will never be satisfactorily answered.

From the time Captain Davis retired to the wardroom until the ship crashed into the reef at 0555—a period of two hours and thirty-five minutes—it is not clear what happened, particularly with regard to the relieving of the watch. We do know that the ship was headed east-southeast (104 degrees (T)) at nine knots—a course and speed that (from the security of armchair hindsight) was far too risky in view of the poor visibility and uncertainty of position. We also know that Ensign Goldfarb turned the watch over to—and was relieved by—Ensign Parkison only five minutes before the ship hit the reef. Neither officer saw land ahead or white water breaking on reefs. Nor did the lookout, who was coming down from the crow's nest at the time of the crash. Goldfarb and Parkison were in the pilothouse at the moment of impact. Apparently no one was actually straining his eyes looking ahead of the ship at the precise moment it hit the reef—unless it was Captain Davis himself. But Captain Davis claimed under oath he was in his berth asleep, was jolted awake by the grounding, and rushed up to the bridge to take charge.

Fifty-three years later, Goldfarb refutes this, stating that Davis not only was topside but was on the flying bridge and had the conn.[6] A copy of the proceedings of the board of investigation indicates no testimony to this effect.

An expert witness at the board testified that strong winds and tides could have played havoc with anyone's estimated fixes, since currents in that area were always capricious, affected by varying phases of the moon, and whether the tide was ebbing or flooding. His calculations, based on a reconstruction of the conditions, placed the 751 as much as fifteen miles farther south than Bobbie Davis's dead-reckoning position. This would explain how the ship could have hit the "thumb" instead of being safely north of its tip.

Ordered to salvage the 751, which was still on the reef, the *Chanticleer* proceeded to Exmouth Gulf with officers Davis and Goldfarb and several crew members of the 751. Beginning on the Fourth of July 1943, they conducted salvage operations from a temporary base camp on the beach three and a half miles away. First they lightened ship by removing the main and auxiliary engines, the echo ranging equipment, guns and ammunition, and all other heavy gear. They tried floating the ship off but failed. The *Chanticleer* returned to Fremantle for additional equipment. When they returned to the scene, they discovered that the winds and tidal currents had moved the wreck a quarter of a mile north. They removed the foremast, mainmast, pilothouse, shafts, struts, rudders, and propellers to further lighten ship. The work was done only when the tide was low or less than mid-tide, in difficult, dangerous conditions, in surf that kept breaking over the fantail and running along the ship's entire length.

Two months passed while they continued with the difficult job. They decided to use the tides to help in the effort. At extreme low tides they brought tractors out to turn the ship over onto its starboard side so that they could repair the holes on the port side. They filled forty empty gasoline drums with water and placed them on the starboard side as ballast. This enabled them to make the hull roll over and expose the damaged port side. They patched the holes and rigged billy pumps to keep incoming water to a minimum.

After several unsuccessful attempts, they were finally able to maneuver the crippled hulk through the reefs by towing it with a landing barge. Twice it grounded again, and twice they got it off. They emptied the drums of water and placed them inside various compartments in the hull to help keep her afloat. Two and a half months after they began the salvage operation, they finally guided her to the *Chanticleer,* hoping to tie her alongside. As they neared the *Chanticleer* it became apparent that the heavy swell and choppy sea made it impossible to tie the hull alongside without the danger of breaking her up and causing her to disintegrate.

They decided to take the wreck in tow. After considerable maneuvering and passing of lines, this was accomplished. Then, just as they began putting strain on the towlines, she began to settle. Within minutes the stern rose up out of the water and the ship quickly dove towards the bottom fifty-five fathoms below. The little subchaser, so proudly commissioned in Boston a year earlier, was gone forever.

Lt. William C. Goldfarb remained attached to the *Chanticleer* and served for two years as her executive officer, navigator, and commissary officer. Today he is a retired insurance underwriter living in good health in El Paso.

Lt. Bobbie C. Davis was transferred to Seventh Amphibious Force and given command of SC 746, operating under Adm. Dan Barbey during MacArthur's advance to the Philippines. But he would never forget his first command and the date of 22 June 1943, when he sailed into a nightmare that must have haunted him for the remainder of his life. Bobbie C. Davis died in Florida in 1995.

13

Kwajalein and Eniwetok

The assault and subsequent takeover of Kwajalein and Eniwetok atolls in February 1944 were orderly steps for closing perimeters and reducing the approaches to the Marianas and the islands of Saipan, Tinian, and Guam. To the west lay Iwo Jima and Okinawa, and beyond those, when the time came, the Japanese mainland itself. While the Third and Seventh Fleets under Adm. William "Bull" Halsey and General MacArthur, respectively, advanced steadily from the south through the Solomons and New Guinea, the formidable Fifth Fleet under Vice Adm. Raymond A. Spruance was closing the gap in similar fashion in the Central Pacific. The noose was tightening. The plan laid down by Admiral Nimitz many months ago, a carefully crafted blueprint based on far-seeing naval decisions, would bring the Pacific war to the shores of Japan herself.

Such manipulations were unknown to all but President Roosevelt and a handful of high-ranking admirals and generals, far removed from the salt-rimed men and their ships, who were only pieces in a gigantic chess game on the vast Pacific. The part that individual ships played would not be understood by those who served on them until many years afterwards, with the help of naval historians who would bring the great plan together.

Subchaser sailors were not interested in grand strategy or the noble enterprise of making war. They were more concerned with the daily routine of begging fresh provisions and water from larger ships, hanging out wet bedding, exterminating cockroaches, scraping paint, boredom, fear, standing their watches, and wishing the war would end so that they could go home. Yet such was their training and experience by now, as well as their sense of patriotic duty, that they were willing to take on almost anything with aplomb.

As the time for the assaults on Kwajalein and Eniwetok approached, three subchasers were picked for significant roles as landing control vessels. Having learned a hard lesson at Tarawa with its long stretches of reefs, the Fifth Fleet command realized that shallow-draft SCs were much better adapted for beach control than destroyers. For the first time in the Central Pacific, SCs would be used for control vessels. Three SCs drew the assignment. Accordingly, on 19 January 1944, SC 997 (recently arrived from the Aleutians), SC 539, and SC 1066 left Pearl Harbor with Task Force 52 under Rear Adm. Jesse B. Oldendorf. They were a sizable armada of escort carriers, heavy cruisers, destroyers, LCI gunboats, LSTs, and troop transports. They arrived at Kwajalein the evening of 30 January.

At the same time a smaller amphibious force, the Majuro Attack Group—under the command of Rear Adm. Harry W. Hill in USS *Cambria*—left Pearl Harbor and headed for Majuro, an island atoll some 250 miles southeast of Kwajalein. Majuro was considered important for use as an advanced base in the seizure of the Marshalls. Information from Naval Intelligence led the attack group to expect about four hundred Japanese on the island. As it turned out, only three were found, and the Majuro takeover was accomplished quickly with a very small force from the 106th Infantry and Fifth Amphibious Force troops. The large transports carrying the troops were never deployed. This unexpected development made it much easier to render support for the landings at Kwajalein and, more importantly, enabled dates for Eniwetok and other landings in the Marianas to be pushed up by thirty days.

Early in the morning of D-Day at Kwajalein, SC 1066, Lt. (jg) Bernard M. Hollander commanding, went alongside one of the transports and picked up a sizable control team consisting of Cdr. Beverly M. Coleman, USNR, head beach master; Lt. Cdr. Richard Black; Lt. (jg) Harry Baker, communications officer; and a number of others, including three army majors (ordnance, medical, and tank specialists) and 1st Lt. Barry Sudgen, a representative of the commanding general. It was "togetherness" carried to the extreme. For several days and nights, the three officers of the 1066 shared their beds in the wardroom with the seven officers of the control team, using a system of "hotbedding," in which each bunk switched occupants every two or four hours, depending on individual degrees of fatigue and the conditions of the watch. Imagine a group of ten sweaty men, living near the equator, sharing the use of three mattresses in a low-ceilinged, windowless, cramped, rolling, heaving room no bigger than a medium-sized bathroom—with one toilet, no air conditioning, no bath, no shower, no laundry, and no linen change—and you have a faint idea of the miasma that must have pervaded the 1066 as she plied her trade as a landing control vessel.

The 1066 proceeded to the western end of Kwajalein Island, where the attack was to take place, and took her position on the line of departure three thousand yards from the beach, dropping her anchor. Extensive bombardment by U.S. bombers had softened the enemy emplacements in preparation for initial landings. SC 539, Lt. (jg) Richard H. Cordell, USNR, commanding, moved into position as backup. Lieutenant Hollander describes the landing, typical of many that took place in the Pacific, as he observed it from SC 1066:

> There was only one point marking the center of the line of departure, it wasn't a wide street or something of the sort. . . . The LSTs and the transports were anchored behind us. The LSTs would launch their amphibious tanks and the transports would lower the troops to the water in LCVPs which were small landing craft and which had a front door that dropped down when they hit the beach. The troops were carried in LCVPs in small numbers, and the tanks and each wave of LCVPs would circle on either side of us until they were dispatched from the line of departure when the Control Officer on our ship would signal them to go at the specified time. It was very carefully timed so they would not run into the support fire that was being thrown into the beach. At Kwajalein where, like Tarawa, there were reefs between the line of departure and the landing beaches, amphibious tanks (LVT(A)s) were used as well to carry the troops over the reefs. They were launched from LSTs.[1]

Hollander notes that this landing was unlike the landing at Eniwetok, made on the inside (lagoon side) of the atoll, in which the tanks and LCVPs went directly to the beaches.

While the southern attack group was thus occupied, a second landing took place on the northern end of the atoll at the islands of Roi and Namur, more than forty miles away. In this operation SC 997 was suddenly called upon to lead a group of LVTs through a shallow, narrow inlet known as North Pass when the destroyer *Phelps,* which first had this assignment, proved to draw too much water. A considerable amount of delay and confusion ensued, since the *Phelps* carried Capt. E. R. McLean, the organizer and controller of the troop landings. Lacking the necessary communication facilities, the 997 had a difficult time, compounded by very high winds inside the atoll, which made the water very choppy. Two amtracs overturned in the surf during the landing, drowning four men and losing two 75-mm pieces. It took most of the day, but by dark they had made it, with minimum enemy resistance.[2]

Kwajalein is an atoll composed of many islets, twenty-seven of which had to be captured during the operation. On at least twelve of them, considerable enemy resistance was expected, so the takeover of Kwajalein became a campaign of many different landings, rather than a strike against a single island.[3]

At 0910 on 5 February, the 539 led the first wave of LVTs to Gugegwe Island, another in the chain, again under heavy sea and air bombardment. The landing was carried out with minimum resistance, although splashes from enemy mortar fire came within yards of the ship. Then, at 1025 Maj. Gen. Charles H. Corlett again came on board, and for the remainder of the day the 539 was his floating command post.

An unexpected but very important bonus at Kwajalein was the capture of hundreds of beautifully drawn Japanese navigation charts. The charts, meticulously and accurately prepared, were not only for Kwajalein but for most of the islands occupied by the Japanese all the way back to Japan. Eniwetok, for instance, was laid out so clearly, with the location of mines and buoys, water depths, and other data about the lagoon, that Admiral Nimitz decided not to have the fleet return to Hawaii to regroup. Instead he sent it on directly to Eniwetok. The charts became a springboard for pushing up invasion dates and were used to advantage at Saipan, Guam, Iwo Jima, and Okinawa.

During the remainder of their days at Kwajalein, the subchasers kept busy with mail deliveries, smaller landings, delivering copies of the newly found charts to various ships, and other miscellaneous duties. The takeover of Kwajalein was about as smooth an operation as any in all the Pacific. Naval historian Samuel Eliot Morison summarized it in classical style: "superbly executed in the glorious setting of deep blue white-capped sea, fluffy tradewind clouds, flashing gunfire and billowing smoke over the target, gaily colored flag hoists at the yardarms of the ships and on the signal halyards of the control craft. One thought of the thundering hoofs and gleaming sabers of a cavalry charge."

After two successful weeks at Kwajalein, SC 1066 and SC 539 joined the Eniwetok Expeditionary Group on 15 February as control vessels for the assault on that island, a large, round atoll 326 miles WNW of Kwajalein. The group, under command of Rear Adm. Harry W. Hill in the attack transport USS *Cambria,* was formidable, with nine transports carrying the 22nd Marine Regiment and two battalions of the U.S. Army's 106th Regimental Combat Team, 27th Division, plus two APD destroyer attack transports, 9 LSTs, and 6 LCIs. The battleships *Pennsylvania, Colorado,* and *Tennessee* and heavy cruisers *Indianapolis, Portland,* and *Louisville* made up the group of "big boys" which, with a screen of fifteen destroyers, were to be used as fire support. In addition, under Rear Adm. V. H. Ragsdale, three escort carriers, four destroyers, a minesweeper group, two oilers, and four tugs were included.

At Kwajalein Admiral Ragsdale had come aboard the 1066 to be ferried over to Admiral Turner's flagship, the *Rocky Mount.* He came up to the flying bridge where Hollander was conning and engaged him in conversation. The admiral wanted to know what ship he had come over on. Hollander said, "This one." The admiral said, "No, I don't mean that, I mean what ship were you carried on?" Hollander replied, "This one." Before Hollander could explain how it was done by refueling several times while under way, they were alongside the *Rocky Mount* and the admiral was gone. Hollander knew the admiral never believed him.

It took two days to make the trip from Kwajalein. Early on the morning of 17 February, Task Group 51.11 stood off Eniwetok atoll at the two entrance passages from the south.

Eniwetok was of considerable strategic importance as a staging point for the Marianas and beyond. Its capture would enable the neutralization—and subsequent bypassing—of Truk, a Japanese stronghold. Consisting of approximately forty islets in the form of a ring around a large lagoon, Eniwetok is the second largest atoll in the Marshalls—388 square miles. At the northern end of the ring lay Engebi Island, the Americans' first target in the atoll because of its good-sized airstrip. Engebi was accessible by approaching it through the lagoon, which had to be entered through channels on the southern end of the ring. At this end lay Eniwetok and Parry Islands, both suspected of having major enemy emplacements with search radar, coastal defense guns, and barracks concealed under a heavy cover of coconut and pandanus.

The entrance of choice, Wide Passage, was full of shoal spots and heavily mined. Shortly after 0700 the minesweeper group began sweeping. It took more than two hours to sweep Wide Passage before the ships slowly passed through, one at a time, in column formation. Everyone knew the enemy was watching, and no one could understand why he remained hidden. He had not replied to the preliminary bombardment of Eniwetok, and the silence was somewhat ominous.[4]

Ten miles ahead, across the lagoon, lay Engebi Island on the northern side of the atoll. The ships made the short passage without incident, although Admiral Hill later said it was the most anxious trip of his naval career. SC 1066 carried the commander of the control units aboard and thus was SOP for the control vessels. Using his recently acquired SF-1 radar and one of the excellent Japanese charts acquired at Kwajalein, Hollander was able to accurately establish a line of departure, dropping his anchor at the center of this imaginary line two thousand yards off the beach. They waved the LVTs in, under supporting fire from the destroyer *McCord* and six rocket-firing LCIs. There was practically no opposition from the enemy, with only an occasional scattering of small-arms fire.

SC 539 was designated to assist in reconnaissance, with Cdr. E. D. Brewster on board. A Japanese battery began shooting at them from somewhere in the smoke and dust on Engebi, to which the 539 responded with 40-mm fire. Although the gunners were unable to see what they were shooting at, they aimed at a section of smoke and dust "on general principles."[5] At 1815 the reconnaissance party returned, having completed their scouting mission with no casualties.

The following day, 18 February, Colonel Walker, USMC, in command of the 22nd Marines, boarded SC 539 with several officers and members of his staff to set up a floating command post while his troops landed on Engebi. Following closely on the heels of the LCIs transporting the marines, the 539 lay to fifteen hundred yards off the beach to observe. A sudden loud explosion close aboard threw every man to the deck, with shrapnel flying everywhere. Lt. Col. E. C. Ferguson, USMC, and Commander Brewster of the command team sustained only minor wounds, but Ens. Francis T. Lavery, USNR, was severely wounded in the stomach. He was treated by F. C. Cassedy, ship's pharmacist's mate, and transferred to the USS *Leonard Wood* nearby.

The rest of the day was spent uneventfully while the two subchasers directed backup traffic for the beaches. Engebi, it turned out, was almost a pushover. In addition the Americans found papers on Engebi that revealed the existence of sizable garrisons of tough, veteran Japanese troops on Eniwetok and Parry Isles, on the southern end of the atoll. This information averted what might have been a disaster, since no signs of life had been noticed when the ships came through Wide Passage the day before, leading

Marine Brig. Gen. Thomas E. Watson to figure he could capture both islands with a small force. As a result of this discovery, he changed his plan and took them one at a time.

The landings, first at Eniwetok and the next one at Parry, from 19 to 23 February proceeded smoothly for the control vessels and the landing boats, but once on land the marines encountered there some of the dirtiest, toughest combat of the entire war. SC 1066 was marking out the line of departure for Parry when suddenly machine-gun bullets began hitting the water all around the ship. They were from friendly planes making a strafing attack on the beach, some of them so close that they gave the men of the 1066 a real scare. Minutes later they watched as one of our carrier planes got shot down in flames when it ran into U.S. artillery fire.

A destroyer, DD 556, USS *Hailey,* laying down fire support in anticipation of a landing on the first day, somehow misfired and hit two or three LCI-R rocket boats that were preceding the landing waves, causing many casualties. A post-invasion inquiry was held aboard the *Indianapolis* to determine the cause of the accident. One of the questions to be settled was the location of the line of departure and whether the lead control vessel had been in its proper location. Lieutenant Hollander testified at this board of inquiry and proved beyond doubt that the 1066 was on station in the proper position. This was confirmed by the commanding officer of the minesweeper USS *Oracle,* who stated that the 1066 had indeed anchored at the proper buoy it had dropped, and that said buoy was at the center of the line of departure. The board of inquiry's finding was that SC 1066 was exactly in the place she was supposed to be.

This discussion affords an opportunity to correct an error that still appears in volume 6 of Samuel Eliot Morison's *History of United States Naval Operations in World War II.* Dozens of authors and historians have relied with considerable confidence on this generally reliable history. The error refers to SC 1066 and the actions of her commanding officer during the landing operation at Engebi. Military histories can fall victim to erroneous information, and Dr. Morison is no longer here to explain his error, but here, at least, we can set the record straight.

Dr. Morison wrote (italics mine):

> The transports arrived in their area at 1230 but in a state of confusion. *A subchaser which had taken no part in the rehearsal had been designated convoy*

> *guide. SC 1066, the one chosen,* had a lucky number for an invasion but she *took station off the wrong islet.* . . . This situation was straightened out . . . but the process took two hours.
>
> All these contretemps brought the tempers of commanding officers to boiling point. *Admiral Hill, regarding the performance of SC 1066 as "completely unsatisfactory," relieved the skipper of his command.*

Only two years ago Bernard M. Hollander, then 83, learned of this statement about his supposed incompetence at Eniwetok, though it has been in print since 1951. Researching another story (about a Japanese submarine that purportedly had launched a float plane that dropped a fire bomb on the U.S. mainland during World War II), Mr. Hollander came across several references to his old command, SC 1066. When his eyes fell upon the startling statement in Morison that "SC 1066 had taken station off the wrong islet" and that he, Hollander, had been "relieved of command," he was utterly aghast. Bristling with indignation, he dropped his inquiry about the Japanese float plane and went to work to correct the defamatory error.

SC 1066 refueling at sea en route from Saipan to Pearl Harbor, July 1944
Courtesy of Bernard M. Hollander

No slouch in the art of investigation (Mr. Hollander still works as a highly respected senior trial attorney in the Antitrust Division of the U.S. Department of Justice), he first wrote a letter to the secretary of the navy, with a copy to the senior historian at the Naval Historical Center, in which he vigorously refuted Morison's statements and requested that the statement be retracted and the record corrected.[6] His three-pronged argument was clear and simple: (1) SC 1066 was at all rehearsals for the landing; (2) SC 1066 was at its assigned position during the landings; (3) the commanding officer was not relieved from command.

He then dug into his personal files and produced a letter of commendation from Adm. Richmond Kelly Turner, stating that Hollander's performance during the captures of Kwajalein and Eniwetok "was excellent, and he carried out assigned tasks in a thoroughly satisfactory manner." He then produced another letter from Capt. D. W. Loomis, Commander Task Group 51.14, which stated that Hollander "did an excellent job during the amphibious assaults on the Islands of Eniwetok Atoll." This letter was duly forwarded by Adm. Harry Hill and, with Admiral Turner's letter, entered into Hollander's service record. The 1066 had not only carried out her duties at Eniwetok but had done so with excellence.[7]

Dr. Morison, commissioned personally by President Roosevelt to write the history, was assisted by many people during the eighteen years it took to complete his highly respected work. Unable to be present during the invasion of Eniwetok, he delegated the task of reporting that operation to one of his assistants, Lt. (jg) Henry Salomon, USNR. Apparently Mr. Salomon accepted rumors instead of checking facts—something quite inexcusable for a historian. We will never know where he got such an untruthful and libelous story, or why it was never cross-checked by Dr. Morison.[8]

The operations in the Marshalls demonstrated the importance of subchasers as well-equipped and well-trained control ships at the line of departure. The capture of Kwajalein and Eniwetok atolls was a far-reaching and valuable step for the Allied Pacific Campaign. Shortly thereafter, the island of Truk, a Japanese stronghold, felt the full fury of our bombers as they flew back and forth from Eniwetok to "bomb the living daylights" out of that strategic enemy outpost. For the remainder of the war the two islands would be major staging areas for campaigns in the Marianas, Philippines, and Ryukyus.

14

This Is No Subchaser

The orders designating SC 648 (my ship) to be the control vessel at Aitape came at a time when we were feeling the effects of an endless series of dull escort trips and harbor patrols—enough to last us for the rest of the war. There had been no interruption in these assignments. No sooner would we return from one plodding, slow-speed, dreary voyage than we would refuel, take on food and fresh water, and go out for another plodding, slow-speed, dreary voyage.

True, we had attacked what we thought was a submarine (it was never recognized as such, like most such attacks), and we had rescued a couple of Australian airmen, but the two weeks in which we played host to a career navy captain turned out to be one of the most memorable periods of my twenty-three months aboard SC 648.

It was during General MacArthur's island-hopping campaign back to the Philippines, and we had been selected to be inner control vessel at Aitape, one of the three landing spots for the Hollandia invasion. The 648 had been with Admiral Barbey's Seventh Amphibious Force for a year by now, beginning in May 1943 in Brisbane, whence we operated up and down the coast escorting all kinds of vessels—Australian merchant ships, oilers, landing craft, slow-moving tugs with heavy barges in tow, floating dry docks, LCTs, and more.

There had been no time between trips to lay up for repairs or normal maintenance. The 648 was long overdue for a dry-docking to clean and apply new antifouling paint to the bottom. The engines had long ago exceeded preventive maintenance measures and were in bad need of overhaul. Only through the skill and ingenuity of her crew did she remain mission-ready and reliable. She had become a dependable drudge, a workhorse. We wondered: Was this the reason why she had been selected for inner control at Aitape—because she was so dependable? We liked to think so.

Curiously, the 648 still had no radar, although most SCs were so equipped, and she would not acquire radar until almost a year later, after the Leyte invasion. Radar was important for navigating in those waters, because many of the charts were outdated and unreliable. The ability to navigate with precision was important for a control vessel. We were to be a control vessel without radar. It sounds improbable but such was the case.

We welcomed the news of our part in the coming landing because it would help relieve the tedium and monotony of the present. But our enthusiasm really soared when we learned that the landing control officer was a navy captain and that we would be his flagship. Everyone aboard felt excitement and nervous anticipation: A four-striper! And our little subchaser was to be his flagship!

No one on SC 648 had ever heard of Capt. J. W. Jamison nor did we have any inkling of his meritorious background and experience. All we knew was that a four-striper was to be the landing control officer at Aitape and would be using our ship as his flagship. That alone was enough to make us work hard to tidy up and get things ready to have him aboard.

Preparations began immediately. Everyone—officers and crew alike—turned to in an effort to spruce things up and make us look more shipshape. We wanted the 648 to look more like a navy ship, instead of looking the way she usually did, which, to be gentle, was less than pretty. The deck gang got busy and holystoned[1] the main deck—something we had never done before—and, although there were a few grumbles during the backbreaking job, it did whiten the deck and greatly improved its appearance. "Junior" Fairlie, Chief Motor Machinist's Mate, decided it was time to spruce up the engine room and gave "Red" Westring, a young seaman striking for the engine room, the job of painting all brightwork in the engine room with aluminum paint. Gunner's mates Jay Green and Lou George began work on all the ordnance, beginning with the mousetraps and depth charges, and then carefully and methodically stripping, clean-

Three subchasers (SC 648 in foreground) dry-docked in a floating LSD at Seeadler Harbor, Manus, Admiralty Islands, 1944

ing, and greasing all guns. They checked, rearranged, and restocked the ammunition lockers and magazine.

There was much scraping of paint, rust removal, application of yellow zinc oxide, and then a fresh coating of battleship gray all over. Rice and Esser rigged a scaffold and painted the ship's "SC 648" numbers in new bright white paint on both sides of the bow. They scrubbed out as much as they could of the white salt stains caused by seawater flowing out the scuppers and down the sides of the hull.

Fagan, ship's cook, took two men over to the submarine tender USS *Fulton* to requisition food items a level better than the Spam, dehydrated potatoes, canned chili, canned beans, and powdered milk diet we had been putting up with most of the time. He came back with a good supply of fresh eggs, sides of beef and Australian mutton, new potatoes, Jell-O, and other delicacies, including an unexpected bonus of two gallons of vanilla ice cream. Everyone was trying to make the ship look presentable for a high-ranking naval officer.

The captain of the 648 at this time was Lt. Paul Allen Spaugh, a tall blue-eyed Texan with clean-cut Scandinavian features and a build earned on the Texas A&M swim team. He was a very good navigator and ship handler and always decisive and fair in his treatment of his men. He loved practical jokes and enjoyed the company of—and kidding with—fellow skippers. In some ways he was a rascal, but his strengths as a leader far outweighed any human weaknesses. He demanded the best effort from everyone, including himself, and he never ordered anyone to do anything he wouldn't or couldn't do himself.

I had just become the executive officer. I had come on a year before as third officer, after swapping jobs with the third officer, Richard E. Vernor, who preferred my former assignment as base gunnery officer on Nouméa. I had longed for sea duty, despite having no qualifications as a deck officer, no SCTC training, and less than three months of formal navy training. But by the time Captain Jamison came aboard, I was considerably more experienced and, along with everyone else on 648, keyed up for Aitape and our real navy captain.

Ours was a happy, tight little ship, and morale was never higher as the day for the landing operation at Aitape approached. The landing was scheduled for dawn on 22 April. On 17 April we were anchored in Langemak Harbor at Finschhafen when we received orders to send a boat to pick up the captain from an LCT a half mile away. Our only boat was a little wherry without a

A few members of the crew of "Yacht 648"

motor. Spaugh dispatched four men with paddles to fetch the captain in the wherry. Two men would have been enough, but Spaugh felt four men paddling would get the errand done more quickly. When they returned with Captain Jamison an hour later, it made quite a picture, with the captain sitting in the stern of the wherry in full regalia wearing his battle helmet, fatigues, and a .45 Colt automatic at his hip. With the weight of five men in the wherry it rode precariously low in the water.

The harbor at Langemak was notorious for its long swells, even on the calmest of days, that kept sweeping across and rocking the ships at anchor. Smaller-draft, narrow, rounded-bottom ships like our SC used to rock like a cradle at Langemak. Some learned of necessity to almost enjoy it, sleeping as though in a hammock high up in a tree on a windy day. Anyway, one of those swells—a particularly big one—came rolling in just as the wherry came alongside, causing it to smack hard into the side of the ship in spite of our efforts to hold it off. Jamison, gripping the gunwales in the stern, didn't look very pleased. There being no ladder or a gangway, hands were extended, and

Capt. John W. Jamison, USN, circa 1941 *Courtesy of John W. Jamison Jr.*

somehow we managed to get him aboard without an accident, but we had been rather lubberly about it and it was a poor introduction for him.

Our first impression of Captain Jamison was that he looked terribly old. He was only forty-two, but most of us were half that age. He was of medium build, with a hint of a paunch developing about his midsection. His hair and mustache and eyebrows were slightly reddish, his complexion ruddy, with blue eyes that could look through you. He was neither pleasant nor unpleasant, his whole demeanor being that of someone who had a job to do, whose stay aboard our ship would be one hundred percent business.

After introducing him to the officers, Spaugh led him into the pilothouse, inviting him for a tour of the ship, which he declined. Jamison asked for coffee and began unpacking things from his duffle bag, one of which was an air mattress. He solved a dilemma for us by announcing he would sleep in the chartroom. We had pondered the sleeping problem beforehand, and since Spaugh and I were old navy hands by now, we had decided to do things the navy way. The lowest-ranking officer would have to give up his bunk in the wardroom and fend for himself. A new third officer, Ens. Glenn Welsh, had just come aboard three days before and would pay the price with his bunk. Captain Jamison showed us how the mattress inflated with an ingenious built-in pump, and we watched, fascinated. This over, the ship returned to its routine and began preparing to get under way. Spaugh took his station on the flying bridge and sang out the orders:

"Light off the main engines! Weigh anchor! Set Condition II!"

Five minutes later we were under way on various courses and speeds, departing Cape Cretin anchorage to rendezvous with Task Unit 76.6 outside the harbor. Our destination for the first leg of the trip was Seeadler Harbor, Manus Island, in the Admiralties, the staging area where the main force would gather for the final run to the invasion of Hollandia, Aitape, and Tanahmerah Bay.

As we were steaming out from Finschhafen to join the other ships, SC 981 was running parallel to our starboard side. Both ships were doing thirteen knots—a pretty good speed for SCs. As if by mutual consent, the two subchasers began converging, gradually coming closer together as they steamed along. Spaugh and the skipper of the 981 were good friends, and several crew members on each SC were friendly, so Spaugh told the helmsman to maneuver us even closer. Soon we were both steaming along side by side at thirteen knots, only fifty feet apart, our bow wakes colliding in an even pattern of white froth. Spaugh was laughing and calling over to the other skipper, and the men on both subchasers were lined along the rails yelling and waving to each other.

I was standing on the quarterdeck just aft of the pilothouse, enjoying the commotion when Captain Jamison emerged from the charthouse and looked across at the other subchaser.

"Treadwell, what's going on here?" he asked, querulously.

"Um, er, well, the captain, uh, we know that ship pretty well, and I guess the captain wanted, uh, you know, to say something to the skipper," I fumbled.

For a full minute Captain Jamison looked across the churning waters, his arms akimbo, the two subchasers racing neck and neck out of the harbor, the men calling across the waves to each other in good-natured banter and cheers.

The captain turned, his expression that of complete distaste. He shook his head, unbelieving.

"This is no subchaser," he said flatly, in a tone everyone could hear. "This is a goddamned yacht!" He returned into the pilothouse.

The men who heard him were doubled over in their effort to keep from laughing out loud, and I had all I could do to stifle my own. Captain Jamison had stamped his appraisal of our ship in words that became immortal on SC 648. From that moment on, whenever something went wrong around the ship, we had the perfect excuse: "For criminy sakes, you dumb jackass, what did you expect? You're not on a subchaser, you're on a goddamned *yacht.*"

Another time, Captain Jamison emerged from the chartroom just as George Green, one of our sloppiest dressers, was passing by on his way to the after crew's quarters. Green, an upstate New York farm boy, was a good sailor, at times a bit cantankerous but very handy with tools—a tinkerer and a storyteller with a good sense of humor. On this occasion he wore ragged cutoffs dragged low by the weight of a long knife, fashioned from an old file, that he always carried in a sheath hanging from his belt on his scrawny backside. He called it his "frogsticker," and it was his trademark. A dirty skivvy shirt hung out of his pants, flapping at the waist. I observed the captain studying Green disapprovingly as he disappeared down the after compartment hatch and made a mental note to myself to speak to Green. Nodding towards him, Jamison said to me, "Is that an example of your dress code?"

I don't remember what I said, but I do recall wondering why I seemed to be the only officer present when Jamison saw or disapproved of something.

Our convoy to Seeadler Harbor was in company with the destroyer *Stockton,* SOPA, and several old faithful workhorse SCs who had been with us for many months, including the 637, 742, 703, 743, and the 981, all providing a screen for a group of eighteen LCTs. The trip took thirty hours and was uneventful, with no breakdowns and no enemy sub or plane contacts. By 1915 on 18 April we had dropped anchor in Seeadler Harbor and were safely nestled among an armada of 215 vessels that had converged on Seeadler as the staging area for the invasion.

The Hollandia invasion was to be the largest yet in the war in the Southwest Pacific. Three separate points on the coast of New Guinea were selected for landing, the Western Attack Group at Tanahmera Bay, the Central Attack Group at Humboldt Bay, Hollandia, and the Eastern Attack Group at Aitape. Seeadler Harbor at Manus, in the Admiralty Islands, had been selected as the rendezvous point for all ships participating.

We spent the next day at Manus refueling and taking on water, making last-minute preparations. A moment of diversion came in mid-morning when we were taking on fuel and water. I was again standing at my favorite spot on the quarterdeck, and Captain Jamison stood beside me, observing. Chief "Junior" Fairlie, in charge of the engine room, came over and showed me the end of one finger, which he held out for me to inspect. The finger had

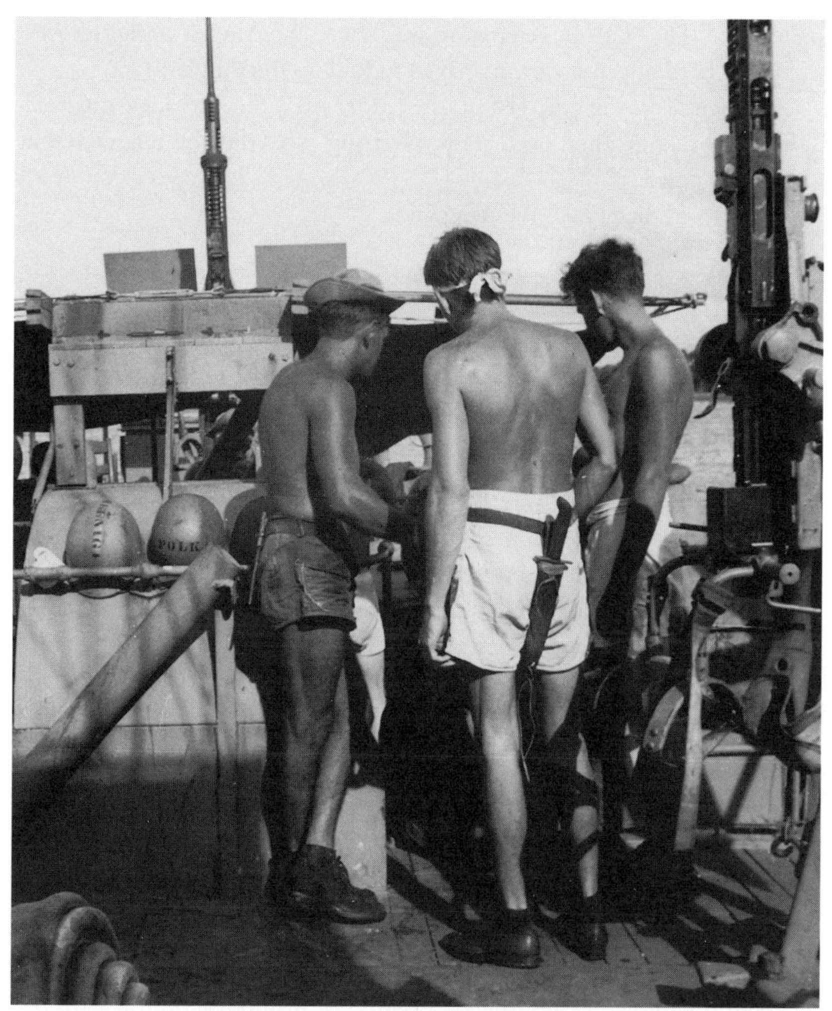

Coxswain Green wears his "frogsticker" while attending a conference on SC 648.

a dab of aluminum paint on it. "Yes, so?" I asked. In those days aluminum paint came in two containers, the contents of which had to be thoroughly mixed. One can held the aluminum powder and the other a lacquer that smelled like banana oil.

He said, "Look at this." He wiped it clean with one swipe of a rag. "The kid painted down there four days ago. It looked great. Just now I wiped my finger along it to make sure it was dry. Everything's as wet as the day he painted it." The "kid" he referred to was "Red" Westring, a youngster who tried very hard but somehow managed to foul up the simplest task.

Just then Westring emerged up the ladder from the after crew quarters. The chief beckoned him over. "Hey, Westring, what did you mix with that aluminum powder?"

"Uh, I used diesel oil," Westring said.

"You used *what*?"

The three of us stared at him unbelievingly. He winced.

"Oooh, gee," he faltered, "I *knew* I should have used lube oil."

Captain Jamison looked at me, rolled his eyes, and walked away. Now it was his turn to laugh. Fairlie took the hapless Westring aside and quietly told him, "Get the hell below and clean it up."

At 1623 on the 19th we were under way in company with eighteen LCIs, five SCs, and two YMS minesweepers, crossing the Bismarck Sea to the shores of New Guinea. We cruised at different speeds and changed courses frequently to throw off any clues the enemy might pick up from our movements. All night and the following day and night we steamed in this fashion. At 1745 on the 21st Task Group TG3 broke away from the others and set course for Aitape. The four SCs in this group were the 637, 648, 742, and the 981. The 703, 738, and 743 remained on course with the Central Group for the landing at Humboldt Bay.

The beauty of the evening before the landing was lost to most of us because of the tension building up over the coming invasion. The wind subsided and the seas flattened. The Southern Cross hung overhead like four bright jewels. We could have imagined ourselves tourists on a South Seas cruise, marveling at such natural splendor. Midnight passed, then the wee hours of the morning, and the sea became even smoother until, with the first faint tinges of dawn, the water was glassy-slick. At 0500 we saw the land, a low, flat smudge on the horizon, slightly out of focus from the faint mist rising from the sea.

Some moments etch themselves deeply within the subconscious. Minute details—the smell, the quiet, the gray, the damp, the chill—stay with you forever. H-hour at Aitape was just such a moment for me.

Close your eyes, old man. Listen.
Hear the hiss of bow through slicksmooth water.
Smell the swamp mist, smell the damp rot,

Smell the stale sweat of 3,000 sons at dawn.
Off the beach at Aitape.

Tremble in the chill air, old man.
Shove dryspit down your throat.
Suck in the roar. Listen.
Hear the death raining down
On the beach at Aitape.

Open your eyes old man. Look.
See the butchery where once
Was the beach at Aitape.

At a point eight thousand yards from Blue Beach we slowed, moving quietly into the Aitape roadsteads that lay between small islands on both sides. The beach, twelve hundred yards wide, was dead ahead. On the flying bridge Captain Jamison studied the approach through his binoculars, and Spaugh leaned into the voice tube, quietly giving orders to the helm. The ticklish business of positioning the 648 correctly in the poorly charted waters had begun. Rice, Signalman 1c, stood on the bow taking soundings, and Beebe, quartermaster, took azimuth bearings in rapid succession, reporting each change in position. The 648 responded easily, as though she herself knew what to do. "Right rudder slowly" . . . "Ease the rudder" . . . "Port engine stop" . . . "All engines stop" . . . "all engines back one-third" . . . "left rudder slowly" . . . "ready anchor detail" . . . "all engines stop" . . . "let go the anchor."

We were anchored fifteen hundred yards from Blue Beach. The dim light of dawn was just beginning to show faintly on the eastern horizon. The 637, outer control vessel, dropped her anchor three thousand yards out. Captain Jamison was satisfied. It was 0623. Further out, nine APDs—one for each wave—carried the assault teams and their landing craft. They began launching the boats and slung over their sides the cargo nets that the troops used for climbing down into the boats. SCs 981 and 742 stood in, ready to fire rockets when ordered. Two AK cargo ships, the USS *Etamin* and USS *Bootes,* made their way slowly down Aitape roads. Farther out, seven destroyers trained their 5-inch guns at Blue Beach, and still farther out the cruisers *Phoenix, Nashville,* and *Boise* brought their 8-inch guns to bear. Somewhere out of sight and over the horizon were the escort carriers *Sangamon, Suwanee, Chenango,* and *Santee.*

At 0630 we felt a whoooossh overhead, so close we pulled in our shoulders and ducked at first, but later got used to it. This was followed by a deep booooom! Then another whoosh, with a second booooom! Then a third, and then they kept coming in, one after the other. The beach began erupting in a huge cloud of black smoke that quickly rose and spread out, covering the sky. The booms and explosions melded into a cacophony of sound, bouncing off the land mass and filling the atmosphere with an odd, supernatural noise, as though you were in a giant echo chamber of drums being pounded by the gods themselves. The roar, mixed with the gloom of dawn and the smoke, resembled something you'd feel all around you while approaching Dante's inferno. It was more overwhelming and more powerful than anything we on the 648 had ever experienced, lasting for twenty minutes, after which the guns suddenly stopped and dive-bombers from the carriers came swooping in to bomb and strafe the beach for ten more minutes. From our ship we saw quite a show—a scene of complete, total, destruction.

The first wave of landing boats with the men from 163rd Regimental Combat was circling our ship. Captain Jamison went back to the stern and held the starter's flag high. It was the black-and-white Navy Negat flag,[2] his own, not that from our flag bag. The men in the boats looked young and tough, their faces smeared with blacking, one smoking a cigar, another waving a small American flag, a few laughing and waving, others just staring. Jamison checked his watch, then brought the flag down sharply. With a loud roar, the boats sprang ahead at full speed toward the beach.

A second group of boats approached and began circling the 648. Again Captain Jamison checked his watch and brought down the flag. SCs 981 and 742 let go with their rockets, raking Blue Beach for a final time just before the first wave of landing boats arrived. Jamison waved in nine groups until all were gone. From first to last wave took only ten minutes.

With the last wave of boats gone and no more bombardment, the ship became strangely quiet, the only sounds the soft hum of our generators and the low rumble of our diesels. Through binoculars we watched the boats as they went into the beach. One boat broached in the moderate surf and another was swamped, but most of the boats beached and disembarked the troops in good fashion. With the beach secured, the LSTs and LCTs wasted no time coming in to discharge their cargoes. A dozen or so of these ungainly but technically correct craft beached themselves, opened their bow gates, and unloaded tanks, artillery weapons, Caterpillar tractors, communication equipment, and other gear. The entire landing was carried out smoothly and was impressive for its show of power and efficiency.

The *Etamin* passed by us close aboard on its way toward the beach. As part of the second wave, it carried a thousand additional combat troops to support the first waves of troops already ashore. In its forward hold were six thousand tons of ammunition, land mines, detonators, and boxed TNT. Its after holds were crammed with drums containing several thousand gallons of high-octane gasoline. Prior to coming in, the *Etamin* had been ordered to assist in the bombardment of Tumleo Island. Had the enemy returned fire from its two pillboxes on Tumleo, a direct hit on the *Etamin* could have blown her out of the water. The *Etamin* was one of the few ships in the Seventh Fleet manned by an all–Coast Guard crew.

Spaugh weighed anchor and maneuvered us alongside the *Etamin* to permit Captain Jamison to board her. As senior officer present, the navy captain was now the beachmaster and the temporary port director at Aitape. His responsibility was to coordinate ship-to-shore activities and make sure the unloading proceeded smoothly and efficiently. The *Etamin* moved in slowly and dropped her anchor about four hundred yards offshore, while she lowered her crane booms fore and aft to begin the task of unloading her cargo. Besides the ammunition and gasoline, the cargo included sections of landing track for the Tadji airstrip. Army stevedores would take over the job of unloading and a Works Wing of the Royal Australian Air Force would make the airstrip ready for use. A number of LCVs (landing craft, vehicle) would assist, plying back and forth from the *Etamin* to the beach. It would be hard, sweaty, dangerous work, and it would take a week or longer to unload all her cargo.

We weighed anchor and moved farther out, where, for the remainder of the day, we slowly patrolled the roadstead. Thus, while everyone was working hard at the beach, we were able to relax somewhat—those of us who were off watch, that is. There was no sign of the enemy, either on land or in the air. By sunset the LSTs and LCTs had discharged their cargoes, backed off the beach, and anchored offshore. Few warships were visible, although they remained in the vicinity, as evidenced by the constant chatter overheard in our radio shack. We picked up Captain Jamison from the *Etamin* and returned to patrol position for the night, sharing this duty with SC 637.

The following day we moved in close to Tumleo Island in company with the rocket SCs and laid down a barrage with our 40-mm and 20-mm guns that set a Japanese oil dump on fire. The fire burned several days, sending up swirls of dense black smoke that covered the sky all the time we were there.

The entire operation so far had gone quite smoothly, and Captain Jamison was pleased. For the first time since coming aboard, he came below and ate evening chow with us, chatting with several crew members. We learned that the beachhead had been secured with only two men killed and thirteen wounded. General MacArthur had been advised by his intelligence corps that there were thirty-five hundred Japanese soldiers at Aitape. With the possibility of shore fire from the outlying islands, and not knowing exactly what submarine or aircraft activity the enemy would use, he wanted to be sure our forces were adequate. It turned out to be an overkill, the only enemy action being some sporadic rifle fire. The surprising lack of opposition was because the Japanese occupation force at Aitape was made up of service personnel instead of infantry soldiers. When we started the shelling, they had been taken completely by surprise and fled inland, leaving their fires going and breakfasts uneaten.

The next several days at Aitape passed uneventfully. By sunset of the second day most of the escort carriers and cruisers had returned to Manus, and by 24 April all that remained at Aitape were the *Etamin,* the 648, the 637, a couple of seagoing tugs, two destroyers, and a scattered few LCIs and LCTs. During this period we spent our time patrolling in alternate shifts with the 637 and taking Captain Jamison wherever he wanted to go, usually to the *Etamin.*

By 27 April, a week after the landing, we were still engaged in this activity. Things had been going smoothly, though slowly, with the unloading operation. By now the *Etamin*'s cargo was more than half unloaded. At 2000 I took over the watch from Glenn Welsh, our new third officer. We were still maintaining antisubmarine patrol, cruising slowly back and forth two thousand yards out from the *Etamin.* Moyer, our sonarman, was at his station below, pinging away. It began drizzling lightly, hardly enough to warrant wet weather gear.

At 2130 Captain Jamison came up to the bridge, followed shortly by Spaugh. The three of us talked about nothing in particular, though I recall the captain talking about his days at the naval academy, answering questions and reminiscing. By now we felt more comfortable with him aboard. With things on the beach going well, he seemed more tolerant of our ship's routine and our quirky, reservist ways. He never interfered with Spaugh's command of the ship and left all operations of that nature to be performed by us, unimpeded and uncriticized, with forbearance that we all appreciated. He stayed by himself much of the time but occasionally would relax and open up a little. That night he was in rare good humor and told us about his family, his life in the navy, the ships he had served on, places he had been, people he had known.

The three of us were thus engaged on the bridge when we heard the faint drone of a single-engine plane, followed by the sudden appearance of a bright light overhead—so bright it was like daylight. You could read a newspaper in it. A second light followed the first and we could see the gray hull of the *Etamin* etched against the dark hills behind it, looking ghostly, like a surrealist painting.

"They're here," Jamison said, "Skipper, you'd better call general quarters."

The enemy had dropped two starshells, and we were lit up like broad daylight. Spaugh ordered Beebe to sound general quarters and have the anchor detail haul up the anchor.

""They're looking us over," Captain Jamison said. "They'll be back."

The captain looked at the *Etamin* through his binoculars. We stood, waiting. It began raining harder. Ten minutes passed. Just as I was beginning to think nothing was going to happen, we heard another droning noise. This time you could tell the plane was much lower, but still we could see nothing. Suddenly, out to seaward, one of the destroyers started firing its 40-mm guns, the white tracers streaming into the night sky. We heard a plane coming in from seaward, passing directly overhead, low, going toward the beach. We still couldn't see it. A second plane came in overhead, this one even lower, but we couldn't see that one, either.

Then we heard a dull boom and we saw a shower of sparks spewing up out of the *Etamin*'s stack like a fireworks fountain display.

"They got her!" shouted Captain Jamison. "They got the *Etamin*!"

Through binoculars I could see the sparks blowing up from the stack, then a billow of white and black smoke and then more sparks. We were facing her starboard side, and as I swept my glasses slowly along her hull I could just make out something black at the waterline that I hadn't seen before. The aerial torpedo had made a perfect hit just abaft the *Etamin*'s center, at the waterline.

Jamison said, "Get under way. We've got to get over there and push her into the beach before she settles."

"Left full rudder, all engines ahead full!" Spaugh ordered. I studied the *Etamin* through my binoculars. It looked as high in the water as ever. I couldn't see any activity topsides. Nobody seemed to be on the deck. Except for the big black mark on her side she looked just the same. We came about in a tight quarter turn and headed full speed for the *Etamin.*

Spaugh let out a cry of pain. He crouched over with one hand at his face, covering one eye. We were steaming full speed towards the *Etamin,* closing fast. Spaugh was in some sort of agony. "Keereist! Damn! Dammit! Goddamn!" He hissed.

"What's wrong, what happened, what's the matter?" I asked him.

He had bent down to pick up something and in doing so had rammed the tip of the antenna from a walkie-talkie left lying on the deck right into his eye, blinding it. He was in excruciating pain.

"God damn! Goddamn!" was all he could say, then, "Ted, make sure they get the lines ready up forward. Jesus! Is it bleeding?" I could see our men were ready. We were two hundred yards from the *Etamin,* closing at full speed. The men on the 40-mm gun up forward looked up at the bridge in alarm. Someone shouted, "Cap'n, Cap'n!"

Jamison bellowed, "Stop the ship, goddammit, you're going to crash it!"

Paul straightened up, leaned into the voice tube. "All engines stop! Left full rudder! All engines back one third!" Luckily, Lou George at the wheel had already begun turning. The 648 slowed, yawing and rolling from its back wake. The *Etamin* loomed over us fifty yards away.

"Back full! Right full rudder!"

Again, Lou George had already turned the wheel. We heeled over, dangerously close. The gray steel wall of the *Etamin* came at us. We braced for a collision. Things happened so fast that no one had time to move from his station (assuming that anyone wasn't too scared to move). There was a violent, shuddering surge as the screws dug in, the reverse wake churning from our stern. The 648 slewed and stopped short of the gray wall by five feet, the water between the two ships heaving up and splashing the men on the 40-mm gun.

Spaugh had done it again. Ever flamboyant in his approaches and dockings, he had by accident surpassed himself, this time with one eye.

Jamison, furious, had no time for talk. His job was to try to push the *Etamin* into the beach so as to save the cargo. He went down the ladder to our quarterdeck and yelled up to the *Etamin* to drop a ladder so that he could come aboard.

Lt. Paul Allen Spaugh, CO, SC 648

Clad in nothing but their skivvies, men were clustered twenty feet above us along the deck of the *Etamin.* We drifted slowly along the starboard side, the steel wall leaning high over us. She had begun settling slightly to starboard, causing her main deck to appear as though it was hanging over our heads. On her deck there was nothing but mass confusion. I saw one officer bawling out orders, with no one listening or paying attention. Men were shouting down to us.

Then we saw it: a twenty-foot-diameter gaping, hissing hole, with a mass of broken, jagged metal, thin wraiths of steam issuing from cracked pipes, and oil drums floating in the water lapping in and out of the opening. The smell of gas was everywhere. Passing slowly aft, we kept yelling for someone to take our lines. A monkey fist went up but no one grabbed it. The men on the *Etamin* were in panic. We heard someone yelling something that I later surmised was "Abandon ship!" Then, like a human waterfall, the trembling, half-naked men scrambled down the side of the steel wall, dropping on our deck until there were about fifty men crowded together shivering, cold and frightened, some whimpering. They were everywhere on the deck, making it hard for us to handle lines. It was still raining.

We finally got lines secured and Spaugh, nosing the 648 against the *Etamin*'s side like a tugboat, gave the order to the engine room for full power. The screws thrashed and churned the water violently and the lines tautened, creaking under the strain. We herded the *Etamin*'s men out of the way, in case our lines let go. The *Etamin* was like a steel pier. She didn't budge. An LCT arrived and began pushing at her bow, but she remained in place. The *Etamin* was immovable.

Fifty years later, while researching this story, I learned that the *Etamin*'s captain had given the order to weigh anchor. A boatswain's mate went below to bleed the anchor winch lines but later reported that the lines "turned over slow and then stopped." The ship could not have weighed anchor in any event. The anchor chain had been almost completely paid out to 120 fathoms, and the ship was anchored so securely that a battleship couldn't have moved her in her present condition.

While all this was going on, Captain Jamison kept hollering up for someone to lower a ladder so that he could go aboard. After much difficulty, a ladder was dropped and he climbed aboard the *Etamin* to assist her captain, George Stedman. The men from the *Etamin* thought we had come alongside to rescue them from their ship, which they thought was sinking. Fagan sent up mugs of coffee and hot soup from the galley and blankets were passed around for the shivering, frightened men still in shock, still in their skivvies. Many of them were army stevedores assigned to the ship for the unloading work. If the *Etamin* was sinking, it was doing it very slowly. I asked someone if anyone had been hurt, and he said he thought someone had been burned but he wasn't sure.[3]

The seagoing tug *Chetco* finally arrived, and we backed away. We disembarked the *Etamin* men into two landing boats that came alongside and took them into the beach. By now someone on the *Etamin* had closed off watertight compartments and had begun pumping out water, and things were holding. It looked as though the ship would not sink, and as it turned out it never did.

For a long time after this I pondered over the reactions of men in crisis situations. My first impression was that the *Etamin*'s crew had not measured up too well, because I had seen so many signs of panic and the scene was extremely chaotic. This initial appraisal was unfair, however. Most, if not all, of the men who scrambled in panic onto our deck were army port battalion stevedores who had been living on the *Etamin.* They had been closest to the blast. They had taken the hit and were very much in shock—which was natural—and they were, with good reason, scared. They knew what the *Etamin* was carrying. With all that high-octane gasoline, she was a floating bomb, apt to go off any minute. If we had thought about that, we would have been just as frightened.

One man on our ship knew the danger, yet without hesitation came to the *Etamin*'s aid and scrambled up a rope ladder to give whatever help he could. For this act, and for his overall commendable effort in the Aitape landing, Capt. John Wendell Jamison received the Legion of Merit.

Two days later the 648 escorted the *Bootes,* with the *Etamin* in tow, back to Finschhafen. At 1645 on 1 May Captain Jamison left our ship. Before disembarking he shook the hands of all three officers and commended the crew for their good performance.

A career navy man, John Wendell Jamison had graduated from the U.S. Naval Academy in the Class of 1921 and for twenty years had served in various sea and shore assignments. When the United States declared war against Japan and Germany in December 1941 he had achieved the rank of commander and was a specialist in amphibious warfare. He first distinguished himself in the November 1942 landing in North Africa, when he was planning officer and beach master for the Casablanca landing at Fedhala. The landing was difficult because of darkness and poor communications. Changes in beach sites and the disposition of landing craft had to be made on the spot. Commander Jamison quickly assessed the situation and boldly changed the original landing plan by diverting the boats to other beaches, despite the objections of several high ranking Army officers. The changes worked to advantage, helped greatly in securing the beachhead, and saved many lives. The ruffled feelings among Army brass subsided when the smoke cleared and General George Patton publicly announced that "Red" Jamison had "saved the whole goddamn operation." Shortly after this, Jamison, a no-nonsense, take-charge officer, was promoted to captain. He was then re-assigned to the Pacific Theater and became Amphibious Training Officer on Admiral Barbey's Seventh Service Force—his status when he came aboard the 648.

Captain Jamison was a fine officer. We never knew whether he ever changed his mind about being on a "goddamned yacht," but in two weeks aboard he made an unforgettable impression on the young men of the 648. In our eyes he had become our very own "General Patton."

15

Those Four-Letter Words

Biak. Mention that word to Leo J. Ranjo of Philadelphia, and he grimaces ever so slightly, the corners of his mouth take on a certain set, and you know something from the past has been permanently etched in his memory. A soft-spoken, elderly gentleman today, fifty-six years ago Mr. Ranjo was a young quartermaster aboard SC 699 when she was struck by a twin-engine Japanese "Betty" bomber. It happened on 27 May 1944 during landing operations at Biak, New Guinea, following Hollandia, the next major step taken by "MacArthur's Navy" in its unrelenting drive toward the Philippines.

The 699 was one of the SCs at Arawe (see chapter 11) and, because she managed to be in the thick of things so frequently, her reputation caught the attention of Admiral Barbey, who called her "The Shootin' 699." Her brushes with danger were not over yet.

The Biak operation[1] took place ten days after a landing at Wakde and only a month after the invasion of Hollandia. Biak, the largest island of the Schouten group just east of the Vogelkop (literally, the head of the bird) of New Guinea, was heavily occupied by the Japanese, who had built three good-sized airstrips within a space of six miles and had established a supply base at Bosnick, the point at which the invasion was planned. Although our intelligence estimated that about two thousand Japanese occupied Biak, there were actually *ten* thousand enemy troops there.

The pre-invasion bombardment was especially heavy and lasted almost an hour. The landing had some hitches, but by noontime the beach had been secured and the first airstrip had been captured. The ships experienced no enemy air activity until late afternoon, when two fighter-bombers came streaking in from behind the hills at low level. They bombed the LSTs at the beach, to little effect.

Shortly after this, four twin-engined planes came in very fast and very low. The entire harbor opened up with intense antiaircraft fire, destroying two of the planes immediately and badly crippling a third, which flew off with smoke streaming out from both engines. Hits were scored on the fourth plane but, instead of disappearing, it made a wide, smoking circle and suddenly began diving straight at Adm. W. M. Fechteler's flagship, the destroyer *Sampson.* The destroyer had anticipated this and was executing a sharp turn as the plane came in. At full throttle the plane overshot the *Sampson,* then banked, causing one wing tip to graze the water. Catapulting, she slammed into the 699 amidships, spraying burning gasoline everywhere. The 699 broke into flames, and an envelope of black smoke puffed skyward, blotting her out from the pilothouse aft.

Trapped inside the pilothouse were Leo J. Ranjo, Quartermaster 2c, at the helm, and Donald Wallace, Pharmacist's Mate 1c, at the engine controls. The last order Ranjo remembers hearing was "Full right rudder!" The two men made a dash to the door aft, which led to the quarterdeck, but the smoke and flames were so intense there was no way they could get through. Their only chance of escape was to break a port of the pilothouse and try to squeeze through. The ports measured 10 inches by 14 inches. One man grabbed a pair of binoculars and smashed the port forward of the engine controls. Helped by the other, he managed to squeeze through, then helped his buddy from outside. Today Ranjo says he was so scared he could have gone through an opening half that size.

They were on the foredeck, where several other crewmen had gathered, stunned and in shock. When the plane hit, Lt. Orville J. Wahrenbrock, executive officer, had been on the flying bridge with the captain, Lt. James W. Foristel. He climbed down the front of the pilothouse and began administering to the injured. Captain Foristel either jumped or was thrown off the flying bridge at the impact, and several men also jumped or were thrown into the water.

SC 699 at Biak (*left*), moments after being struck by a "Betty" bomber. Note the men clustered on the bow. *Naval Historical Center*

The 699 had been inner control vessel for the landing and was carrying the landing control officer, Lt. Cdr. P. C. Holt, USNR. He took charge, organizing one group of men to put out the fire and another to administer to the burned and wounded. In the meantime the men who had landed in the water climbed back aboard. The ship, though badly damaged, stayed fully afloat.

There were two fatalities. Allen Hagmann, Motor Machinist's Mate 1c, was just coming up the engine room ladder to see what was going on when the plane struck. He was killed instantly.[2] William Henry Harrison, Radioman 2c, who remained at his 20-mm gun station and fired until the plane crashed into him, died in his firing crouch position. They had to remove his charred body, rigid, from his gun station.

After assisting in extinguishing fires topside, Leo Ranjo went below into the smoke-filled engine room to turn off the engines, which someone had noticed were still running. Unable to find the switch, he found electrician's mate David B. Bennett, who also went into the same inferno, managed to find the switch, and secured it. Millard Stone, Gunner's Mate 1c, Francis Ward, Radioman 1c, and Fred Seveny, Gunner's Mate 3c, all grabbed hot ammunition and threw it overboard. Stone rescued a man trapped in flames. Lt. (jg) Henry Reents, third officer, though badly burned and thrown in the water at impact, helped keep a crew member afloat and was able to get back aboard and assist the others. Joseph Hare, ship's cook, dove in the water and rescued Merle Smith, Fireman 2c, who was drowning.

Throughout the episode the landing control officer, Lieutenant Commander Holt, coolly impervious to the smoke and flames and the danger of explosion and falling debris, directed the men in saving the ship. In a brief report he wrote later, his reason for assuming command was that "the captain had gone overboard without leaving any orders." For his valor in the face of this extreme emergency Lieutenant Commander Holt was awarded the Navy Cross.

Five minutes after the crash the navy seagoing tug USS *Sonoma* came close aboard and used fire hoses to help extinguish the flames. Several men in the water were picked up by SC 734, the injured transferred to LST 459 and the uninjured to the 699 to assist the others. Fifteen minutes later the flames were out, and it became obvious that the subchaser was not sinking. LCI 31 came alongside to assist, and the 699 tied alongside her for the remain-

A downed enemy plane at Biak

der of the night. The following day the "Shootin' 699" was towed to Hollandia and the crew were transported to Cairns, Australia, for a much-needed R&R. Three months later the 699 was back in action with the Seventh Amphibious Force at Leyte.

Jim Millholland, Gunner's Mate 1c, was one of the men who remained at his battle station until after the plane crashed, and then he rendered assistance to injured shipmates. His father had served as a chief machinist's mate on SC 225 in the Adriatic during World War I and had written a book about it.[3] When young Jim was ready to go to war in World War II, it was his father, Ray, who inspired him to join the navy and try to get on a subchaser. As a courageous survivor of that little holocaust aboard the "Shootin' 699," Jim more than lived up to his father's expectations.

Incidentally, SC 699 was the victim of the first officially planned Japanese suicide attack against an American ship.[4]

"Guam" is another four-letter word permanently stamped in the minds of the men who were there during its recapture in July 1944. Beginning on W-Day (the designation of D-Day at Guam) on the 21st until the island was secured two weeks later, the retaking of this American possession was a pure bedlam of noise and destruction.

An hour before the first amtracs clattered across the reefs and onto the beach, the big guns of six battleships and eight cruisers, plus fire support closer in from numerous destroyers and rocket-equipped LCIs, enveloped the beaches in a continuous roar of billowing smoke and debris, followed by bombs dropped by carrier-based planes, all for the purpose of softening the enemy strongholds. Historian Samuel Morison described it:

> LSDs disgorged tank-filled LCMs; DUKWs loaded with artillery milled around; and over all there was the terrific din of gun and rocket fire, of air bombs bursting, of diesel and gasoline engines roaring, of LST and landing-craft ramps clanking, while flags striped with the beach colors gave the whole spectacle the air of an utterly confused and inconceivably noisy motorboat race enlarged several dimensions.[5]

Several subchasers were in the thick of it from the beginning. For the first two days, SC 1319 under the command of Lt. Jean Reed Keith, USNR, operated as assistant control vessel at the transfer line, a task which, Keith said, "was well within our scope." On the 23rd things suddenly changed. The plan originally called for the destroyer *Ringgold* to be primary control, first for the landing of the assault troops and then for the reserve troops. When it became apparent that the reserve troops would land abreast of the later echelons of the assault troops, a separate control vessel had to be assigned for their beach. Rear Adm. L. F. Reifsnider, commanding the task group, selected the 1319 for this sudden, daunting task.[6]

Within minutes, motor launches and boats from the *Ringgold* had pulled alongside the 1319, and nine officers and twenty-nine enlisted men climbed aboard.[7] Lieutenant Keith found himself with not just two or three additional men on his little subchaser, but a grand total of thirty-eight! The landing control and beach-master parties outnumbered his own ship's roster. To make this situation even more unbelievable, the thirty-eight extras were aboard for *seven days.* Having lived on a subchaser, I still can't imagine what it must have been like: one whole week, as sixty-seven men managed to eat, sleep, shave, and attend to bodily needs on that little ship with its tiny galley, three heads, and only twenty-seven mattresses. Yet not only did they adapt but they, along with SC 1328 (which performed similar exacting duties at other beaches at Guam), received high praise and letters of commendation from the admiral.

The bow of SC 648 smashes into a heavy sea. Note the mousetraps loaded with projectiles.

Seconds later, the entire foredeck is awash.

Notwithstanding the terrific bombardment that took place right up to the actual beaching of the boats themselves, the tenacious Japanese had dug deep tunnels that kept their lines of communications open. Moreover, although many rebutments and blockhouses were demolished, there were still enough pillboxes left to give them plenty of wallop from the heights overlooking Agana and Apra harbors. One subchaser would find this out only too well.

At 0515 SC 1326, Lt. Howe G. Wheelock Jr. commanding, was prepared and ready for action with fire hoses laid out, men at Condition 1, and pumps ready to use if necessary. Also a control vessel, she proceeded to APA 43, the *Fayette,* to pick up Lieutenant Commander Baggs, USN, TransDiv beach master, and his party, consisting of Lt. Lindsey. C. Claiborne, USN, and a group of enlisted men. This done, she proceeded to station, where she awaited the launching of LVTs from their mother LSTs. At 0728 she guided the first wave at two and a half knots toward the line of departure.

Arriving there thirty minutes later, she continued with the first wave toward shore. Ahead of her were the rocket-equipped LCIs, which, after they had reached the proper distance from the beach, commenced firing. The 1326 moved into position and also fired from her 40-mm and 20-mm guns a total of 750 rounds until the LVTs were about two hundred yards from the beach. It was now 0825. Gunners on the 40-mm reported that the barrel had warped from heat generated from the rapid rate of fire, so they replaced it.

From somewhere on the beach the enemy was beginning to fire on the LVTs as they were making their approach, the splashes quite visible to the men on the control ship. No one could determine exactly where they came from. Commander Baggs asked Captain Wheelock to move the ship in closer, and he complied, until they were about sixteen hundred yards from shore. Shells continued to splash among the LVTs, and as they approached Wheelock noticed the splashing was getting uncomfortably close to the 1326. When one hit the water only seventy-five yards off their bow Wheelock knew they were being targeted. Ordering full left rudder and kicking the engines up, he was in the middle of the turn when a 3-inch mortar shell struck the water twenty yards off the port beam, spraying the pilot house and flying bridge with shrapnel. This was followed by a second shell that landed squarely on the 1326 just forward of the pilothouse, killing three men on the 40-mm crew instantly and fatally wounding two more. Eight others were wounded, five seriously. Four cases of ammunition broke out in

A 40-mm gun crew at work

Remains of a downed enemy plane

flames but were quickly extinguished. Two members of the control party were hit by shrapnel.

Damage to the 1326 was listed as "extensive but superficial," with lots of holes in the deck, the hull planking, ready boxes, and pilothouse. Six of the twelve ports in the pilothouse were shattered. The wounded men were transferred to the USS *Zeitlin.* The bodies of the three men killed were so badly mutilated and dismembered that it would have been impossible to preserve them for later burial on land. They were, therefore, buried at sea the following day, with appropriate ceremonies.

After retreating to a position about two thousand yards from the beach, the 1326 was able to continue its job of control satisfactorily. For the next four days she stood patrol duty and provided communication and dispatch service among the transport ships scattered about the harbor. On 25 July

SC 742, flag at half mast, after her action at Arawe and Biak

she departed Guam in company with other ships for the return to Eniwetok and hull repairs.

Those four-letter words, Biak and Guam, spelled death for many Americans. Every subchaser sailor knows what they meant to the Splinter Fleet and shares the loss.

16

Subchasers as Gunboats

Late in 1943, in response to requests by PT commanders in the southwest Pacific, eight subchasers were selected to be converted into gunboats. PT boats had proven effective at inshore patrol but were limited in range and firepower. Much of their activity was concentrated on impeding or preventing movement among the islands by Japanese barges. Their range and firepower limitations were a hindrance to this mission, and SCs seemed likely alternatives.

A gunboat is classified as a small, well-armed vessel, commonly used for river patrol. In 1943 the navy's complement of gunboats consisted of a number of miscellaneous vessels in a wide range of sizes and types, including former private yachts, commercial surveying ships, cable ships, and old gunboats. Most of them were too big for the purpose for which the SCs were converted. PG 51, for instance, the USS *Charleston,* was 328 feet long, carried a seaplane, and resembled a light cruiser.

The SC subchaser hull, it was believed, lent itself admirably to the qualities needed in a gunboat. Its shallow draft and good maneuverability were two important characteristics that would be useful for patrolling small harbors and rivers where Japanese barges might be lurking. Consequently, by early December 1943 eight SCs had been converted as follows:

Formerly	*New Designation*
SC 644	PGM 1
SC 757	PGM 2
SC 1035	PGM 3
SC 1053	PGM 4
SC 1056	PGM 5
SC 1071	PGM 6
SC 1072	PGM 7
SC 1366	PGM 8

The SCs selected were equipped with GM 16-184A "pancake" engines, an ingenious lightweight 16-cylinder diesel that used four layers each of four cylinders stacked radially around a vertical crankshaft. Over half of all SCs built were equipped with these engines. Gunboats had to have them instead of the straight eight-cylinder engines because ships so equipped were much more maneuverable and could attain speeds of over twenty knots. The maneuverability of the converted SCs was enhanced by the use of variable-pitch propellers and twin rudders.

The reputed speed of over twenty knots is questionable. Lt. (jg) Ed Thorney, executive officer on PGM 2, writes in a postwar letter to a minesweeping buddy: "You mentioned your ship could hit 'only' 28 knots. Our good old PGMs had to struggle to reach 20 knots, only possible with all of the crew at the oars, the wind and sea at our backs, and going downhill!"

PGM 6, formerly SC 1071 *National Archives*

The converted SCs certainly looked like gunboats. Their low silhouette, green camouflage paint, and heavy armament gave them a mysterious, somewhat sinister look. I remember how startled I was upon viewing one for the first time in the South Pacific. I recognized the SC hull but was baffled by the changes to its superstructure. The PGM looked like a true fighting machine. The familiar pilothouse was gone. In its place was an austere, open cockpit backed by a short, folding radar mast. As on a PT boat, the topside was open for complete horizontal and vertical visibility all around. It was armed to the teeth with a 3-inch/50 gun forward and a twin 40-mm mounted aft. In between there were twin .50-caliber machine guns and either one or two 20-mm Oerlikons, one 60-mm army mortar, a multi-barreled bazooka with sixty rockets, and two smoke generators. The gun stations and the cockpit were protected with quarter-inch steel shielding.

The eight converted SCs, now designated PGMs, underwent shakedowns at Terminal Island, formed themselves into a group called PGM Division 1, and set out for Pearl Harbor, ultimately to join the PT boats in the Solomon Islands. With them was a small tanker for refueling underway. No sooner had they left San Pedro than the weather turned sour and they found themselves in a three-day gale of almost hurricane proportions.

The captain of the tanker was a mustang with no knowledge of celestial navigation, and this proved to be a problem because few if any of the green officers on the PGMs had any practical experience in navigation. With the ships rolling as much as 67 degrees in turbulent water, it took a half hour to go from the officers' cabin to the bridge ten feet away. To take star sights, a line of three or four men had to be formed from the radio shack, where the chronometer was kept, to the officer taking the sights. The sights were shouted down to the quartermaster standing by the clock. The ships were heaving and tossing so much that it took an hour of painful work to record and plot the sights.

Three PGMs decided to turn back, since they were taking in more water than their bilge pumps and billy pumps could manage. Their action alarmed the tanker skipper, who, violating strict orders to maintain radio silence, began sending messages on the emergency frequency to determine their position. The PGMs tried to answer him by blinker, but the pitch and roll of the little ships were such that lights shone on the water or up in the sky most of the time. They finally decided that the danger to the PGMs from submarines was minimal, since they drew only six feet of water and a torpedo would pass underneath. The danger to the tanker was serious, but that was that captain's responsibility. He evidently felt that everyone's chances of surviving the hurricane were small. As a result the convoy's position was broadcast for all to know, including the enemy.

With the disappearance of bad weather, the five PGMs refueled from the tanker and encountered no more problems until they arrived in Pearl Harbor. The commanding officers of each ship were questioned thoroughly about their violation of radio silence, but the PGM skippers were exonerated after explaining the circumstances. The results may not have been as satisfactory for the captain of the tanker.

Upon their arrival at Guadalcanal, the five PGMs were rejoined by the three sister ships turned back by the hurricane on the way to Pearl Harbor. They were then deployed among several PT bases and individually, or in pairs, began their duty of working with PT boats patrolling the islands and inland waters of the Solomons.

Much of our information about the PGMs has been generated from the recollections of two men who served aboard these vessels. Bill Prechtl of Bridge City, Texas, former radioman, says the time he served aboard PGM 4 would have put "McHale's Navy" to shame but adds, "I wouldn't have traded the experience for a million dollars." George Puente of Yonkers, New York, former coxswain aboard PGM 5, was a "plank owner," having served from the day she was commissioned as SC 1056 in June 1943 to her decommissioning in the Philippines two and a half years later. Mr. Puente is a veritable storehouse of incidents and tales about the PGMs, many of them quite funny. Underneath the humor lies the undeniable element of risk entailed with each mission.

The PGM 5 saw a lot of action and was commended for carrying out more than eighty missions and destroying seven enemy barges. Once while based at Treasury Island MTB Base #9 in the Solomons, PGM 5, in company with two other PGMs, sailed steadily for two days, rendezvoused at night with twelve PT boats, and moved in very close to shore, forming a long line parallel to a beach. Japanese ground troops were supposed to be there. The fifteen vessels opened fire on the beach with all of their guns, setting several fires. They kept this up for twenty minutes. Mr. Puente says he doesn't remember if this took place at Bougainville or in New Guinea, and he's not even sure of the date, but he can still visualize how eerie it was after they ceased fire. "It got very quiet and the smoke seemed to hang there close to the ground and the odor of gunpowder was sharp and clean. The fires went out one by one, it got dark again, and we left this place as we came—silently, a few boats at a time."

Another incident that Mr. Puente recalls occurred when PGM 5 was on a five-day reconnaissance of Japanese-held Choiseul Island. They were looking for five Australian scouts who had been landed on the island a few days earlier. Uncertain as to their location, the PGM 5 nosed slowly into the beach and sent most of their men into the bush to locate the five Australians, leaving only four men aboard. A lone U.S. PBY spotted the gunboat and made several parallel passes, each one a little closer, until finally the plane made a fast diving run at the ship. The four men had refrained from using signal flares, thinking they would look like unfriendly tracers. As the plane got closer three of the men started moving, not knowing what else to do. A fourth yelled, "Stand still!" Grabbing a U.S. flag from somewhere, he held it straight out. The pilot saw the flag just in time, pulled out of his dive, and was forced to fly over land through Japanese gunfire. Mr. Puente doesn't remember which crew member had the presence of mind to grab Old Glory, but "he saved that mission and our asses. Sure would like to thank him for that."

On another occasion all ships in Bougainville were given priority orders to get under way and out of there as quickly as possible. PGM 5 was ordered to patrol duty offshore and to challenge any and all ships encountered. In the dead of night they were thus engaged when an enormous hulk of a ship appeared, stacks low in the water, bristling with big guns fore and aft. The little PGM 5 bravely challenged the monster with its signal lamp, "Who are you?" The hulk replied in turn with: "Little man, we is the cruiser *Tuscaloosa,*" at which the relieved little gunboat flashed, "Thank God."

Another time the routine at Treasury Island was interrupted by the unannounced appearance of Bob Hope and his troop of entertainers. Some of the men on PGM 5 first saw them early in the morning boarding a PT boat to go for a ride. The PT was maneuvering backward and forward, turning to leave the little harbor with Patti Page, Frances Langford, and Jerry Colonna aboard. A PT boat was moored next to PGM 5, nose to the beach. It was customary for the men on the PT to use a one-inch-thick board with a hole in the center for toilet purposes. The board was hung over the fantail. One man, apparently oblivious to the visitation by the entertainers, went to the fantail, dropped his pants and sat down on the board, opening a newspaper and lighting a cigar in full view of everyone. Men on PGM 5 yelled to him, "Hey, there's women around." He ignored them and they repeated, "Hey you, there's women here!" He said, "Stop bothering me, there's no women on this island." Someone said, "Turn your head." He did, amid plenty of laughter from the entertainers and everybody else, as he quickly spat out the cigar, pulled up his pants, and exited.

During the early morning hours of 18 July 1944, PGMs 8, 5, 4, and 7, in that order, got under way from Treasury Island and headed for patrol duty in the dangerous waters that formed a channel between New Britain and New Ireland. The seas were very rough, and the four vessels were pounding so badly it was virtually impossible to maintain speed and position. Each boat would climb up a wave, reach the crest, then fall off sideways. On PGM 4, Bill Prechtl, Radioman 1c, who also filled in at radar watches, found the sea conditions so rough that the radar was sweeping the sky more than the surface. Every second or third sweep they might get a bearing on the two PGMs (8 and 4) ahead. They never got a return from PGM 7, following them, but didn't think much about that since their main objective was to keep track of the two vessels ahead. They believed that PGM 7 was cresting at the wrong time and their radar was probably missing her.

Lt. (jg) Myron C. Dickes, commanding PGM 4, asked Prechtl to go aft to the galley and light the range. Prechtl respectfully replied that he didn't know how to light the range. The seaman at the helm spoke up, saying he knew how. The captain told Prechtl to take the helm and sent the seaman aft to light the range. At this time the captain was braced forward of the wheelhouse splinter shield, attempting to observe sea conditions so that he could advise the helmsman when to ease off. Shortly after Prechtl took the wheel, the ship's gyro began spinning wildly. Prechtl, who had been following the gyro, quickly switched to magnetic compass in order to keep the ship on course. At that moment they all saw the PGM 7 crossing their bow from their starboard side. The captain only had time to give two orders, "Stop all engines!" and "Stand by for collision!"

The PGM 4 struck PGM 7 amidships, broadside to, on her port side. Her bow ripped through the 7's engine room, tearing the port engine loose and stacking it on top of the starboard engine—a fortunate thing, as otherwise the 4's bow would have cleaved PGM 7 in half.

The two gunboats hung together in a giant T, the violent sea tossing them about while men on both ships came running up from below. Prechtl switched on lights on PGM 4 to see if anyone had been injured or thrown overboard. The OTC on PGM 8 radioed orders to PGM 4, "Douse your lights," to which the 4 replied, "We've had a collision." PGM 7 was flexing. It was apparent her keel had been broken. Prechtl had gone below to the radio room to call the base for assistance when someone on PGM 7 told them to secure and that they would take over communications. PGMs 8 and 5 came back and began circling the two ships. Two P-38 planes were sent out to provide air coverage, and a minesweeper was dispatched to take PGM 7 in tow.

Miraculously her fore and aft engine-room bulkheads had held, and she was able to remain afloat. PGM 4, her bow considerably damaged, was ordered back to Treasury Island. The collision, though unfortunate, was an eloquent demonstration of the truly seaworthy construction of the SC hulls.

The usual board of inquiry followed. One issue, discussed at length, was whether the sea conditions were too rough for the speed the tactical commander (PGM 8) was trying to maintain. However, no one was blamed, there being too many unanswered questions about speed, sea conditions, station keeping, and possible errors in judgment.

Lt.(jg) Ed Thorney, mentioned earlier, joined PGM 2 in September 1944 as executive officer. He wrote the following about PGM duty in the Solomons:

> We worked with Australian coast watchers. Our first mission was to land Lt. John Andresen, RANVR, on Choiseul Island with some native scouts and their radio gear. This took place in broad daylight on a Japanese island reported to contain twenty to thirty thousand troops. John was very nonchalant about the whole thing but the rest of us had grave doubts and were feeling pretty edgy. Thick jungle grew right to the water's edge and we would have been beautiful point blank targets. Of course John knew exactly what he was doing and nothing happened. We nosed the bow up to the beach and he didn't even get his feet wet.
>
> Another mission was to bombard Porapora, Choiseul, along with PGM 3 on Christmas Eve, 1944. Porapora was a Japanese army encampment in and around a cave that opened to seaward. The cave was hidden by trees and vegetation but was vulnerable to fire from the water. This was a daytime strike, commencing just after dawn. It was led by "Snowy" Rhoades, RANVR, a legendary coast watcher who wrote a couple of books about their exploits after the war. We came within five hundred yards of shore and fired everything we owned at seemingly unoccupied jungle. It was impossible to tell at the time if we were doing any good, but later reports indicated we were most successful. Apparently we caught the enemy completely by surprise, and if there was any return fire their aim was bad. It was the first time I had ever seen a 3-inch/50 firing with a burned-out barrel. We saw 3-inch shells starting to go in all directions, up, down and to both sides.

There was no way to control them. After we had fired everything available in our ready boxes, including star shells, we retired unscathed.

Long after the war had moved to the north and into the Philippines, a few U.S. ships had to remain in the Bismarck Archipelago, not only to maintain our presence but to block any attempts to supply bypassed islands still occupied by Japanese. It fell to the PGMs, SCs, PTs, and other vessels to fill this need, much to the frustration of those gung ho sailors who wanted to be in more forward areas.

In January 1945, PGM Division 1, now seven ships instead of eight, proceeded in convoy to Leyte and other Philippine locations, where for several weeks they were given miscellaneous assignments, mostly patrol work of a routine nature. One mission deserves recounting, since it provided a taste of adventure for four PGMs.

Mindanao, originally General MacArthur's first target in his plan for Philippine liberation, actually was the last island to be occupied by American forces. Mindanao was a rugged and mountainous island covered with many rain forests. Roads were limited, most of them little more than improved trails incapable of supporting modern military vehicles. Although there were over forty-three thousand Japanese troops on Mindanao, Filipino guerrillas controlled 95 percent of the island and were able to confine the Japanese largely to the towns and principal roads. In retrospect, there was little reason to risk American troops for an island of such small strategic value. The capture of Mindanao, therefore, may have been an operation undertaken for reasons of prestige and to please our Philippine allies.[1]

On 17 April a landing was made near the mouth of the Mindanao River on the western shore of the island. There was no opposition, and the landing proceeded smoothly. The troops moved rapidly inland and along Highway No. 1, which led to Davao on the eastern coast. Knowing that the highway was nothing more than a widened trail and most of its bridges had been destroyed by the Japanese, they decided to exploit the Mindanao River as a water route to the interior. The army knew it was navigable at least as far as Fort Pikit, thirty-five miles inland, and just beyond that was Kabakan, an important junction with a highway leading to Cagayan in the northern part of the island.

Army engineers had a flotilla of LCMs that had been converted to gunboats and rocket boats and planned to use them to go forty miles up river and capture Fort Pikit. In need of additional firepower, four PGMs and two LCI(G)s were designated to lead the expedition up the river. Consequently, at 1010 on 19 April, PGM 4, PGM 5, PGM 6, and PGM 8 arrived at the mouth and proceeded six miles up river to the town of Cotabato, where, shortly after midnight, they moored alongside LCI(G) 61 and LCI(G) 66.[2]

The next day a few men from PGM 5 had an opportunity to look over Cotabato, a town now occupied by the U.S. Army and in shambles. George Puente and some sailors were talking to some army men at their post. A tall, thin man, wearing black shorts and twirling a big black opened umbrella on his shoulder, sauntered towards them. An army man called, "Halt!" The man kept coming. Other men called, "Halt!" He still kept coming. A third time they yelled "HALT!" He said, "You can't stop me, I'm the mayor of this town." A sergeant aimed his cocked .45 automatic at him. "One more step and you're the dead mayor of this town," he said flatly. The man looked at him, turned around and went away fast.

Mr. Puente, of PGM 5, tells about exploring Cotabato. The sailors continued their walk around the village and stumbled upon a deep, wide hole leading into a cave. They spotted many wooden crates inside the cave "needing attention." Puente and another sailor went down into the cave to investigate. Breaking one of the crates open, they discovered it packed with small squares of something wrapped in wax paper, "light brown in color and soft." Thinking them to be some kind of Japanese food or soap, they broke open a few more crates and found the same mysterious square objects. They tossed some up to the other sailors to examine. One of them asked a passing soldier, "What's this?" The soldier replied, "Dynamite." Puente got up out of the cave pretty fast, and "after we finished shaking and exchanging 'what ifs' with each other, we continued exploring."

The day passed and it began to get dark, so the sailors started back to the ship. As they approached the area near the dock, they heard someone say, "Halt. Say the password." They didn't know the password, but they remembered what had happened to the "mayor" earlier in the day. They tried to figure out what to say. The guard called out again, the sailors heard them loading a machine gun, and they whispered to each other, "These guys ain't kidding." The five of them yelled out together, "We're sailors and we don't know the fucking password!" As they came forward the sergeant and a couple of his men recognized them. As they passed by, the sergeant looked them over and said, "You guys are pretty goddamn dumb, but you're lucky."

Early the next morning the flotilla proceeded up river, an army LCM leading, the two LCIs next, and PGMs 4, 5, 8, and 6 following in that order.

Both sides of the narrow, dirty, muddy yellow river were a tangle of dense jungle from which noises—the screech of a parakeet, the chatter of monkeys—carried across the water. On PGM 5 a crewman sighted a man with a rifle peering out at the passing ships. He was in uniform. The crewman pointed him out to his skipper. Without hesitation the captain said, "Shoot him." The sailor looked at his captain. The captain repeated, "I said, shoot him." The sailor raised his rifle, aimed, and fired. The man disappeared. The ships kept moving.

They passed a clearing in which there was a small village with houses close to the water. Children were bathing, families sitting on grass, all in colorful garb. It was a sudden, dazzling, surrealistic scene from another world. The ships passed, the sailors staring silently and the villagers staring back just as silently.

That afternoon the ships anchored at a sharp bend in the river. One of the LCI(G)s was having engine trouble, and the army commander decided that everyone should remain there for the night to allow the disabled ship to make repairs. The ships anchored in such a position that the two LCI(G)s were on one side of the sharp bend, hidden from the PGMs, who were on the other side of the bend. Dense growth hid the two groups of ships from each other.

When the dark of night came, the men, used to the open sea, felt hemmed in, claustrophobic. It was eerie, mysterious, and only added to the tension already building up. There was a sense of being trapped. The river was too narrow to turn around. They were surrounded by jungle behind which the enemy could be lurking and even at that moment preparing to attack.

Someone on one of the LCI(G)s thought he detected movement. He cocked his rifle, raised it, and waited. Again something moved. He pulled the trigger and fired. Someone fired back. A third rifle fired. PGM 8 came to general quarters, thinking they were under attack. They began firing at the rifle fire. Tracers streaked horizontally at each other, a furious enfilade, with all ships blazing away at each other, each thinking they were under attack. It kept up until, just as suddenly, it ceased. It was at that instant everyone realized they were shooting at each other. The LCI(G)s, on one side of the sharp bend had been shooting at the PGMs and these, thinking they were being attacked by the enemy, returned fire. When daylight came the cause of the commotion—and the sole casualty—turned out to be a stray water buffalo.

While getting under way that morning, PGM 5 fouled her propeller in an underwater log, damaging the shaft enough to prevent her from remaining with the expedition. She was pushed, stern to, back to the mouth of the river by one of the LCMs. The other ships got under way with orders to proceed at best possible speed and not to stop for any individual ship. PGM 4, Lt. R. A. Pickering in command, led the column, and PGM 8 and PGM 6 followed in that order, with the LCI(G)s bringing up the rear. The formation caught up with the advanced units of the army engineers at Lomopog, from whence it proceeded with a small army support boat in the lead. This boat had made a preliminary reconnaissance as far up as Inogog the previous day and knew the conditions up to that point. The enemy was known to be just beyond.

When they reached Inogog, the three contingents—the infantry, army engineers, and ship's captains—held a conference. They knew that the enemy, about five hundred in all, held the river at Balumis, from which they could fire downstream and across stream near the bridge just south of Fort Pikit. A plan was devised by which two PGMs abreast would lead the army LCMs upstream and commence firing at Balumis as soon as they reached a sharp turn just below it. Since many of these turns did not appear on the charts, they were using two Filipino guerrillas who were put aboard PGM 4 as spotters. An army lieutenant with a radioman came aboard also for liaison. PGM 8 was selected to proceed astern of the whole formation and to anchor at the first curve in the river to act as a guard, or proceed upstream as the situation dictated. Meanwhile the infantry was to march up the west bank and join the river-borne forces at Fort Pikit. PGM 4 and PGM 6 were to divide, one to stay anchored just north of Balumis, the other to continue to Pikit itself.

At 1455 on 21 April the two PGMs got under way and proceeded upriver abeam at a speed of five knots. It was difficult to maneuver in this fashion since the channel was very narrow, causing the PGMs at one time to be only three feet apart. The trip lasted over an hour. Disaster threatened when, just before making the last crucial turn, PGM 4 went aground. By backing down full, then coming left into PGM 6 and going ahead fast, Pickering was able to proceed. Balumis lay twelve hundred yards ahead. PGM 6 fell astern and both PGMs opened fire with their 3-inch/50 cannons, continuing the barrage intermittently until Balumis was passed to starboard. When they reached the bridge below Fort Pikit they ceased fire and, after a pause, proceeded through and anchored just south of Fort Pikit, which stood on the left bank on top of a hill. Both PGMs concentrated their 3-inch/50 fire on the fort, the noise in the confined spaces of the jungle deafening. The barrage continued for a half hour, during which the LCTs joined them and the infantry went up the hill. The ships stopped shelling, and the troops swarmed into Fort Pikit. The enemy had fled, as they had done at Balumis, leaving dishes of hot food still on plates in their mess hall.[3]

The ships remained at Fort Pikit until 24 April before returning downriver, which turned out to be not all that simple. First they had to turn around. PGM 4 made the first attempt, backing down to a bend just below Fort Pikit and then easing sternwise into a riverbank to let the current push its bow around. Everything worked fine until they tried to go forward and found themselves hopelessly aground. PGM 6 and PGM 8 both managed to turn around and head downstream. However, it was much more difficult to control headings because the flow of current was the same as their forward movement. Consequently, both PGM 6 and PGM 8 also became hopelessly stranded. Word of the PGMs' plight was sent to Rear Adm. A. G. Noble, in USS *Wasatch,* in charge of the entire task force. He sent back a message to Pickering to put a marker on the bank of the river opposite his ship and, when the river rose to a certain point, to notify the admiral, who would send an expert up to bring them down.

Pickering had little confidence in this plan, since there was no assurance the river would rise again, nor did he believe he needed an "expert" to help them. The admiral, however, proved to be correct. In a few days the water did rise. An expert in the form of Lieutenant Commander Bullard, executive officer of the Coast Guard ship USCGC *Spencer,* arrived, and with the help of some LCMs that he used as ramplighters, managed to free all three of the stranded PGMs. He then attached two LCTs on either side of each PGM and they maneuvered safely back down the river. Three days later they were ready to take on new missions.

The PGMs were sent to Luzon, where they kept busy patrolling the coast, ferrying personnel, and occasionally strafing enemy trucks, supply dumps, and anything else that looked suspicious. They encountered and sank several Japanese one-man suicide boats. They participated in landings at Iwo Jima and Okinawa. At the end of the war the seven PGMs reported to the commander of the Yangtze Patrol in Shanghai, where their busy careers ended. In 1947 they were sold to China and the Philippines by the Foreign Liquidation Commission.

Opinions regarding the effectiveness of the PGMs have been mixed. The PT sailors liked them for their superior firepower but complained that their slower speed held everyone back. The PGM "rolled too easily and rapidly."[4] Nevertheless, the PGMs made up for this with three times the range and endurance of the PT boats. The fact that they were SC subchasers to begin with makes them worthy of note here. Although several PGMs received Unit Citations and Lieutenant Pickering of PGM 4 was awarded the Bronze Star for his leadership in the Fort Pikit operation, the PGMs did a lot of dirty work for which they received scant recognition.

17

Leyte

SC 991 saw plenty of action in the Pacific. After serving as beach control vessel in a vicious landing at Peleliu from which she emerged unscathed, she was reassigned to the Seventh Fleet. Accordingly, in September 1944 she proceeded to Hollandia, New Guinea, where she learned she would be inner control vessel in the invasion of the Philippines at Leyte.[1]

Leyte, the biggest of all the landings thus far in the Pacific war, had a special significance for General MacArthur, for it would fulfill his famous promise to the Philippine people, "I shall return." Humiliated by being forced to leave the Philippines, which the Japanese took over shortly after Pearl Harbor, MacArthur had been waiting almost three years for this moment. Liberating the Philippines was not only a personal crusade; it would also mean that U.S. military and naval power would be within striking distance of Japan itself.

The date for the invasion was set for 20 October. A full-scale practice was held at Manus in the Admiralty Islands, complete with troops, landing boats, and full air coverage. Then, on 13 October, Task Force 78, the Northern Attack Group under the command of Rear Adm. Daniel "Uncle Dan" Barbey, formed up and left Hollandia. Several destroyers and PCs and the lone subchaser SC 991 provided a screen for the transports, which were carrying troops of X Corps, 24th Infantry Division, and 1st Cavalry Division. A drenching rain storm and high winds extending well into the night made it difficult for the ships to maintain station, but conditions improved by the second day, and for six days the convoy steamed north with no problems, changing course frequently and maneuvering in various zigzag patterns to disguise their movements from enemy spotter planes. At midnight on 19 October, the Task Force had arrived off the entrance to Leyte Gulf.

Picking their way carefully between the two islands[2] flanking the entrance to the Gulf, the ships had to be on the lookout for mines. The day before, the destroyer USS *Ross,* which had been screening the pre-invasion minesweeping operation, had struck two mines in succession and suffered many casualties. On the 991, for Lt. (jg) Irving N. "Hep" Hepner and his men, traversing the channel in pitch dark was a white-knuckle event, all hands topside and no one sleeping. Samuel Eliot Morison described it thus:

> During the night the men snatched a few hours of restless sleep and then left their sweaty bunks for the fresh air topside . . . No one talked much, for there was not much to say, but all hands had plenty to think about. Few episodes in the war were more vivid in the minds of American sailors than the story of heroism and death on Bataan. Yet if any of these men felt like avenging angels or crusaders they kept it very much to themselves. More important to them was the fact that this was a big step along the road to Tokyo and the end of the war.[3]

The passage was made safely nevertheless, and once inside Leyte Gulf the convoy formation quickly dispersed and SC 991 began a run for its position on the line of departure at the beachhead. The landing was planned for 1000 because the high tide and broad daylight were most favorable for the large transports to make their way through the channel. At 0845 the 991 had reached her position five thousand yards off White Beach and dropped her anchor. Soon after she began receiving radiomen aboard who directed the waves of LCVPs that hit the beach, using their SCR radios to talk directly to the boat coxswains of each wave. There was little or no enemy resistance during the landing, things proceeded quite smoothly, and at 1150 the 991 got under way and moved in closer, anchoring twelve hundred yards from the beach.

That afternoon, the men of SC 991 were eyewitnesses to a historic moment. A landing barge passed close aboard, and standing in it dressed in fresh suntans, braided hat, and sunglasses was Gen. Douglas MacArthur himself, with several members of his staff and the president of the Philippines. The general was making good his "I shall return" promise to the Philippine people. The barge scraped on a reef in shallow water and the General and his party waded ashore to the beach where an American flag flew from a coconut palm stripped of its foliage by the pre-invasion shore bombardment. The dramatic return took place in full view of the men on SC 991, who would never forget that moment.

There was only light resistance during the day of the landing. That evening a lone Japanese airplane dropped a bomb on a large ammunition dump, causing a huge explosion and fireball that lit up the sky for a long time. Two nights later a large number of Japanese aircraft swooped over, some of them intentionally diving into individual ships. Vague and undefined reports kept coming through about Japanese surface ships in the area, and ships' radios crackled with ominous messages about Japanese surface ships. The recurring Flash Red signals[4] kept everyone on the alert, and it was necessary to lay smoke almost constantly, a task relegated to a few LCIs equipped with smoke generators.

On the fourth day a Nelly passed fifty feet over the 991's mast and crash-dived LCI 1065 anchored a hundred yards astern; a second Nelly dived into a seagoing tug nearby. The LCI sank, but the tug was able to get under way and beach itself. Amid the garbled radio communications on the 991 they heard an urgent and clear message: "All ships this station stand by for a naval bombardment."

As it happened, no such bombardment took place inside the Gulf. History has recorded the action of the U.S. Navy in the great battles of Surigao Strait, the battles off Samar, and Cape Engano, all of which combined to save the landing and virtually destroy the Japanese navy—the largest naval action in history.

Enemy planes continued to harass the ships inside the Gulf nevertheless, and in the days that followed the 991 expended a lot of ammunition, successfully shooting down a twin-engine Betty and a Val dive-bomber. A few days later the 991 opened fire on a smoking dive-bomber that crash-dived SS *Benjamin Ide Wheeler* anchored to starboard. The plane dived straight down into the after cargo hold of the ship, causing it to explode and sink. Portions of its superstructure still showed above the surface after it settled to the bottom.

With the stress and excitement of Red Alerts and air attacks, the 991 had little need for other problems, yet toward the end of October the ships in the

Gulf found themselves in a full-blown 120-knots-per-hour typhoon. The third officer, Ens. Roy Johns, describes the experience thus:

> All the ships had their running lights turned on and the concept seemed to be "Every man for himself." Rain was streaking horizontally. I saw one man on the bridge with a navy raincoat streaming out from his neck at 90 degrees to his body with all buttons and clasps stripped and useless. Ships appeared from every possible angle out of the darkness and rain, some looming directly at our ship. Thus, frequent commands of "All Ahead Full" or "All Back Full" in short bursts of power were used to avoid collision. It was a true nightmare! "Hep" (CO Irving Hepburn) relieved me shortly before 0400. I told him we were definitely dragging anchor and using both engines to steer clear of other ships. He saluted and took the conn. I was exhausted and went below to hit the sack, but I could hear every change in engine speed and direction. In twenty minutes I heard Hep go from "Full Ahead" to "Full Astern" to "Full Ahead," and then a loud crunch on the starboard side. I went topside and saw a very large Australian ship parallel to our starboard side with both ships banging each other with each surging wave. The ships parted and the Aussie ship hit our bow and cut our anchor chain. Thus, anchor and chain were lost along with other damage to the ship. Within minutes two men went forward to the violently heaving bow, opened the deck plate to the chain locker, pulled out a spare anchor and a coil of wire rope, and successfully got the anchor in the water with the wire rope secured to a deck fitting. Each plunge of the bow covered the men with sheets of water while they were doing this . . . When the storm had subsided late the following day we were some 15 to 20 miles from our beachhead anchorage.

Early in November they were hit by another typhoon with conditions identical to the first storm. Again, Ensign Johns had just gone below when he heard contradictory orders repeated to the engine room in quick succession, followed again by a heavy crunch on the starboard side. This time an LCI had hit the ship and knocked a hole in its side. Fortunately the hole was mostly above the waterline and they were able to make temporary repairs. When that storm finally ended, the ship had run out of food except for sacks of sweet potatoes and the ingredients to make pancakes. The pancake-and-sweet-potato diet continued for several days, three meals a day. To supplement this diet the crew removed all sea rations from both life rafts. Finally, during a lull in Flash Reds, they were able to tie alongside an LST and draw fresh rations.

On November 7th, amid gunfire, storms, kamikaze attacks, and the stresses of shipboard life, Ensign Johns quietly turned twenty years of age, with no cake or celebration or mention of it by ship's personnel.

In time, SC 991 received orders to escort several LSTs back to Hollandia. While proceeding through the same channel marking the entrance to Leyte Gulf, the convoy was attacked by one group of low-flying fighters and a second group of high-altitude medium bombers. The fight was short and furious, resulting in a hit on one of the LSTs, killing eighteen men. The OTC signaled all ships to steam hard all night to get away from the land-based planes. Late the next afternoon, under gray, somber skies, all ships closed ranks. Cruising slowly, the ships, fifty to seventy-five yards apart, attended as the stricken LST conducted burial-at-sea ceremonies. One by one, as the names were read, the body of each sailor, wrapped in a white sheet with a length of anchor chain, was placed on a board and slid over the side.

From the time SC 991 had been tied up at a wooden dock at Tulagi to the time she tied up to a wooden dock at Hollandia, she had been at sea for seventy-eight continuous days. The ship had served as a landing control vessel at Peleliu, had rescued a float plane off a reef and returned it to a cruiser, had discovered a mine field and had it dismantled, had participated in night retirement operations and convoy work for all ships at Peleliu, had convoyed the amphibious forces to Leyte, had served as control vessel at Leyte, had survived two typhoons, and had survived two collisions.

18

The Subchaser and the Zero

Silhouetted in the orange light of dawn, hundreds of ships lay quietly at anchor in Leyte Gulf. They made an awesome display of sea power, a sight that must have caused concern to the Japanese warlords, who by now were having second thoughts. The attack on Pearl Harbor may not have been such a good idea after all. The conquest of the Pacific was backfiring, with thousands of Japanese troops left to starve in New Guinea, Rabaul, Truk, and the Philippines. The ghosts of Pearl Harbor had returned tenfold.

The peaceful scene at Leyte early on the morning of 27 November 1944 was deceptive. Night after night the Japanese were sending planes over, and night after night the ships, so peaceful now, were shooting up a storm of fire so deadly and so concentrated it defied description. Whole blankets of tracer fire streaked up and blended together in one gigantic fireworks display, lighting up the harbor and dulling one's senses with the noise. A plane would explode in midair, or get hit and start coming down. Ships kept firing at it until it crashed into the sea, or a ship. The tracers would level out as the plane came down, until they made a horizontal line and ships fired through each others' rigging. Men were killed and wounded by such friendly fire.

At 0730 on this quiet morning SC 744 lighted off her engines and got under way, slowly threading among the ships anchored in Tacloban Harbor, heading out from San Pedro Bay to rendezvous with tugboat TP 114 with a heavy barge in tow. The barge was loaded with drums of high-octane gasoline for use at a PT base being built at Liloan on the western side of Leyte. The sea was calm, there was only a slight breeze, and the sky was clear and blue, with high, wispy clouds. The little convoy moved out slowly, the 744 taking station three hundred yards ahead. Once clear, the 744 began zigzagging according to plan. The convoy's speed was five knots.

In command of the 744 was Lt. Donald S. Stroetzel, USNR, a twenty-year-old Princeton graduate from upstate New York. He had reported aboard in July and by September had relieved the previous skipper, who had served his overseas tour and had been ordered back to the States, in a routine transfer of command. His executive officer was Ens. Aldine A. Rosser, USNR, from Tifton, Georgia, a few years older than Stroetzel. The third officer was Ens. Lewis Morris Jr., USNR, from Amsterdam, New York. Just before 744 left Tacloban, Lt. (jg) John A. Doane had come aboard as a passenger. He had orders to report to the PT base in Liloan.

Under way, everything went routinely that morning. Men off duty were in their compartments sacking out, writing letters, reading, or playing cards; Ensign Rosser had the watch on the flying bridge, Stroetzel chatted over coffee with Lieutenant Doane in the chart room. A couple of men were doing their laundry on the fantail. It was a nice day to be on the water, and for the next two hours everything was routine.

At 1133 a large puff of black smoke was sighted eight miles away on their port quarter, followed by a muffled boom like that of an explosion. The radio crackled. It was an alert to all ships that enemy planes were in the vicinity. Nine Japanese planes had attacked a group of warships entering the Gulf. The battleship USS *Colorado* and two cruisers were already damaged.

Captain Stroetzel, observing the smoke and plane activity, set Condition I (general quarters), ordered the speed increased to twelve knots, and began zigzagging in an irregular pattern. U.S. fighter planes had intercepted the enemy planes, and a dogfight lasting several minutes followed, watched by everyone on the 744. Three planes dropped lower, crossing the convoy's wake about four miles astern. From their gun positions they watched as the planes turned and began flying toward them, bearing on the starboard side of the convoy. They streaked by at about twenty-five hundred yards, and they could see it was a P-38 fighter in hot pursuit of two Zeros. They held fire so as not to endanger the P-38.

The Zero in the lead began climbing. The second one kept flying straight, the P-38 in close pursuit. The first Zero kept climbing, then banked to the left until it was about five thousand feet up. It circled, hovered; then they could see it was straightening out and coming directly at them. The 744 sprang alive, opening fire with all guns blazing, the plane in a steep dive. They could see its wing guns flickering. Their 20-mm and 40-mm shells smashed into it, but it kept coming. "Left full rudder!" The plane roared in, starboard side forward. A bomb exploded off the bow. The Zero hit the ship aft with a sickening crash, while the men at their guns blazed away.

The plane's tail hung crazily in the air, then came down, slowly toppling backwards over the ship's side into the water. It disappeared almost immediately. A cloud of smoke rose up from just aft amidships. There was no fire. Moans could be heard in the quiet that followed.

Stroetzel and Rosser came down from the bridge. Men stood staring, in shock. Albert H. Angelini, Pharmacist's Mate 1c, was the first to reach two badly wounded men at the starboard 20-mm. One of the plane's wings had struck the barrel of the gun, uprooting it from its mounting and scattering it onto the deck. The man was strapped to the gun, his left arm twisted into a knot with raw bone protruding. His bowels were exposed from a gaping wound in his abdomen, a jagged piece of aluminum in the middle of it. Blood, still flowing, puddled under him on the deck. Angelini kneeled over him, gently removing the eight-inch piece of metal and applying pressure to stop the bleeding but Glenn O. Flanders, Motor Machinist's Mate 3c, USNR, died before he could apply an I.V. Next to him the loader, Dale Lee Brown, Machinist's Mate 3c, lay unconscious, multiple wounds over his entire body. Six men of the 744 were missing. Their bodies were never found.[1] The passenger, Lieutenant Doane, was wounded superficially.

The tug TP 114 came over to assist. On their way they saw a man struggling in the water. It was Leo J. Marino, Seaman 1c, who had either jumped or been thrown into the water when the plane struck. Men on the tug pulled him aboard. His clothes were gone except for his skivvy shorts. Aside from a lacerated right arm, he was unharmed. When Angelini got to him, Marino, very excited, said, "Doc, don't worry, don't worry, we're going to be all right. When I was in the water I could see my mother's face in a halo of light above me, and she told me we would be OK." Angelini said to him, "Calm down, Marino, how could that have been your mother, you told me that she had died when you were two years old." But Marino kept repeating the story to anyone who would listen.[2]

They cleared some of the debris. A quick inspection of the 744 showed the hatches and watertight bulkheads were holding, and it appeared that the ship would stay afloat, although it was down badly by the stern. The fantail was barely above water. Someone found Ensign Rosser's battle helmet, split, lying on the deck aft. It had blood in it. No one, including Rosser—who was unscratched—could figure out how it got there.[3] The deck was full of holes from the strafing, particularly on the flying bridge where the officers and two or three men had been. Yet no one in that group had been hit.

After they determined that the ship would stay afloat, at least for the time being, they carefully placed the body of Flanders and the badly wounded Brown aboard TP 114. Then all but four of the remaining men boarded the tug and were taken into Dulag. Captain Stroetzel and third officer Ens. Lewis Morris remained aboard with two enlisted men, Donald P. Schrader, Coxswain, and Clarence C. Lee, Seaman 1c, to await a tug that would tow the 744 back to Tacloban.

Angelini considered himself the luckiest survivor of all. Only a week before, the 744 had replaced its forward 3-inch/50 cannon with a 40-mm antiaircraft gun. Angelini's battle station had always been amidships, to avoid the deafening noise of the 3-inch/50. As the ship's pharmacist's mate he could choose his station because, in an emergency, he might be needed anywhere. After the 40-mm was installed, with its less intrusive bark, he offered to assist that gun crew during general quarters in breaking out ammunition. This meant his bat-

SC 744 waits for assistance after being struck by a kamikaze plane, Leyte Gulf, 27 November 1944.

tle station would be just forward of the pilothouse on the port side. Had they not replaced the 3-inch/50 with the 40-mm he would surely have been standing aft amidships—in the plane's path—at the time it crashed.

With the TP 114 steaming off towards Dulag, Captain Stroetzel and the three men busied themselves with clearing debris and further assessing damage. Satisfied that they had done everything possible, Stroetzel and the others stood around on the flying bridge, not knowing whether their ship would still be afloat by the time help arrived. There was little more anyone could do.

At about 1400 a subchaser escorting several LCTs appeared. The subchaser was SC 749, Lt. Henry G. Reents, USNR, commanding. When he saw the 744 standing by itself in what appeared to be a sinking condition, Reentz told the LCT to stand by. Coming close aboard the 744 and learning what happened, he passed over some additional damage control equipment and had some of his men cut away wreckage and shore bulkheads. They made a big kettle of hot chicken soup for Stroetzel and his men that they lapped down with gratitude.[4] Reentz radioed the base to expedite their sending a tow since, in his opinion, the hopelessly wrecked vessel would not remain afloat for long. This done, he rejoined his convoy of LCTs.

An hour later my command, SC 648, on our way to relieve the harbor patrol, spotted the 744 and came close aboard to see what had happened. Don Stroetzel was a fellow skipper and friend with whom I had played poker the night before. After telling us what happened, Don said they had just learned by radio that a tug was on the way. Help being imminent, we proceeded on our way but not before snapping a picture of the stricken vessel.

Help for the 744 finally arrived in the form of an army tug, which took her in tow and brought her into Tacloban. There they tied her securely to a cluster of pilings. Stroetzel reported to the base and asked for some experts to come down and inspect the ship to be sure it would remain afloat. This was done, with a Seabee officer and an officer from BuShips who, after looking it over, assured Stroetzel she would hold fast for several days.

In the meantime Ensign Rosser and the survivors on T 114 were taken to Dulag, where an ambulance took the body of Glenn Flanders and the wounded men to an army field hospital unit. Angelini and Ensign Rosser stayed with critically wounded Dale Brown for a long time.[5] That night they joined up with a convoy of army vehicles bound for Tacloban.

Because of the possibility of encountering Japanese raiding parties along the way, the GIs gave them all rifles. Once on the trip the convoy stopped to take cover on a report that Japanese patrols were near. The sailors got out of the trucks and took positions with rifles at the ready, as directed by the foot soldiers. No raiders appeared, and they reached Tacloban safely in the wee hours of the morning. The men were taken to army tents and Rosser found quarters with some army officers.

The next morning Rosser found Stroetzel and the rest of the crew at the ship, which was still tied to the pilings. Three navy officers, including a lieutenant commander, were standing around with Stroetzel, discussing the condition of the 744 and what might be done with her. No one was happy with her condition, but the experts believed she would stay afloat until they decided what they were going to do with her. Someone suggested she could be repaired enough to use for a pilot boat in San Pedro Harbor. This meeting ended and Stroetzel and Rosser spent the remainder of the day making arrangements for feeding and sheltering the crew.

Stroetzel drew up a schedule of watches, assigning four men per watch to stay aboard and guard the safety of the 744. He faced a lot of paperwork as a result of the attack. An official report of the attack itself had to be written and sent through the proper channels, along with a list of the missing and wounded, the extent of damage to the ship, ammunition expended, letters to the families, and many forms to be filled out. Two days went by.

On the evening of 29 November Stroetzel assigned Rosser and four enlisted men to night watch aboard ship. Rosser made a thorough inspection and determined conditions to be the same as they had been earlier, although he had one of the men secure the ship better by taking two extra turns around the pilings. At 0100 on 30 November one of the pilings supporting the ship aft broke and fell into the water. Upon inspection, Rosser determined that the tide was causing the ship to swing, causing the piling to break. Since there was no apparent change in the ship's condition and the salvage officers had opined that the ship would not sink, he didn't think it necessary to summon aid. He checked again at 0130, and everything was the same.

At 0405 one of the men reported to Rosser that the engine room had sprung a leak by the port muffler and was taking on water. Rosser took a quick look and realized she was flooding fast. They stood on the quarterdeck and yelled at the top of their lungs for assistance. A small craft moored at a buoy nearby heard them and came alongside and evacuated them. Rosser directed them to get them to the beach as quickly as possible. The boat took them to the rear of a beached barge, where they clambered off and started running for help. All of a sudden Rosser heard a sound in the direction of the 744. She was sinking at her pilings, stern first. At 0420 she sank in thirty feet of water. When she came to rest, about five feet of her mast was sticking up out of the water. Rosser and his men returned to the small craft. At 0630 he reported the sinking to Captain Stroetzel.

I can still remember coming in to Tacloban Harbor from patrol duty the day I saw the 744 in her stricken condition. Around noon on 30 November I debarked my ship and went over to where the 744's mast was sticking up from the water by the pilings. Standing there, looking at it sadly, was Don Stroetzel. We talked for half an hour while he told me what had happened—the attack, the aftermath, and now this. He was very much down in spirits, having lost his first command and facing, he was sure, a full-fledged navy investigation into the matter—an investigation which, he felt, could end up in a court-martial and place the blame for the sinking directly on him. I tried to assure him that I doubted this would happen, since he and Rosser and the crew had done everything possible beforehand to save the ship. The experts had assured him that it would not sink. They had to share the burden if justice were to prevail.

I didn't see Don again. The image of him standing at those pilings, disconsolately looking at the mast of his once proud little ship now barely sticking out of the water, remained in my mind for a long time. In the years to follow whenever I thought of those days and nights at Leyte Gulf, I would wonder what had happened to my friend Don Stroetzel. Was he found guilty of a commanding officer's dereliction of duty or something equally abominable, or did he get through it and live out a life of peace and accomplishment?

Fifty-two years later, while surfing the Internet in connection with research for this book, I got my answer. I learned that Don lived only ten miles away from me in a neighboring town. A quick phone call renewed our friendship, we got together, and I learned what happened after I had last seen himstanding on the dock at Tacloban on the other side of the world, wondering what was going to become of him.

There had been an investigation, as there always is in such cases, but no one was blamed for what happened. Indeed, Stroetzel received a letter of commendation from Commander, Philippine Sea Frontier, for keeping the ship afloat and having it towed into port and for maintaining good discipline and organization on his ship.[6] Under dire and stressful conditions, the men of SC 744 proved they could react with courage and fortitude. There were no single heroes that day. They were all heroes.

19

The Sea Rover

When some unseen hand dealt out the various assignments for subchasers, it was the lot of some to receive more than their share of adventure and excitement, while others plodded through the war in a mind-numbing sequence of days, weeks, and months of what one subchaser veteran called a "boring, dirty, stinking life." In her three-year tour of Pacific duty, SC 521 was an odd mixture of both, setting a few records along the way. For sheer distance traveled and number of ports visited, she may have seen more of the Pacific Ocean than most ships in the navy—certainly more than any other subchaser.

The 521 was one of the first SCs to come off the ways after Pearl Harbor, and one of the first on the scene in the Pacific. She saw arduous duty in the Solomons until March 1944, when, badly in need of an overhaul, she was sent independently to Dunedin, New Zealand, for repair and R&R for the crew. On the way they battled and somehow survived a violent storm in the vicinity of Norfolk Island, arriving at Dunedin, New Zealand, on 10 March, the first U.S. naval vessel to appear there since Admiral Byrd's expedition to the Antarctic in the early thirties.

After a month spent mostly in dry dock, the 521 was declared fit for sea and returned to the Solomons. From there she escorted a convoy to Kwajalein in the Marshalls where, on 17 June 1944, she survived an attack by three Japanese torpedo bombers. From Kwajalein she went to Eniwetok, joining the gigantic armada being assembled for the recapture of Guam. Used as a control vessel on the morning of 21 June 1944, she was still a bit heady from the success of that experience when, in the afternoon, she was assigned to the lowly duty of delivering officer-messenger mail among the big ships. She pulled alongside one battleship to hand over several sacks of mail and, as her crew was casting off, a seaman on the giant warship hollered down,"Take her away, coxswain," much to the chagrin of Lt.(jg) Frederic W. Freeman, CO, on the flying bridge.

That evening they were ordered into Agana Harbor to intercept any Japanese barges trying to escape (none were sighted), and the following morning they were ordered to go up to the docks of Agana and strafe the streets, which they did. According to what they were told later, this act made the SC 521 the first American vessel to reoccupy American territory.

From Guam the 521 steamed alone to Ulithi atoll. On the way she encountered a fierce hurricane, which she survived by dropping both anchors, letting out a lot of chain, and pulling on them at full speed on the engines. This ordeal over, she proceeded to Hollandia for badly needed repairs, arriving there on 17 November 1944. Her logbook verifies that in the seven months between her departure from Tulagi early in May until her arrival at Hollandia in November, the men never set foot on land; the ship anchored only twice, at Guam and Ulithi. She was supplied with fuel, food, and water continuously while under way by tankers and LSTs.

In January 1945 the 521 was used again as a control vessel, this time in the landing at Lingayen Gulf and then at a small landing near Manila. On the way to Lingayen Gulf in Suragayo Straits, she was sent ahead of the huge convoy to seek out any Japanese PT boats lurking along shore, but saw nothing. During this voyage she got caught in crossfire between an Australian cruiser and a U.S. battleship while both were shooting at a wave-skimming kamikaze. The crossfire destroyed the 521's wherry on its davits at the fantail, sending it up in a shower of splinters. Fortunately the wherry was the only casualty.

Throughout her career, breakdowns on the 521 were so common they became accepted as normal. Because she had been among the first SCs to be launched, much of her gear was one of a kind, requiring much Yankee resourcefulness to overcome the lack of spare parts. When native ingenuity failed, the men resorted to "moonlight requisitioning," a polite term for stealing. In March 1945, after discovering that her false keel had become badly worm-infested, they took her back to Hollandia for dry-docking. Here she was tenderly restored to health by Seabee shipwrights and carpenters. By April, afloat once again, she steamed over to a "homecoming" at Tulagi, her first port of assignment three years earlier.

In May 1945, Lt. (jg) Chester R. Partridge, who had come aboard the 521 as third officer a year and a half earlier, took command. By now everyone, including the enemy, knew America was winning the war and it would be just a matter of time before the Japanese capitulated. The war-weary men of the 521 hoped it would end while they were still in the Solomons, where it was nice and quiet, far behind the action, now hundreds of miles north. Much to their happy surprise, they received the most welcome news of all—SC 521 was ordered to return to the United States!

Accordingly, at dusk on 9 July 1945, SC 521, in company with SCs 1047 and 1327, in that order, departed from Guadalcanal on a course due east at a speed of ten knots, destination Pearl Harbor via Funa Futi in the Ellis Island group, the first leg of their long-awaited homecoming. The four subchasers proudly flew their pennants and Old Glory from their mainmasts, and their officers and crews alike jubilantly talked and reminisced about going home, what they would eat, what they would do, where they would sleep and with whom, and other happy things. So happy were they on the 521 that they didn't even mind that the master gyro had developed a 5-degree westerly error, a petty annoyance solved by relying on the magnetic compass.

By daylight, however, the seas got angry, and the ships were pounding into fifteen-foot waves. Everything and everyone aboard was jarred and thrown around. The seas crashed and tumbled over the bow in foamy white torrents, washing down the decks from fore to aft and causing the ship to take on water. The jarring loosened the radar tubes, throwing it out of calibration. The column formation was switched, with the 1047 taking the lead position.

On the 521 seawater kept pouring into the forward compartment through the goosenecks, chain pipe, and other openings, soaking everything below. Water in the forward bilges began rising, so they switched the engine-room pump to the forward compartment. They tried using a handy billy, but it quickly drowned out. They were being buffeted so badly that it was dangerous for the men to come topside. At 1605 C. W. Knight,

Quartermaster 2c, had just come up the forward ladder when he was thrown overboard by a heavy wave. After several minutes of jockeying and maneuvering on the part of all four subchasers, he was miraculously recovered by the 1047.

The little ships struggled along, the 521 struggling harder than the others because she was slowly becoming waterlogged. In her forward compartment, water had risen so high in the crew's head that it was unusable. The radio room and wardroom were soaked. Water began trickling down the forward bulkhead just aft the peak. This meant the peak tank was full. By 2200 water had risen above the deck in the forward compartment. Captain Partridge ordered a bucket brigade and signaled the 1047 to let them know they were rapidly taking on water. He requested the convoy speed be reduced to seven knots. The bailing helped for a while, but by 2330 water was covering the footlockers, rising at an estimated rate of fifteen inches an hour.

At 2345 they began emptying the magazine compartment, a tough job even in smooth waters, and now almost impossible under their present conditions. They jettisoned the 40-mm ammunition and began passing the 20-mm ammunition through the emergency exit into the radio room, up the radio-room ladder to the wheelhouse, and through the wheelhouse to the quarterdeck, while the ship was violently corkscrewing and taking on green water.

The men kept working feverishly in the forward compartment, in the magazine, and on the handy billies. Electrical circuits began shorting out. The water kept rising until, at 0200, it was four feet deep in the forward compartment. They were losing. Water in the radio room and wardroom was twelve inches deep. The only dry compartment on the ship now was the lazarette.

Captain Partridge had managed to notify the OTC (Officer in Tactical Command) on the 1047 of the serious condition of his ship. At 0230 he passed the word for all hands to stand by to abandon ship if necessary, with the only men remaining at their posts the ones working handy billies, shifting ammunition, or at helm and engine controls. Their efforts were greatly hampered by their having to slosh in water. They were exhausted and dizzy from fumes from electrical shorts. Someone attempted to get at the safe in the wardroom to remove classified and registered documents but failed because of fumes, water, and floating debris.

Partridge knew the danger of their situation and asked the 1047 to come alongside to take everyone off. The 1047 came close aboard, and the 521 fired a line that got fouled in the 1047's screws. The seas were too rough for transferring. Partridge decided to tough things out until dawn, and the 1047 stood off. Heading away from the sea, Partridge hoped to ride it out. It was very hard to steer because the ship was down by the bow and the stern was being lifted out of the water. The ship pivoted and wallowed on its heavy bow; each wave causing it to nose and scoop up more green water. Everyone stood by in life jackets, not knowing what was going to happen. It looked as though she would start sinking. The hours went by.

At the first sign of dawn the wind and sea began to abate. The ship was now down by the head 15 degrees. The water in the radio shack and wardroom was four feet deep. The screws were out of the water most of the time. There was no freeboard forward of the pilothouse. The 521 was sinking. At 0630 the word was passed to abandon ship. The other three subchasers lay to on the leeward side and the 521 stopped her engines. They launched the starboard raft, and the 1327 shot a line over which they fastened to the raft. The 1327 towed eight men over. They then launched the port raft, filled it with eleven men and one officer and let it drift over to the 1047. Partridge remained aboard with one officer and four men to completely destroy secret and confidential gear and to save the logbooks and other records. They were going to open the sea cocks, but these were inaccessible. Instead they removed the strainer on the bilge pump and knocked free the drains in the after head.

SC-502 nosed her bow up to the 521's quarterdeck, and Partridge ordered his men to jump across, one by one. When the 502 came in the second time, the captain jumped, thinking he was the last man to leave. Seconds later someone realized that Dale D. Pearmain, Motor Machinist's Mate 1c, was still in the engine room. Pearmain came running topside, mounted the one remaining rubber boat, and was picked up by the 502 a few minutes later.

The tired old 521 labored and wallowed in each deep trough, rode up the crests, and plunged crazily down again. She was a sorry sight. Captain Partridge asked the skipper of the 1047 to sink her by gunfire. As the guns raked her from bow to stern, splinters flying everywhere, she just lay there and took it, gradually sinking lower and lower until her whole deck was awash. At 0852 on 10 July 1945, brave little SC 521, after having seen so much and traveled so far, slipped under the waters, her pilothouse, flying bridge, and mast disappearing into the depths, gone forever. Her exhausted crew watched in silence from their sister subchasers, some choking back tears. The jubilance they had felt about going home evaporated as they watched their ship—the beloved little ship that had shared so much with them—vanish.

Two days later a narrative report was filed by Chester R. Partridge which, with the addition of personal correspondence between May and June, 1996, enables us to know how her journey ended.[1]

She rests 2100 fathoms below a point 350 miles east of Guadalcanal. In her short life of only three years, she may have traveled and seen more than she bargained for, but no subchaser bore her commission pennant more proudly than USS SC 521.

20

Conrad Young's Secret

We all know that plans to invade the Japanese mainland in World War II never materialized because President Harry S. Truman made the decision to drop the atomic bombs on Hiroshima and Nagasaki, thus ending the war many months ahead of schedule. His decision, one of the most agonizing decisions a president ever faced, spelled doom for thousands of innocent Japanese people, yet was more than justified by saving the lives of tens of thousands of American *and* Japanese fighting men who otherwise would have been slaughtered in the final battle.

Dr. Thomas E. Hamilton, aboard SC 1297, expressed these sentiments and those of most SC veterans in a letter to the editor of an Atlanta newspaper a few years ago:

> When the *Enola Gay*, at the instruction of one of our great presidents, Harry Truman, dropped the bomb and essentially ended World War II, my tiny submarine chaser SC 1297 was training for a new job. Because our draft was only 6-½ feet, we were chosen to be one of the many minesweepers whose duty would be to remove mines in front of the invasion fleet. What chance would our crew and wooden ship have had, running parallel to the Japanese coast only a few hundred yards offshore? I most likely would have been killed, and all my children and grandchildren never born. . . . The

Japanese had agreements with Germany and Italy to partition the world, and were almost successful, had it not been for practical, commonsense people like Harry Truman and, yes, like the officers and crew of SC 1297.[1]

Early in 1945, long before President Truman's decision, the navy conducted an experiment with a subchaser that today seems so far-fetched as to be almost unbelievable, yet the photo (below) reproduced from files in the National Archives shows that it truly did happen. At first glance the picture appears to be a photo of a CVE escort-type aircraft carrier, but if you look more closely you will see that something does not seem quite right about that superstructure on the starboard side. And those airplanes—are they for real?

You have a right to be suspicious. That flight deck is only thirty-seven yards long and those planes are six-foot wooden dummies. The superstructure is only large enough for one man (usually the skipper) to poke his head and shoulders into to take a look around when conning the ship. The ship is actually a subchaser that has been made to look like a baby flat-top. Kind of a crazy, cockamamy idea—right?

Wrong. This was a carefully planned, top-secret experiment in wartime deception that might have been used in the final stages of the war with Japan. It was but one of many pieces of an elaborate puzzle being studied by our naval strategists after regaining Leyte and the Philippines, when it was

The ultimate in deception: SC 449 disguised as an escort carrier, Ocracoke, North Carolina, February 1945 *Naval Historical Center*

obvious that we were winning the war. From the standpoint of the conditions existing at that time, it was an ingenious, brilliant concept that, but for the atomic bomb, would have been of considerable military significance.

With the almost complete destruction of Japanese air and sea power during the Leyte campaign, it was apparent to everyone, including the Japanese warlords themselves, that the tides had turned in our favor and we were winning. The Iwo Jima and Okinawa campaigns were planned and ready for early 1945 and after those conquests we would be on the doorstep of Japan herself—the only islands remaining to be taken. For the Japanese people, it was a time of painful awakening to the realization that they were fighting a lost cause. History has shown how bitterly they fought at Iwo and Okinawa because they knew that the only target left after that was the Japanese mainland itself.

And what a bloodbath that would have been! Desperate though the Japanese were, their fighting men had proven time and again how fierce, stubborn, and courageous they could be in battle, especially when up against superior odds. Their suicide attacks with planes, boats, and land vehicles had proved that they would not hesitate, nor were they afraid, to die for their emperor and their country. If and when the enemy set foot on their soil, they would fight to the last man, woman, and child in what certainly would have been the bloodiest and most costly battle in the history of warfare. Tens of thousands of American and Japanese lives would have been lost in a bitter struggle of unimaginable fury and violence.

How, then, to make an amphibious landing on the mainland of Japan that would accomplish all the objectives, yet with the least cost to American lives? This was the problem faced by Adm. Chester Nimitz and his Pacific Fleet commanders early in 1945. Solutions to the question, slow in coming at first, took shape during the Okinawa campaign when a bold and imaginative plan was drawn up by Vice Adm. Richmond Kelly Turner, Commander, Amphibious Force, South Pacific Force, a brilliant leader who had accumulated plenty of experience in amphibious warfare.

Admiral Turner's inspiration was part of a top-secret plan named Operation "Olympic," which was to be the invasion of the Japanese mainland—or possibly of the Kurile Islands—on 15 November 1945.[2] His idea was to set a trap by making a fake landing two weeks before that date that would look so realistic and so much like a genuine assault that it would move the Japanese into throwing their entire force against it. The "cherry blossoms,"[3] their weapon of last resort, would be wasted in such huge quantities on this fake landing that they would be left empty-handed and powerless to defend themselves when the real landing took place two weeks later.

Turner's idea ignited after he saw his amphibious fleet at Okinawa being decimated by kamikazes and *baka* bombs,[4] not on D-Day but in the days and weeks afterwards. The Okinawa operation had been very costly to the United States, with 26 ships sunk, 368 damaged, and almost ten thousand men killed or wounded. But if the Japanese had counterattacked with kamikazes and a massive force of ground troops during the first hours of the landing, the U.S. assault could have been crushed from the very beginning. Instead, they waited four days before they counterattacked—a serious mistake, because it gave Turner's forces enough time to bring ashore all the guns, munitions, food, and supplies necessary to firm up and hold their beachhead. The only opportunity for the Japanese to drive their enemy back into the sea was when the Americans were in their weakest and most vulnerable position, which was in the first critical hours of the landing. Knowing that the Japanese would not repeat this mistake was the inspiration for Turner's ideological strategy.

His plan called for a D-Day fleet of four hundred ships with enough transports to carry half a million men and their equipment, landing boats, and vehicles, plus escort ships, control vessels, fire support ships, and all the paraphernalia of a full-fledged amphibious landing force. Boats would be in the water, dive-bombers and rocket ships would bombard the beach, and radio waves would be crackling with faked messages. But the entire spectacle would be counterfeit—a phantom fleet carrying no troops and with only skeleton crews—and several hundred miles away from where the real landing would take place two weeks later.[5] The Japanese, backs to the wall, would throw their only remaining arsenal into the fight—the kamikazes and baka bombs—in one last desperate effort to save themselves. The kamikazes would self-destruct or be destroyed by antiaircraft fire. In either case the result would be a rainstorm of falling steel and shrapnel.

Granted, in such a scenario the risk of casualties to American ships and their skeleton crews would be high, yet these would be nothing contrasted to the costs of a real landing. That one, two weeks later, would be virtually painless—or so Turner reasoned—because the kamikaze would no longer be viable, having destroyed themselves in their assault on the phantom fleet.

It was in this frame of mind that our naval strategists ordered SC 449, operating out of Ocracoke, an Amphibious Training Base on the outer banks of North Carolina, directing her to Portsmouth, Virginia, in December

1944. There she was placed in dry dock and systematically stripped of almost everything topside—the flying bridge, her mast, her guns, depth charges, mousetraps, ready boxes, racks, and other gear. This done, she was loaded with a huge cargo of lumber, including a large number of 7/8-inch exterior plywood sheets, and directed to proceed back to Ocracoke. Upon arrival there she was again dry-docked for a major piece of cosmetic surgery that transformed her from an SC subchaser into a mock CVE escort aircraft carrier, complete with camouflaged hull, a flight deck with three wooden dummy airplanes, and fake starboard superstructure.

"CVE 449" and the sea trials that followed were given the code name Operation Swiss Navy. In certain Bureau of Ships correspondence it was referred to as the "B-J Project."[6] For two months the mini-carrier went through a series of sea trials in highest secrecy, attended by high-ranking officers on board and in a PBY flying overhead, to take pictures and to observe the ship under different weather, wind, and sea conditions. It was obvious early on that the large sail area of the CV type caused the vessel to roll dangerously in winds over ten knots, and recovery time was so slow as to run the risk of capsizing. The tests, therefore, were conducted only on days when wind and weather permitted. At the end of two months the tests were completed. Although they were considered successful for the valuable information gained thereby, the Bureau of Ships recommended that future conversions be made on larger, more stable vessels such as the PCE (Patrol Escort).[7]

No files have been found by this author directly linking Swiss Navy to Admiral Turner's project "Olympic," but the war rooms in both Washington and the Pacific were privy to and had free exchange of all information regarding such projects. It seems safe to assume that the use of deceptive vessels such as were countenanced by Swiss Navy would have played no small part in Operation Olympic.

The idea of disguising a little subchaser to make it look like an aircraft carrier is not as absurd as it first might seem. Viewed from an airplane, it would be quite realistic. At sea level, distances and perceptions when looking out at the ocean can be deceiving. Imagine yourself sunbathing on the New Jersey shore on a nice day. You begin to see a fleet of what appear to be several aircraft carriers emerging on the horizon. It would take time to figure out they were not real aircraft carriers but small-scale "fakes," because the visual sighting and your brain's interpretation would not connect quickly enough to sort the real from the ridiculous. In that interval, if your country were at war and you felt threatened and you had a cannon, you would start shooting.

SC 449, as noted in chapter 2, was built to the experimental design selected for production just before World War II. She had approximately 50 percent greater stability than the production models based on her design, which probably explains why she was chosen for the test. She looked more like a World War I subchaser, with her wooden pilothouse beveled at the corners and portholes in her sides for ventilation in the forward crew's compartment. Her ordnance was obsolete, a 3-inch/23 cannon decorating her bow and a .50-caliber machine gun on her flying bridge and no 20-mm guns or K-guns. Her career prior to Operation Swiss Navy had been rather humdrum, mainly that of working as a training vessel for the Fleet Sound School in Key West. Nevertheless, in those two months at Ocracoke in 1945, the 449 made an important contribution to the global drama being played out in the Pacific.

So guarded and secret was Swiss Navy that for fifty-five years the 449's commanding officer, Lt. (jg) Conrad S. Young, said nothing about it to anyone, not even his wife. When I asked Mr. Young, who is in good health and living in Omaha, why he waited so long to talk about it, he explained that the navy had drummed the importance of secrecy into him so thoroughly that he never dared speak about it and simply pushed it out of his mind. "Moreover," he added, "if I had ever told anyone they wouldn't have believed me anyway."

21

The Western Pacific, 1945

From the bridge of a battleship a navy subchaser was a speck on the ocean, hardly bigger than a canoe, but SC 1272 worked its way from south to north, threading its way through its share of hot water and joining everyone else in the Iwo Jima invasion fleet.[1] The 1272 arrived in the Pacific in the middle of 1943 and, like her sister SCs, made many a patrol and many an escort trip guarding convoys against Japanese submarines. At least twice she dropped depth charges on underwater targets, but like many such attacks they were false alarms—attacks on a school of fish, a whale, or an underwater object other than a submarine. And, like her sister SCs, the 1272 was lucky that no Japanese sub ever surfaced and aimed at her, because the sub's deck guns could have blown her out of the water. She kept coming close to the edge of the world but she "never quite sailed over."[2]

Like many other subchasers, the 1272 went back to Pearl Harbor to be refitted and made into an SCC—a landing control vessel—with added communications equipment, berths for an extra enlisted man and officer, and three-inch-high numbers painted on her bow to make her easier to identify in the smoke-filled air of an assault. Her first major landing operation as a control vessel was at Iwo Jima on 19 February 1945.

• • •

Iwo Jima. What more can one say about this little island that, for three months, was a living—and dying—hell for the brave young men who were there? The island "that never looked more aesthetically ugly than on D-day morning"[3] was under constant bombardment for three days prior to the landing, but the Japanese cozily sat it out in their deep underground shelters. Although the boats beached quite easily, the terrain was full of rocky terraces, making it difficult for the marines to move forward. The resulting heavy concentrations of men made easy targets. The Japanese opened up with point-blank mortar and machine-gun fire so withering that the marines were literally chopped to pieces.

Robert Sherrod, veteran correspondent, described it thus:

> Nowhere in the Pacific war had I seen such badly mangled bodies. Many were cut squarely in half. Legs and arms lay 50 feet away from any body. In one spot on the sand, far from the nearest cluster of dead, I saw a string of guts 15 feet long. Only legs were easy to identify; they were Japanese if wrapped in khaki puttees, American if covered by canvas leggings. The smell of burning flesh was heavy. . . .[4]

The men on the 1272 were witnessing this carnage from offshore when an LVT amtrac accidentally came too close and banged into her, tearing a gaping hole in her hull at the waterline. The water was choppy, and with every roll of the ship green water poured through, flooding the crew's quarters. Men rushed to the spot, stuffed the hole with canvas, nailed boards over it, and continued with their control duties. For twelve days throughout the invasion, she directed traffic, delivered mail, patrolled, and fulfilled the rest of her duties at Iwo, patch notwithstanding.[5]

SC 724, in the South Pacific since July 1943 and a veteran of the Guam landing, was also sent back to Pearl Harbor for conversion into a control vessel in preparation for Iwo. On D-Day at Iwo she carried Capt. Carl E. "Squeaky" Anderson, beach master, so-named for his high pitched voice, described by one observer as "an extraordinary character as wide as he was tall who delivered his commands in amazingly blasphemous language with a strong Scandinavian accent."[6] Taking station three hundred yards from the beach under heavy mortar and machine gun fire too close for comfort, after the boats were dispatched the 724 withdrew to an area five hundred yards southwest of Suribachi. She quickly became a target for mortar fire, one shell dropping fifteen yards off the port beam, scattering shrapnel over the flying bridge. For ten days she hovered around the landing area, performing various missions for Squeaky Anderson and coming under enemy fire numerous times.

Once, when they were anchored off Red Beach near the southwest tip of Suribachi, photographer Joe Rosenthal boarded the 724 and spent a few hours aboard observing and taking pictures. In conversations with the crew he announced his intention to photograph the Stars and Stripes being raised when the marines reached the summit of Suribachi. A few days later this memorable event occurred, permanently stamped in history by Rosenthal's famous photograph.

In due time Iwo Jima was taken at a staggering cost of 6,812 American and 20,703 Japanese lives, with 19,189 Americans wounded. By the middle of March, all but a handful of the amphibious assault ships had departed to prepare for the next big landing, which was to take place in the Japanese Ryukyu Islands at a place called Okinawa. As for their stay at Iwo Jima, Bill Root, crew member on the 724, summed it up in one short sentence: "It was Hell and nobody was sorry to leave."

While these activities were taking place in the Central Pacific, General MacArthur and the Third and Seventh Fleet were concentrating on the liberation of the Philippines. Leyte had been the first step, but the enemy was strongly entrenched in other islands—Luzon, Mindoro, Palawan, Mindanao, the southern Visayas, Panay, Negros, Cebu, and others. These were methodically and relentlessly pursued in a series of landings and assaults, some tricky and difficult, others relatively easy. Manila finally was reclaimed, after bitter, fierce, house-to-house fighting in a month-long battle during which the city was reduced to rubble. The job of clearing Manila Bay and the retaking of the Bataan Peninsula and Corregidor was daunting since the bay was heavily mined and over five thousand Japanese were garrisoned in Corregidor alone. But by the end of March most of Luzon had been liberated, including the outlying islands of the bay.

Early in February American troops had reached the infamous Japanese prison camps at Santo Tomás and Bilibid, freeing 4,724 starving and emaciated Allied prisoners whose appearance alone told of the cruelties inflicted upon them during their years of captivity. These atrocities were highly publicized, with chilling, graphic photographs and stories in the press, and were not lost on the American men still fighting there. To say it embittered them somewhat would be an understatement.

SC 698, like so many other SCs, had come across and through the islands, participating in the assaults at Arawe, Hollandia, Cape Gloucester, and Leyte and seeing her share of gunsmoke, fire, blood, and death. Her war-weary officers and crew had seen and done it all. They were tired and homesick, and they longed to be anywhere else but where they were, which, on 21 March 1945, was on antisubmarine patrol at the entrance to Manila Bay.

At 0900 on that day they were steaming between Limbones Island and Cochinos Point when the lookout spotted a raft with three Japanese soldiers on it, some five thousand yards seaward of Corregidor Island and twenty-five hundred yards from the 698. Lt. Hamer S. Culp Jr., USNR, commanding, immediately called the ship to general quarters, notified his task force commander, and asked for instructions. The answer was, "Take prisoners if possible. If they show resistance kill them." Kicking his engines into full speed, Culp headed straight for the raft. When he was seventy-five yards away, he slowed down and circled the raft, noting that one of the men was an officer and the two others enlisted soldiers. Each was holding hand grenades. He ordered them to swim away from the raft, telling them if they did so they would be saved. The men completely ignored his offer. He repeated his command. They ignored him. He ordered, "Fire." Two 30-caliber machine guns opened up with direct hits, mowing the men down and spattering blood in all directions. Coming alongside, the crew found personal effects tied to the raft, including an up-to-date diary among the officer's papers. Patrol was resumed.

At 1020 a second raft was spotted carrying two men. The 698 made the same approach and began circling at seventy-five yards while Lieutenant Culp repeated the same orders as before. Someone on the 698 tossed a life ring to the raft which the Japanese soldiers refused. Again Culp gave the order to fire. One man was killed instantly; the other was wounded in one arm. He dove overboard and began swimming away from the raft, then turned and waved to the ship. The 698 approached him cautiously, while the men trained their small arms at him. They pulled him aboard and stripped him, and the pharmacist's mate treated his wounds. The man's uniform bore the insignia of the Japanese Imperial Marines. The 698 proceeded to LCI 690 and delivered the prisoner and his compatriots' effects on orders from task group commander.

At 0815 on the following morning a third raft was sighted at approximately the same location off Corregidor. This raft carried three men, one of whom must have been an officer, for he carried a sword that he brandished menacingly as the ship approached. The same verbal procedure ensued, a line was shot to the raft and refused, each Japanese carried hand grenades, and all were killed by ship's fire.

At 0840 that same morning a fourth raft was sighted. They refused rescue, displayed hand grenades, and were shot and killed.

Finally, at 0945 a fifth raft was spotted with two Japanese marines aboard who refused rescue. They were shot and killed. The men of the 698 did what they were ordered to do and what they had to do.

To the east lay Okinawa, the largest island in the Ryukyus. On Easter Sunday, 1 April 1945, an enormous force of ships, a "most audacious and complex enterprise" [7] appeared along a ten-mile stretch of shoreline on the west coast of southern Okinawa. Operation "Iceberg," the vast amphibious landing on this island, the largest island in the Ryukyus, dwarfed anything previously seen in the Pacific. Under the guiding hand of Vice Adm. Richmond Kelly Turner, ships and landing craft as far as the eye could see began moving to their positions. Wave after wave of LVTs, LCVPs, LCMs, and LSTs made their majestic procession into the beaches, churning the water into parallel wakes that, from the air, looked like laying stripes across a giant football field. But what distinguished Okinawa from previous landings was not so much its gargantuan size, but the degree of sophistication that went into its planning and execution. The experiences of Saipan, Peleliu, Guam, Kwajalein, Eniwetok, and Iwo Jima all bore fruit at Okinawa.

Twenty-three subchasers were used as control vessels and escorts in a landing that extended almost fifteen miles along the southwestern coast. Color coding, an innovation for landing control, was used prominently. SC 1066, control vessel at Purple Beach, bore a purple banner, while SC 1049, at Orange Beach, flew an orange banner with one black vertical stripe marking the northern edge of the boat lane; SC 1312 flew an orange banner with two vertical stripes to mark the southern edge.

For six days prior to the main landing, Amphibious Group Seven was busy with landing and securing the Kerama-rettō, a small group of islands off the mainland of Okinawa. SCs 1338, 1341, 1349, and 1350, along with four PC-type vessels, formed part of a task unit for guide and control of landing ships. No enemy opposition was encountered except for a few sporadic air attacks too far away to do harm.

On L-Day after the waves of boats had been landed Cdr. Lawrence C. Leever, USNR, beach master for one sector, came aboard SC 1272, asking the skipper to get in as close to the shore as possible. Lt. Lewis M. Walker, CO, slowly and cautiously brought the ship in toward the beach. He and his men could feel themselves being tracked by enemy scopes on the bluffs nearby. Leever kept demanding that she get even closer. When her bow scraped on sand, Walker turned to him and said, "Are we close enough, sir?" The commander, single-minded in his task and oblivious to the sarcasm, thought this was great. They remained there a good half hour, Walker and his crew feeling as exposed as if walking stark naked onto the concert stage at Carnegie Hall. If the Japanese had been on the spot, the 1272 could have been blown to bits. But it never happened. The tide came in just enough for the ship to pull back into deeper water and the men had those few moments of suspense to remember for the rest of their lives.[8]

Enemy opposition on L-Day at Okinawa was almost nonexistent except for occasional desultory mortar and sniper fire—an unexpected novelty for the invasion forces. This lack of resistance during the most critical hours became the key to Admiral Turner's strategy for the planned invasion of the Japanese mainland. But the Okinawa invasion is best remembered less for the events of L-Day as for the onslaught of kamikaze planes that began four days after the landing and continued without letup for six weeks. This was Japan's "Last Hurrah," the fight of her life—to her death.

The heavy kamikaze activity at Leyte was, it turned out, merely an introduction to the carnage at Okinawa. During the afternoon of 6 April alone, a total of 335 kamikaze planes and 341 Japanese bombers attacked the expeditionary force. Thirty-five were shot down by ship's antiaircraft fire and twenty-four crashed into the sea, but at a cost of three destroyers, an LST, and two ammunition ships, all sunk, and damage to many others, with hundreds of human casualties.

Night and day thereafter the Japanese pulled out all the stops, using not only planes and *bakas* but *kaiten* (human torpedoes) as well. The routine was the same, beginning with a Red Alert warning of approaching "bogeys" on the radar, then the furious bursts of antiaircraft fire from destroyers on the outer picket line, followed by similar bursts from the inner pickets as the kamikazes, threading their way through this withering fire, picked their targets and made their final fiery plunge down onto a ship, exploding on contact, causing indescribable damage and mayhem on board. No ships were safe—there was no place to hide; the kamikazes kept coming. The men were under constant strain, standing general quarters for days and nights on end until sleep became a rare commodity, a luxury.

The destroyers on the picket lines suffered the most in lives and damage. The navy's bottom-line price for Okinawa was heavy. Thirty-two ships were sunk and 368 ships were damaged. Over four thousand sailors were killed and an additional 4,824 were wounded—the heaviest loss incurred in any naval campaign in the war.

The twenty-three SCs and their sailors who survived Okinawa escaped, miraculously, without a single casualty. Their small size may have been an advantage, but in those flak-filled, turbulent, nerve-wracking, and dangerous six weeks it was the "luck of the draw" more than anything else that spared them. Still to come at Okinawa was typhoon "Louise"—more terrifying to the subchaser sailors than anything they had ever witnessed in combat. But that was in October, after the surrender.

By the end of June 1945 Okinawa was secured, and our victory in the Pacific was certain. The Japanese navy was hopelessly crippled, her air power destroyed, her island outposts bypassed, with thousands of Japanese troops left starving and her mainland in shambles by steady bombardment from Admiral Halsey's Task Force 38 carrier planes. The drubbing continued through July, bringing Japan to her knees even before the first bomb was dropped on 6 August. With the second one at Nagasaki three days later, all hope in Japan vanished. She capitulated 14 August 1945.

On 2 September 1945, an armada of 254 Allied warships gathered in Tokyo Bay to witness the ceremony ending hostilities between the United States and Japan. It was held aboard the giant battleship *Missouri* with Gen. Douglas MacArthur officiating, accepting the humble surrender of the Japanese. It was a most solemn and auspicious occasion, carefully designed to impress the entire world with the awesome power that can be unleashed whenever and wherever freedom-loving countries are threatened. From mighty battleships and aircraft carriers, heavy and light cruisers, destroyers, submarines, frigates, attack transports, cargo ships, repair ships, tankers, oilers, seaplane tenders, hospital ships, landing craft, PC patrol ships, minesweepers, and lowly tugboats, all the different classes of ships were represented.

All, that is, except the lowly SC subchaser. The valiant little ships—which had been so much a part of the war in dozens upon dozens of landing assaults, landing control operations, mine sweeping, smoke laying, beachmaster assistance, ferrying, surveying, escorting, patrolling, and rescue—were not only not in Tokyo Bay, they weren't even missed. Not one subchaser was invited to share in that memorable ceremony just by being present. The ragtag kid brothers, the "little fellas," were simply ignored. And do you know what? The men didn't much care, because they were very tired and all they wanted to do was to go home.

My old ship, SC 648, witnessed her own mini surrender. I had been relieved of command at Hollandia early in February 1945, after almost two years aboard, and had returned to the States, where I finished my naval service in Miami as an Afloat Instructor at SCTC. My relief was Lt. (jg) John W. Storrs Jr., USNR, who, after several weeks of dry-docking and repair at Manus, took the ship back to Leyte for routine escort and patrol duty. At the end of June she was ordered to Tawi Tawi to escort a slow convoy of oilers and yard ships to Brunei Bay, Borneo, and after this she did escort duty between Brunei Bay and Balabac Island that continued through August 15, the date of the surrender.

Shortly thereafter the 648 was ordered to Kuching, Borneo, where, on 11 September, she went up the Sarawak River for the purpose of transporting POWs, missionaries, and other detainees who had been held by the Japanese in a compound outside of Kuching. Edward Furman, Quartermaster 3c, wrote a letter (much abridged, below) to his family describing the trip upriver and his impressions of the sights and sounds he saw:

> Kuching, Borneo, 13 September 1945 . . . The larger ships were not permitted up the river due to their deep draft so the leading officers and Aussie personnel boarded our ship and the H.M.A.S. Kapunda, with the senior officer present. . . . We didn't know what to expect so all our guns were loaded and cocked, ready at a moment's notice.
>
> About seven miles upriver there's a junction where the Sarawak leads off to another river. It was here that we met the Japanese representatives. . . . Each Nip had his long sword at his side and didn't bat an eye. Everyone stood at attention during the surrender ceremonies, which took approximately fifteen minutes.
>
> After that we headed upriver towards Kuching. . . . The Japs were to leave town within 48 hours after the surrender but when we arrived some were still in town. . . . Malayans and Chinese were along the entire river dressed

in their Sunday best, cheering and waving their hands. We had not entered the town as yet so the Jap military police were still having their last few minutes of fun with the populace. Two of them drove up in a bantam car and chased the people off the dock, apparently for no reason except that they were waving at us. When the Japs returned to the car the people returned to the dock. . . . [w]e came across some educated Malaysians who told us where the Japs were camping and how they had been treated. The Japs issued invasion currency, food became scarce, and they had to print more invasion dollars. One cigarette cost five dollars. There was no electricity in town because the Japs were unable to import diesel to run the generators. Very few of the natives wore shoes and most are down to their last piece of clothing. The Japs had taken their cars, refrigerators and anything else they wanted.

. . . [Y]esterday we took aboard our first load of prisoners to turn them over to larger ships and convalescent camps in Brunei Bay. I wish people back home could have seen this pitiful parade of officers and enlisted men as they walked down the road to our ship. We had to help them they were so unsteady. They could hardly find words to express themselves—it almost brought tears. Many of them had been prisoners for three and a half years, what a sad sight! Six hundred men died from starvation or were killed in that camp, beaten with clubs. Red Cross packages never found their way to the prisoners. The Japs kept them. The prisoners lived on a few ounces of rice, vegetable leaves, dog and rat meat. One major told me he hid his personal papers, pictures of his wife and child, in an empty bottle which he kept in the ground, out of sight. They kept their spirits up with a small radio which they hid in a stove. Every time the Japs made a search they would start a fire in the stove. They had the receiver protected somehow so it wouldn't burn. Another group hid their radio in a bucket of oil and every time there was a search it took days to clean and dry all the parts so they could listen to news broadcasts.

On the 14th we rented bikes for some cigarettes and rode out to the prison camp. . . . An Aussie PW offered to take us around. There are four sections in this camp, one for women, one for enlisted men, one for officers and one for civilian men. All of them were captured in China. Most who were able to move about had already left the camp. Those remaining were so weak and thin they had to be fed in order to gain strength. Our guide first showed us the storeroom where the PWs themselves rationed food to make it last until the end of the week. He showed us the bins of filthy rice which seemed to have been swept up from the warehouse floor. I have a matchbox full of that stuff and will send it along. We saw what seemed to be fish entrails crawling with maggots. The PWs cooked and ate it. Salt and pepper were in raw form, rock salt and pepper kernels. Their ration of rice was five ounces per day, very few vegetables.

Next we went to visit the men who remained in the camp. . . . Six or seven of them gathered around me, not one weighing more than 110 pounds even though some were tall and elderly. They had ulcers on their feet and said that the Japs liked to kick their bandaged legs. Their beds were hard boards. Some of them who had worked in the fields managed to get strong weeds which they nailed between two boards to form a type of spring. . . .

The women's camp had a female doctor who showed us around. She showed us how they had to use the same dressings over and over, after washing them, for even though the Japs had plenty of fresh dressings they wouldn't give her any. There were a number of Roman Catholic nuns and a few Carmelites in this camp. I met Sister Superior, a Dutch nun who could speak English quite well. As we walked through the women's barracks the women started to get up as was their custom when the Japs entered. Our lady doctor guide had to tell them differently. The ladies were given much more food than the men and found ways to use certain leaves of flowers as vegetables. They were also allowed to have a garden. The Japs didn't stop at striking men only, however. The doctor told us that she had been beaten on the head simply because she had taken one of her patients to a dental office. . . .

Well, it's about time I close this letter and get to addressing envelopes. Hope you are all well!! Love and Kisses, Brother Ed.

On 1 October 1945 SC 648 departed Victoria Harbor, Kuching, for Subic Bay, Luzon, carrying an army officer with nine soldiers looking for transportation to nearby Batangas Bay. Dry-docked for repairs at Subic, she remained laid up until 26 October. On 5 December Lt. John W. Storrs was relieved of command by Lt. (jg) Philip Kelber, USNR, and on 13 December she began the process of decommissioning by jettisoning all her ammunition in 175 fathoms of water, eleven miles from shore. On 26 January 1946 the few remaining crew members were transferred to billets on the beach, their compartments secured. Finally, on 5 February 1946 in Subic Bay, SC 648, the storm-tossed home for the best subchaser crew who ever sailed the seas, was decommissioned. On 30 June 1948 she was transferred to China. The plucky little ship, my first and only command, was gone. Where she is or whether she even exists is not known, but, since half of the goods within China today are shipped via inland navigation, it is definitely possible that she is still afloat. If so, the souls and spirit of seventy-five brave American boys sail with her.

22

Buckner Bay

Mention Buckner Bay to anyone who happened to be there on 9–10 October 1945 and you'll get an instant reaction. That was where "Louise," the worst and most deadly typhoon in our navy's history, struck with winds gusting up to 150 knots, tossing subchasers about like matches, hurling nineteen of them onto rocks or reefs, and damaging four of them so badly that they had to be scrapped. In less than twenty-four hours, a total of 265 ships were damaged or grounded. Four fifths of all houses and buildings on Okinawa were destroyed or rendered uninhabitable. Food stocks were reduced to ten days' supply. Medical facilities were so incapacitated in the area that a hospital ship was borrowed to support shore activities. Fortunately, considering the extreme violence of the storm, the casualties were low: 36 dead, 47 missing, and approximately 100 men seriously injured.

After the securing of Okinawa in late June, Buckner Bay[1] had become a bustling anchorage and facilities station for thousands of navy ships as they went about their business of war. Then came the halcyon weeks following the surrender, with everyone savoring the sweet smell of success. The worries of combat were over, the peaceful occupation of Japan was beginning its remarkable seven-year existence under Supreme Commander General MacArthur, and the ships and men of the fleet were looking forward to going home. Although Okinawa had warning of a tropical storm north of Rota in the Marianas on 4 October, it came too late for ships to get under way and escape the typhoon's terrible violence.

Until the evening of 8 October, Louise followed a fairly predictable track, which would have taken her between Formosa and Okinawa into the East China Sea. But when she began to veer easterly, Vice Adm.Thomas F. Wilkinson, on the flagship *Mt. Olympus* in Tokyo Bay, issued an all-ships' warning: Louise was expected to pass near or through Okinawa. She passed through, all right, never slowing down; in fact, she increased her intensity, developing into one of the most violent storms ever to hit Okinawa, before or since. The center passed less than fifteen miles east of the island's southeast coast.

The bay, on the east coast of Okinawa, was jammed with vessels of all sizes. By 1000 on 9 October the wind had risen to forty knots, the barometer had fallen to 29.50 inches, visibility was less than eight hundred yards, seas were rising, and rain, liberally mixed with salt spray, was coming down in torrents. By noon visibility was zero and the wind blew at sixty knots from east and northeast, raising towering seas that hurtled high over moored ships and crashed down on them with deadly force. Larger vessels precariously held on by running their engines full speed. By 1400 the wind had risen to eighty knots, with gusts of even more intensity; the driving, horizontal rain was more salt than fresh. The bay, blacked out by the heavy overcast and rain, turned into a scene of indescribable confusion as dragging ships collided or barely missed each other by skillful use of their engines, then disappeared into the murk. Hundreds of ships were blown ashore. Several ships at a time drifted into a mass of wreckage on the beach, their crews working desperately to maintain watertight integrity and to get a line on anything at hand in order to stop the pounding. Many ships had to be abandoned. Some crews were taken on board other ships; others made their way ashore, where they spent a miserable night in the open or huddled in caves; many men were drowned.

By 1600 Louise had reached her peak. The glass dropped to 29.15 inches as the center passed, but then the winds continued in unabated strength for another two hours. The wind, backing into the north and then northwest, began blowing ships off the formerly lee-shore reefs where they had grounded, and across the bay to the south shore, dragging their anchors the entire way. These wild voyages by helpless, damaged vessels caused another nightmare series of collisions as well as a few providential escapes.

The shore afforded no sanctuary. Twenty hours of torrential rain soaked everything, turning roads into quagmires, ruining virtually all stores, destroying most of the tents and flooding the rest. Some Quonset huts were lifted bodily and moved hundreds of feet; others were torn to bits, the galvanized iron sheets ripped off, the wallboards shredded and the curved supports torn apart. Officers and men, driven from their housing, took shelter in caves and the big Okinawan tombs and in trenches and ditches in the open fields to escape the tents, boards, and sections of galvanized iron hurtling through the air. By 2000 the wind had subsided from super-typhoon to mere typhoon strength, but it was not until 1000 the following morning that it dropped to forty knots and the rain began to abate.

If you were a sailor on a subchaser caught in the middle of Buckner Bay that awful night and you lived to remember it, you went through an experience more terrifying than a kamikaze attack or anything else you had ever seen or would do in your lifetime. Say "Buckner Bay" now and you would be right back there, living it again:

You can't go topside cause you'd be a goner—swept away by wind and raging water. So below, in your compartment, you feel a fear go through your whole body like you never felt before. Everything wet, the water coming in like through a sieve. You cling white-knuckled to your pipe bunk while the ship plunges and rocks crazily under and around you. You lose your balance and fall in a confusion of bodies, ramming your elbow and forearm deep into someone's stomach, and he yells and curses you, and the deck comes up and smashes you hard and then everything rolls over and hangs there—oh God, just hangs there—and you think it's going over and then you fall against the bulkhead and something cracks inside your arm and you broke your wrist but you don't even know it and the mess table is like your wall next to you and you grab at it like everyone else and it comes down on top of you, knocking the wind out of you. "God, is this the way we're going to die?"

All the while you can't hear anything except a banging, crashing, hang-on-here-it-comes-again noise like a giant smashing us from outside or somewhere—you can't tell where. Your buddy's face is bleeding. He grabs the upright and his eyes are wide open, with fear written all over them, and so are yours. You're so scared you want to die. This is it. This is the way you die. That awful howling noise is the wind and rain hitting against the ship; someone near you is yelling something but you can't tell what. "Oooooooh, ahhhhhhh." You suck in your belly, you hang on, you wonder, will the wind ever stop?

Now you feel the pain; your wrist hurts real bad. Get down, hold fast. Oooooh, there she goes again. Hang on, you son-of-a-bitch, with your arm around the stanchion, oh God, dear God, let me die.

In the pilot house two men grab the wheel with all their strength. It's only noon but it's as black as midnight. Salt rain cracks like a bullwhip against the ports. The air is filled with a dreadful howling, a wailing banshee noise that blows loud and soft and never stops. The ship rides up, then falls down crazily into an abyss as though it were being swallowed up in a black hole. You hear an awful crunch as the ship smacks the water sideways, and you wonder how long it can be before she starts coming apart. The ribs, the bulkheads, and the planking creak; you can feel them move under your feet. The ship heels over and hangs there for an eternity, then plunges down into a deep trough, then swiftly rolls over and just as swiftly rides up the crest of another towering wave. The captain, hanging on for all his might, wonders when the really Big One will come and she actually broaches. . . .

Charles E. Clauser, Radioman 2c on SC 633, remembers seeing seawater seeping through the small port above his head in the radio shack. Being in that little cubicle was like hanging on inside a crate on a giant sling rocked by an earthquake. He was feeling very seasick. It had taken twenty minutes to make it from the forward compartment to the radio shack, hanging on for dear life, the wind grabbing him, sucking the breath out of him with every gust. Twice the heavy water almost washed him overboard. Once below, he stayed by the key, transfixed by the messages, hardly believing what he heard:

goodwife 8 we are aground but in good condition near berth l-128x
horsethief is aground and breaking up near buoy 13x
this is yms 424x we are abandoning shipx
o-a-chancellor central any ship this circuit able to proceed vicinity berth b-99 do so immediately to pick up survivorsx
vgoodwife 8 firestone broke away from shore are now 5 degrees l-122x most of crew abandoning shipx both engines inoperativex
yms 275 v respect-0 we are adrift and out of controlx
vnaked bt we are on reefx
v7yms4 - all hands are abandoning shipx
vrespect we have already collided with one lsmx
center monia island is adriftx anchor chain has partedx

-0-goatfish 86 firestone we are aground in berth 126x taking water amidshipsx will you revolve a very bright light so that we may find our position from youx

respect we have just passed red nun buoy no 6x we are trying to hold up into the wind but unable to do sox

goatfish 86 we are under way again heading on course 000 heading into beachx we are taking on waterx badly need assistancex

lanyard 3 we are lost and dragging up on the beach unable to tell positionx

vrespect bt we are still afloat no serious collisions as yetx we do not know where we arex we may be at seax

vrespect bt we are aground and are going to abandon shipx

vtanager 9 we are drifting down on next 15x if help does not reach us soon we will abandon shipx

following ships listed aground as of 1045z x atr53, lci69, lci992, yms299, 6ms442, yms292, sc1338, sc1372x

lanyard 3 aground believed near tsuken shimax listingx power gonex rescue of most personnel immediately advisablex will fire very lights on the hour to show locationx

horsethief aground west of berth b209 reportsx she must abandon ship in ten minutesx any small craft able to assist proceed to her rescuex

goodwife 8 to the rescuex

go getem sugar charliex[2]

When Clauser got back to the forward compartment after the storm he found it completely flooded. All his clothing and personal belongings were gone. When a small boat came alongside to transfer him and his fellow crew members to a tender, he left the ship stark naked—something he can't believe he did but which, at the time, seemed perfectly reasonable. On the tender they were issued skivvies, shoes, and miscellaneous clothing, Clauser an officer's uniform. He removed the bars and wore it until he could get to ship's stores for a new sea bag, ditty bag, and wardrobe.

There had been a typhoon that September that SC 724 had attempted to ride out at anchor. When the anchor began dragging, they got under way. The anchor winch was manual, requiring two men to operate handles on either side of the winch. While two men were working the handles with all their might, a handle suddenly flew off and struck one of them in the face, breaking his jaw. The captain ordered the anchor to be let go, got the engines up to full power, and almost rode it out—until the wind drove the ship into

SC 1012 stranded in Buckner Bay, Okinawa, as a result of typhoon Louise, 10 October 1945 *Courtesy of James K. Myers*

a shallow mud bank, bending the tips of both screws. That typhoon was a good dress rehearsal for Louise, because in October the 724 managed, by dexterous use of her engines and superhuman efforts at the helm, to ride it out—the only subchaser in all Buckner Bay that did not founder or collide.

The earlier typhoon caused the loss of SC 636 when all hands had to abandon ship. Late in the afternoon of 16 September the 636, skippered by Lt. (jg) W. H. Jackson, USNR, and unresponsive to engines and helm, had grounded on a shoal off Brown Beach and was rapidly taking on water in the after crew's compartment. Thirty-foot waves were breaking over the ship, and she was lurching violently. SOS radio messages and firing of the Very pistol garnered no assistance, since all other ships were too busy with their own problems in fighting the storm. At 2100 the ship began lurching from reef to reef, first afloat, then adrift, her engines dead. At 2350, she broke from a reef and began drifting fast towards the Tatsu entrance to Buckner Bay, still taking on water. Finally, LSM 391 appeared out of nowhere and maneuvered alongside in an effort to take her in tow. Firing lines and jockeying about in the raging seas, the two vessels collided, bashing the 636's stern badly, but they finally managed to get hawsers secured. Five minutes later the hawsers parted. The 636 began drifting fast toward a reef. LSM 391, under the direction of her skipper, Lt. J. M. Libaire, USNR, despite a propeller fouled by a hawser, was able, by superhuman effort, to come alongside and remove everyone from the subchaser. The abandoned SC 636 was last seen at 0540 on 17 September, drifting out to sea, down by the stern. There were no casualties. Lieutenant Libaire justly received a letter of commendation for his outstanding display of seamanship and shiphandling under frightful conditions.

That was a *small* typhoon, three weeks before Louise.

Louise killed two men of SC 727, Willard D. Goosby, Ship's Cook 1c, USNR, and David F. Mack, Seaman 1c, USN-I, and swallowed up two men who were never found, Herman R. Graff Jr., Motor Machinist's Mate 2c, USNR, and Van M. Mendenhall, Gunner's Mate 2c, USN-I. The log entry is dated 9 October:

> 1055—Under way from astern of LST 568. LST has broken loose from buoy.
>
> 1220—Moored astern IX 135 near buoy #12.
>
> 1330—Under way from IX 135 proceeding in Buckner Bay having parted two eight-inch hawsers. Visibility not over 10 yards. Terrific winds. Trying to maintain a westerly course of 250 degrees T.
>
> 1335—Radar out of commission.
>
> 1400—Helm would not answer to control due to heavy seas and high winds. All hands at General Quarters in life jackets.
>
> 1435—Requested tug to take us in tow. Tug itself disabled. Asked ARD to take us in tow. No answer.
>
> 1510—Requested tug to take us in tow. Tug answered she was in distress.
>
> 1525—Sighted reef close aboard. Backed down.
>
> 1527—Ship taking on water showing this vessel had evidently already struck reef and damaged bottom.
>
> 1530—Ship aground. Men being washed overboard. Ship rolling approximately 90 degrees to either side. Starboard ready box on quarterdeck broke loose and tore away starboard life rail. Several men washed overboard.

> All but six were recovered at once and every effort made to recover all of them.
>
> 1540—Received line from grounded LCI 399 to our bow and ship's company abandoned ship across bow line. Immediate muster taken. GRAFF—missing. MENDENHALL—missing. Life jacket was recovered along with billfold on afternoon of 10 October 1945.

Like all the other small ships in the anchorage, SC 1368 was in a bad way. On 8 October, the day before Louise struck, she had been ordered out of Buckner Bay to seek safer anchorage. After proceeding fifteen miles up the coast, her captain, Lt. Ingmar Molde, USNR, decided that this course of action was even worse than staying put, so he turned her about and fled back to Buckner Bay. The executive officer on the 1368 was twenty-year-old Pierre Salinger, a child piano prodigy who had enlisted in the navy on his seventeenth birthday while a student at San Francisco State College. He made officer candidate school and in due time went aboard the 1368 at Kwajalein in August 1944 as third officer. Salinger stood five feet nine, weighed 165 pounds, and played a good game of poker. He wore the perpetually impish look of a youngster about to play a joke on somebody—but there was little to smile about on this day.

The 1368 squeezed back as far as she could into Buckner Bay before putting out two anchors with all the chain she carried. By now the wind was a steady howl, and the rain, driven horizontally, made it impossible to see more than a few yards. A huge freighter completely out of control bore down on her but Captain Molde backed out of harm's way just in time to avoid collision. The freighter went aground, and the 1368 snapped her own anchor chains in the maneuver. As she began drifting toward disaster, the winds miraculously died down to a whisper, the rain stopped, and blue sky could be seen overhead. They were passing through the eye of the storm.

In every direction there was devastation—ships with cracked hulls grounded, flotsam and jetsam of every description floating in the bay. Knowing that in a short time it would start again, Captain Molde decided to drive the ship hard between two grounded steel pontoon barges. Quartermaster Daniel E. Kennedy brought her skillfully in, grounding her solidly. The 1368 had been converted to a shallow-water minesweeper in preparation for the invasion of Japan, and fortunately she had miles of cable aboard. The cable was made fast to the grounded barges on the theory that they were too heavy to be swept away.

The sea was running angrily some six feet over the sand spit on which the 1368 had grounded. Ensign Salinger and Lieutenant Molde were standing on the bridge, sweeping their surroundings with binoculars, when they spotted a group of men waving frantically at them from a tiny area on the sand spit still above water. A short time before a Liberty ship had rammed and sunk the USS *Southern Seas,* a PY converted yacht used by the navy as a floating hotel. Salinger and Molde surmised, correctly, that the six stranded men were survivors of that sinking.

Without hesitation Ensign Salinger asked for volunteers from the crew. He and three men stripped to their shorts and dived overboard carrying a heavy line, one end of which was made fast to the deck. Salinger took the lead, with the others spaced out a few yards behind him, holding the line under their armpits and swimming slowly toward the little piece of ground. Waves broke everywhere over the sand spit except for the small unflooded spot where the survivors stood. It was slow going. The usually warm waters of Buckner Bay were amazingly cold, and the swimmers' arms and legs grew numb as they struggled through the heavy surf. The water was slightly more than chest deep in the trough of the waves, a bit too deep for wading.

Salinger, in the lead, swam a crawl stroke, but the normal breathing to the side was almost impossible in the rough surf. When he finally crept up on the sand, he had more water inside than out. The rescue party found a broken spar on the little piece of ground and drove it deep into the sand, then tied the line to it. The six exhausted sailors awaiting help were too weary to make it back to the 1368 unassisted. Salinger placed one of the rescued beside each of his own men and the group made its way back to the ship, hand over hand, along the line. Salinger, accompanied by one of his volunteers, then made his way back along the line and brought over the remaining pair of survivors. The distance from the ship to the spot of land was about 150 yards, but the operation required almost an hour because of the surge of water and the constant danger of being swept away by heavy wreckage swirling by.

Rescued and rescuers were wrapped in blankets and warmed up with coffee from the galley. They got off the sand spit just in time. Soon the second half of the vicious storm struck, with a violence more frightening than ever. The day soon faded into a night of terror.

For his part in the rescue Ens. Pierre Salinger was awarded the Navy and Marine Corps Medal, a medal awarded to anyone serving with the navy or marine corps who distinguishes himself by heroism not involving combat with an enemy. Salinger moved up to captain of the 1368 a few weeks later and stayed on as skipper until she sailed into San Francisco Bay in the summer of 1946.

Best known now for his role as President Kennedy's press secretary, Salinger became a newspaper reporter after the war. At the age of twenty-five, he was the night city editor for the *San Francisco Chronicle* and later joined *Collier's* magazine as an investigative reporter. After a subsequent stint as a U.S. Senate investigator, he was Kennedy's press agent in the 1960 election campaign. A life member of the Patrol Craft Sailors Association, Salinger now lives in London, where he is still active in public affairs and still remembers Buckner Bay.[3]

Epilogue

On 2 September 1945 a total of 254 warships gathered by invitation in Tokyo Bay to be present at the historic surrender ceremony conducted aboard the battleship USS *Missouri.* Most of them were from the United States, but ships from Great Britain, Australia, and New Zealand were also present. Battleships, aircraft carriers, heavy and light cruisers, destroyers, destroyer escorts, frigates, minesweepers, submarines, patrol craft, gunboats, landing ships, tenders, tugs, oilers, transports, repair ships—all classes and types of warship were there.

All, that is, except one.

And two months later, on 27 October 1945, millions of people celebrated America's victory with a grand event in New York harbor, a tremendous Navy Day celebration. Over fifty of the navy's fighting ships were there, fresh from the war, anchored in a line that began at Battery Park and stretched as far up the Hudson River as one could see, even beyond George Washington Bridge. The *New York Times* headlined it "Seven Miles of Sea Power."[1] President Harry Truman came up from Washington amid ruffles and flourishes to commission the giant aircraft carrier USS *Franklin D. Roosevelt* and to be piped aboard the battleship USS *Missouri* for lunch with Adm. Jonas Ingram. That afternoon he boarded the destroyer USS *Renshaw* and commenced steaming slowly up the river in a processional review that took many hours.

It was a majestic and impressive sight, the throngs on shore cheering, the men of each ship in their dress white uniforms snapping to attention and saluting smartly as the president passed, and the ships exchanging salutes by dipping their colors. It was long after sundown by the time the president arrived at the PC 1264, the last ship in the long line of ships.

Not one SC subchaser was invited to share in these momentous events, the signing of peace in Tokyo Harbor and nation's celebration in New York on that bright October day—oh, how long ago! Overlooked? Scorned? It doesn't really matter. Now, having come this far, we know that the doughty little wooden ships of the Splinter Fleet and those iron men who sailed them were indeed "Too Good To Be Forgotten."

Appendix A

Postwar Disposition of Subchasers

From 1943 to 1945, seventy-eight SCs were transferred to the Soviet navy: SC 500, 537, 538, 634, 643, 646, 647, 657, 660, 661, 663, 673, 674, 675, **685**, 687, 713, 719, 720, 721, 752, 754, 756, 774, 986, 997, 1007, 1011, 1021, 1031, 1060, 1073, 1074, 1075, 1076, 1283, 1284, 1285, 1286, 1287, 1295, 1324, 1364, 1365, 1475, 1476, **1477**, 1478, 1479, 1480, 1481, 1482, 1483, 1484, **1485**, 1486, 1487, 1488, 1489, 1490, 1491, 1492, 1493, 1496, 1497, 1498, 1499, 1502, 1503, 1504, 1505, 1506, **1507**, 1508, 1510, 1511, 1512, 1517.[1] Boldface indicates SCs reported lost in action. The remainder were returned to the U.S. Navy, to be scrapped or scuttled by 1956.[2]

From 1943 to 1944, fifty SCs were transferred to France: SC 497, 498, 503, 506, 507, 508, 515, 516, 517, 519, 522, 524, 525, 526, 529, 530, 532, 533, 534, 535, 638, 639, 649, 651, 655, 666, 676, 690, 691, 692, 693, 695, 697, 770, 771, 977, 978, 979, 1029, 1030, 1043, 1044, 1331, 1335, 1336, 1337, 1344, 1345, 1346, 1359.[3] They were put to good use by the French navy in various duties, including minesweeping, auxiliary patrol, support ships for divers and commandos, etc. By the end of the 1960s all but one had been stricken from their list. SC 497 (Fr. Chasseur *.96*) remained in service until October 1980.[4]

On 2 July 1948, fifteen SCs were transferred to the Philippines: SC 699, 731, 732, 736, 739, 742, 743, 747, 750, 769, 982, 1267, 1269, 1274, 1278.[5] Their present status is unknown.

From 1942 to 1943, eight SCs were transferred to Brazil: SC 762, 763, 764, 765, 766, 767, 1288, 1289. By December 1951 they had been decommissioned.[6]

From 1947 to 1948, seven SCs were transferred to the Republic of China: SC 648, 698, 704, 708, 722, 723, 735. No information has been received about the fate of these vessels.

In October 1945, SCs 683, 718, and 1061, originally loaned to occupied Norway for use as *Shetlandsbussen,* were officially transferred to Norway. They were sold to private owners in 1958. In 1987, SC 718 (KNM *Hitra*) was fully restored to her wartime condition as a floating museum. (See appendix B.)

In 1947 thirty-four SCs were transferred to the Foreign Liquidation Commission: SC 527, 528, 637, 644, 650, 652, 664, 703, 727, 734, 737, 738, 741, 745, 746, 748, 749, 757, 768, **1000,** 1001, 1014, 1018, 1035, 1053, 1056, 1066, 1071, **1280,** 1290, **1291, 1301,** 1350, 1366. A temporary postwar agency, the Foreign Liquidation Commission no longer exists. Boldface denotes four SCs transferred to Cuba, no longer in service.[7]

SC 679 transferred to Indochina on 14 March 1951; SC 1309 transferred to the Sea Scouts, Boy Scouts of America on 26 September 1946; SC 1316 transferred to the U.S. Army on 11 December 1946; SC 1358 transferred to the U.S. Department of Interior on 30 September 1946.[8] The present status of these four SCs is unknown.

From 1946 to 1948 the U.S. Maritime Commission received by transfer 117 SCs. as follows: SC 502, 504, 505, 513, 514, 520, 531, 539, 540, 628, 629, 630, 631, 640, 641, 645, 658, 667, 669, 680, 681, 688, 689, 701, 702, 705, 706, 707, 712, 724, 725, 726, 728, 729, 730, 733, 755, 759, 760, 761, 773, 980, 983, 990, 991, 992, 993, 994, 995, 998, 1002, 1005, 1006, 1008, 1019, 1020, 1025, 1026, 1034, 1036, 1039, 1040, 1041, 1042, 1045, 1046, 1047, 1048, 1050, 1051, 1052, 1058, 1059, 1065, 1266, 1268, 1270, 1271, 1272, 1273, 1275, 1276, 1277, 1279, 1281, 1282, 1292, 1293, 1294, 1299, 1300, 1302, 1303, 1304, 1305, 1308, 1310, 1311, 1312, 1314, 1315, 1317, 1318, 1319, 1320, 1321, 1322, 1323, 1325, 1326, 1327, 1328, 1330, 1332, 1333, 1334, 1338.[9] Most of these were sold or auctioned at prices ranging from a low of $1,160 to a high of $13,125, many of them at $10,000. The original cost of a subchaser was $325,000.

From 1946 to 1948 the U.S. Coast Guard received by transfer seventy-three SCs: SC 449, 453, 499, 511, 512, **536,** 539, 540, 541, 635, 642, 653, 656, 659, 662, 670, 672, 682, 684, 710, 711, 714, 715, 717, 753, 758, **772,** 775, 985, 987, 988, 989, 996, 1003, 1004, 1009, 1010, **1013,** 1015, 1016, 1017, 1022, 1023, 1027, 1028, 1032, 1033, 1037, 1038, 1054, 1055, 1062, 1063, 1064, **1068,** 1069, 1070, 1296, 1297, 1307, 1329, 1339, 1340, 1347, 1348, 1355, 1356, 1357, 1361, 1362, 1367, 1369, 1373.[10] Intended to be used for Air-Sea Rescue service, they were given the names of birds, prefaced with the word "air," the Air-Sea Rescue radio call sign. Many were never fully operational in the Coast Guard and were, most of the time, on "in commission in reserve" status due to a lack of personnel. SC 453 was sold to Haiti in 1947 and was struck from that country's list in 1977. Boldface indicates SCs whose hulls are still afloat. (See appendix B.)

From 1946 to 1950 the following SCs were "sold" or "disposed of": SC 501, 665, 668, 671, 677, 678, 716, 981, **1057,** 1341, **1342,** 1343, 1349, 1351, 1352, 1353, 1354, 1360, 1363, 1368, 1370, 1371, **1372,** 1374, 1375, 1474.[11] Boldface indicates SC hulls still afloat. SC 1371 may be, but its status is not certain. (See appendix B.)

The following hulls were destroyed by the U.S. Navy: SC 518, 632, 633, 654, 686, 999, 1012, 1049, 1298, 1306, 1349, all but two of them as a result of grounding and damage suffered in typhoon Louise.

Appendix B

Subchaser Hulls Still Afloat

As a genus of historic and/or classical ship, SCs have almost vanished. After World War II, as is often the case, economics took precedence over sentiment, no matter how distinguished the wartime record or how beloved the ship by her sailors. Only a handful of SC hulls have survived and are still floating, thanks primarily to the tender loving care of their owners or to groups interested in their preservation.

Now known as *Hitra,* SC 718 was the Shetlands Bus described in chapter 8. The story of her discovery in 1982 and the restoration that followed is almost as exciting as her war record. After the war, the three *Shetlandsbussen, Hitra* (SC 718), *Hessa* (SC 683), and *Vigra* (SC 1061), remained in service as patrol craft until 1958, when they were sold to private owners. The three vessels moved from one short-lived ownership to another, until *Hessa* wrecked on the coast of Sweden, *Vigra* sank as a too heavily laden sand barge, and *Hitra* was towed to a ship's graveyard to be left to vandals and the savagery of the elements. She would have disappeared altogether but for an incident of global significance that occurred during the height of the Cold War.

On 27 October 1981 a Soviet Whisky-class submarine ran aground near the Swedish naval base at Karlskrona. The event rocked the international community and was highly publicized. A Swedish naval officer, Capt.

Y. Rollof, wrote an article about the incident titled "Whisky on the Rocks" in which he concluded humorously that "not only the Russians were infiltrating Karlskrona waters, the Norwegian *Hitra* has been here for years." The article, printed in a Norwegian magazine, was brought to the attention of the director of the Royal Norwegian Navy Museum. He and Ingvald Eidsheim, *Hitra's* old skipper, hurried to the site and confirmed that, sure enough, the *Hitra,* though in sad shape, was there. "A sorry sight," Eidsheim commented as he gazed at the once proud vessel, only her bow and foredeck visible above water, her equipment and fixtures gone. An organization was formed called "The Friends of the Shetland Bus" for the purpose of reconstructing *Hitra.* The campaign mounted quickly and was overwhelmingly successful. Two-thirds of the funds were raised by public contribution, and the remainder was furnished by the Norwegian government.

To everyone's surprise, when *Hitra* was tenderly lifted onto a barge and brought to Norway for reconstruction, it was found that much of her wooden hull was sound and usable. It took four years to restore *Hitra* to her wartime condition.

Today *Hitra* is based at Haakonsvern, Norway's major naval base near Bergen. She is owned by the Royal Norwegian Navy Museum and leads a charmed life as a living reminder of her wartime role. She has earned a special place in the hearts of all Norwegians, especially those who knew of her during the Occupation. In the summer she cruises to towns along the coast where people are told about her World War II adventures. Veterans enjoy visiting her for reunions and story-swapping. *Hitra* is the only SC subchaser still in existence fitted out and equipped exactly as she was during the war. And for anyone who may doubt her authenticity, a close look at her highly polished ship's bell reveals ever so faintly the engraved words "U.S.S. SC 718."

SC 1372 is now a luxury yacht named *Cairdeas,* moored at Orcas Island in the State of Washington and owned by David Baxter, a hands-on builder and restorer of wooden boats. In 1949 *Cairdeas* first emerged as a company yacht for General Construction Company; then in 1967 she was sold to Patrick and Maureen Dickson, who lavished twenty years of loving care on her while making her available for charter. Actress Julie Andrews and her family used *Cairdeas* several summers for relaxing and fishing in the Desolation Sound area. Mr. Baxter has recently remodeled the interior quarters. In addition to captain's quarters, *Cairdeas* has a library room, a dining salon, a main salon, five staterooms each with heads and shower, and crew's quarters

KNM *Hitra,* formerly SC 718, after being raised from her muddy grave at Karlskrona, Sweden, 1983 *Courtesy of Royal Norwegian Naval Museum*

KNM *Hitra* fully restored, in her home port of Bergen, Norway, 1998

forward with six single bunks. She mounts a helipad on her afterdeck. Equipped with two V-12 Deutz MWM diesel engines, she carries five thousand gallons of fuel and three thousand gallons of water.

SC 1068 is alive and well in Ketchikan, Alaska. Transferred to the Coast Guard after the war and named *Air Snipe*, she was purchased by Mr. Kent Halverson, who owns and operates a fleet of tugboats in Ketchikan named Boyer Towing, Inc. For three or four years she was used for towing small oil barges, until Mr. Halverson, realizing she was "not a very happy tugboat," decided to keep her for family use. *Air Snipe* is Mr. Halverson's pride and joy and is beautifully maintained.

SC 536, named *Moonlight Maid*, is owned and operated by Pat and Kelley Warga, a husband-wife team from Bainbridge Island, Washington. Each year from March to September they take her to Valdez, Alaska, where she is used in the fishing industry as a packer boat and tender. The Wargas keep the *Moonlight Maid* in excellent working condition. Early in the war SC 536 had an incident worth reporting. Operating out of Astoria, Oregon, one night, she was ordered out to a point ten miles off the coast to investigate a possible Japanese submarine sighting. Upon reaching the area, a good underwater contact was made with her echo ranging equipment, and she made several depth-charge attacks, using up all her charges. An observation blimp overhead claimed that

The yacht *Cairdeas*, formerly SC 1372. Note the helicopter. *Courtesy of George Baxter, owner*

The yacht *Air Snipe,* formerly SC 1068, in Ketchikan, Alaska, her home port
Courtesy of Kent Halverson, Boyer Towing Co., owner

her depth charges had definitely sunk a submarine. When the acting captain, Lt. (jg) Edward F. Kroepke, USNR, triumphantly took his report to Commander, Northwestern Sea Frontier, the admiral cut him down fast. "So you think you sunk a Jap sub off the coast of Washington, eh, Kroepke? Let me show you a map of the Pacific. Here is Astoria, and there is Hawaii and out there are the Marianas and down there is Guadalcanal. What do you think would happen if I called Washington and reported that a Jap sub had been sunk off the Washington coast and this news hit the media? The people aren't going to panic on my watch. So, now, you forget about sinking a sub and have some breakfast and get some sleep." Lieutenant Kroepke left the admiral's office so crestfallen that he never said another word about the sub to his men until they had a reunion forty-four years later. It's a nice story, but the hard fact is that no enemy submarine was ever sunk even remotely near that location or date.[1]

For many years after the war SC 1013, converted to the *Mount Independence,* was a familiar sight as a sightseeing and tour boat on Lake Champlain in upstate New York. In November 1989, Bruce P. Keller of Baltimore purchased the *Mount Independence,* her topsides in poor condition but her hull still sound and waterborne. He and his brother David brought her down from Plattsburg, New York, in eight days of sub-zero cold, encountering frozen locks in the New York state waterways and shivering in the wheelhouse around a cantankerous kerosene heater. ("The locals said we wouldn't make it but they didn't know the Kellers.") Today the *Mount Independence,* a pretty, well-kept yacht, is moored

The fishing tender *Moonlight Maid,* formerly SC 536, Prince William Sound, Alaska *Courtesy of Pat and Kelley Warga, owners*

in Baltimore Harbor, from whence Captain Keller and his family take her out for fishing and just plain fun. During the war, as SC 1013, she had the distinction of being the ship that escorted the German U-505 back to Bermuda after her capture by three destroyer escorts and the carrier USS *Guadalcanal.* She also participated as a control vessel in the Normandy invasion.

SC 772, the *Lady Goodiver,* has recently been acquired by Craig Brezden who operates a sportsfishing tackle shop on Vancouver Island, B.C. Her previous owners, a husband and wife team, operated her for several years as British Columbia's "largest live-aboard dive boat," accommodating up to twelve divers per charter. Mr. Brezden states he has no firm plans for her but "I sure have grown fond of her."

In 1977 Richard Lindsey of St. Paul, Minnesota, an enterprising young man unafraid of hard work, spotted the remains of SC 1342 on the Wisconsin side of the St. Croix River. She had been towed there from New Orleans several years before, stripped of everything of value, including her pilothouse and deck planking, and abandoned. There, for over a decade she remained, half sunk in the mud. In December 1977 Lindsey purchased salvage rights and hauled her out of the ice and up onto a hill, where he and a neighbor, Brian Larson, worked in their spare time repairing the hull and making it refloatable. After two years

The *Mount Independence,* formerly SC 1013, as a sightseeing vessel on Lake Champlain. Today she is berthed in Baltimore. *Courtesy of Bruce Keller, owner*

MV *Lady Goodiver,* formerly SC 772, British Columbia's largest live-aboard dive boat *Courtesy of Bill and Verleen Coates, owners*

she was relaunched in the nearby Mississippi, and Rick Lindsey has lived aboard ever since, making improvements with Brian's help as they go. Today, although a lot of work remains, parts of the vessel are looking quite respectable. Her damaged bow has been replaced with a long, metal prow. This, plus the fact that her exterior lines have been given a slanted, forward thrust, and all exterior surfaces have been painted a gleaming white, presents the appearance of a vessel considerably larger than a subchaser. Indeed, the extended prow adds almost twenty feet to her original length. Mr. Lindsey, somewhat a free spirit in nature, has mounted a four-foot diameter wagon wheel for a helm, but this is a mere detail in the midst of potted plants, a washing machine, a porch swing, a pet dog and cat, a den with hardwood flooring, and other interesting things aboard his ship. The ship has not been given a name because for Rick Lindsey she will always remain SC 1342, one of the very special company of subchasers who braved the Normandy invasion of 6 June 1944.

There is no more likely candidate for restoration as a historic SC subchaser than the *Bonner Lee* (ex-*Palace II*, ex-USS SC 1057) now registered as "SC 1057" and floating at anchor in Crystal River, Florida. During the war she was stationed at Key West, making numerous convoy-escort trips to Cuba and other ports in the Caribbean and the Gulf. In 1945 she was sent to New York for similar duty up and down the Atlantic seaboard. As the war ended she was under conversion to SCC, for use in the event that we invaded the

The SC 1342, still known by that name, at her mooring on the Mississippi River, St. Paul, Minnesota *Courtesy of Richard Lindsey, owner*

Japanese mainland. Her condition today is generally good; the hull is sound, she has her original GM-286 engines, but her deck and superstructure need to be replaced. For many years after the war she was the *Palace II,* a fishing vessel berthed in Hoboken, New Jersey, from whence she ran daily deep-sea fishing trips off the Jersey coast, often carrying a hundred or more sports fishermen. She changed ownership in the 1980s and became the *Bonner Lee,* ending up in Galveston, Texas, in 1996, for sale. In 1997 she was purchased by Paul Purdum and his wife Maria, who sailed her from Galveston to Crystal River. Mr. Purdum, born in St. Petersburg, Florida, has spent most of his adult life restoring older wooden boats in his spare time. The Purdums are deeply aware of the vessel's historic significance and have committed themselves to a long-range restoration effort. In order to embark on a full-fledged project, however, they will need lots of interest and lots of help, both physically and financially. Nowhere in the United States is there a World War II SC subchaser on display as a historic artifact. SC 1057, if restored and displayed indoors or afloat, would preserve an important and little-known segment of naval history, reminding people—especially young people—about what the SCs accomplished during those eventful years, while at the same time serving as a means for education, information, ceremonies, and reunions.

The *Bonner Lee,* SC 1057, moored in King's Cove, Crystal River, Florida
Courtesy of Paul and Marie Purdom, owners

Appendix C

Patrol Craft Sailors Association

The Patrol Craft Sailors Association (PCSA) is a naval veterans organization dedicated to preserving the history of patrol craft and crews who served during World War II and the Korean War, and of the Cyclone-class Patrol Coastals of today's navy. Their motto, "Too Good To Be Forgotten," speaks for itself.

In 1986 two former PC sailors, Wesley Johnson and Patrick Ward, along with Rear Adm. Alban Weber, USNR, a former PC skipper, saw a national organization of small craft sailors as the best way to keep the wartime patrol fleet's service record alive. They formed the nucleus of the PCSA, giving their time and money to create an organization of former sailors "too good to be forgotten" whose experiences might otherwise be lost to the passage of time. Membership has grown to over two thousand active members, and PCSA membership files now hold some four thousand names of former patrol craft crewmen from fifty states, Canada, Australia, and the Philippines.

The *PCSA Newsletter,* published quarterly, contains wartime anecdotes, sea stories, research studies, and news contributed by the membership. Reunions are held in a different city each year. A library and museum containing the PCSA collection of memorabilia, books, paintings, models, and archival reference documents are located in the Historical Museum of Bay County in Bay City, Michigan.

Although membership in PCSA is divided among several types of patrol craft, there are over four hundred subchaser sailors, representing 220 SC subchasers of World War II, on its rolls. For additional information about the Patrol Craft Sailors Association, write to: James W. Heywood, 7005 Bridges Road, Cincinnati, OH 45230.

Appendix D

Scale Model Subchasers

At this writing, if you want to make a model of a World War II SC subchaser, you will have to build it from scratch. No kits of any type—plastic or wood—exist for this class. Maybe this is in keeping with the lowly, unwanted status of subchasers in general—even the model companies don't want them. In the world of ship modeling, the Splinter Fleet has become the "Forgotten Fleet."

This gloomy pronouncement notwithstanding, anyone truly interested in building a model subchaser can do it, if only to prove that nothing is impossible. A scattered few ship modelers have crafted beautiful subchasers of museum quality. One of these is in the U.S. Naval Academy Museum in Annapolis. Two fine models are exhibited at the PCSA Collection located in the Historical Museum of Bay County in Bay City, Michigan (the "Birthplace of the PC").

There are several good magazines that can get you started with ideas. These contain ads for all kinds of interesting sources for model makers. Scale drawings, authentic navy plans, scale kits, molded hulls, deck fittings, guns, and books galore are available for just about any navy ship that ever saw service—except, of course, for subchasers. But don't lose heart. If you have the patience and skill to try making a World War II subchaser from scratch, scale drawings may be purchased from: Taubman Plans Service International, 11 College

Drive #4G, Jersey City, NJ 07305, telephone (201) 435-5205. Be prepared to wait a minimum of four weeks for delivery. Charges are nominal.

The Scale Shipyard of Long Beach, California, has been working on master plans for the World War II subchaser hull and expects a fiberglass hull in 1:48 scale to be in production by mid-2000. This source is a large supplier of fiberglass hulls for the scale modeler, with about 140 to choose from. In addition, they manufacture an extensive line of polymer resin fittings and weapons to compliment their hulls. For more information, contact: The Scale Shipyard, Internet Responses, 5866 Orange Avenue #3, Long Beach, CA 90805-4146.

You would also need photographs—lots of them. The best sources for photos of subchasers are: National Archives II, 8601 Adelphi Road, College Park, MD 20740-6001; Naval Historical Center, Washington Navy Yard, Washington, DC 20734-5060; U.S. Naval Institute, 291 Wood Road, Annapolis, MD 21402-5034, telephone: (410) 268-6110.

Several sources are available for fittings, guns, ordnance, and general supplies for ship modelers: HR Products, Inc., P.O. Box 67, McHenry, IL 60051, telephone: (815) 477-4636; The Dromedary, 6324 Belton Drive, El Paso, TX 79912, telephone: (915) 584-2445; Bluejacket Shipcrafters, P.O. Box 425, Stockton Springs, ME 04981, telephone: (800) 448-5567.

If you have neither the time, ability, nor inclination to build a model subchaser but would like to own one, there is an outfit that will make one for you. Fine Art Models in Birmingham, Michigan, produces exquisite, museum-quality, limited-edition scale models as fine as any you have ever seen. Their models can be found in museums and private collections around the world. They have reproduced a World War II subchaser in a 3/8:1 model measuring slightly more than forty-one inches in length. The hull is made from high-definition resin, the wood that shows is real wood, and everything above the deck is hand-fabricated brass. The interior of the pilothouse is finished off. The mousetrap rails can be raised and lowered. The model comes mounted on a shipping cradle complete with walnut display base and Plexiglas cover. The model is expensive, and the delivery time is long—but isn't this true of all things worthwhile?

Notes

Prologue

1. Sigrid Arne, Associated Press, circa 1942.
2. Albert Angelini, Pharmacist's Mate 1c, letter to author, 18 October 1995.
3. Francis R. Walsh, letter to author, 4 December 1995.
4. *U.S. Naval Vessels 1943,* ONI 54 Series (Annapolis, Md.: Naval Institute Press, 1943).

Chapter 1. World War I Subchasers: The First Generation

1. W. W. Nutting, *The Cinderellas of the Fleet* (Jersey City, N.J.: The Standard Motor Construction Co., 1920), p. 2.
2. *(Taunton, Mass.) Daily Gazette,* 29 October 1955.
3. Paul G. Halpern, *A Naval History of World War I* (Annapolis, Md.: Naval Institute Press, 1994), 399.
4. SCs 210, 220, 294, 300, and 431.
5. This account of SC 127 and *Lizzie Ann* is abridged, with his courteous permission, from Robert M. Daly Sr.'s article, "From Subchaser to Block Island Ferry—The History of the Lizzie Ann," *Block Island (R.I.) Times,* 3 January 1998.

Chapter 2. World War II Subchasers: The Second Generation

1. *Dictionary of American Fighting Ships* (Washington, D.C.: Department of the Navy, Naval History Division, 1977), 6:732.
2. For a detailed list of boatyards and the SC numbers of keels laid, launched, and commissioned, see ibid., 6:711–42.
3. Department of the Navy, *Specifications for Building Subchasers* (Washington, D.C.: Bureau of Ships, 1941), pp. 628–56.
4. Norman Friedman, *U.S. Small Combatants* (Annapolis, Md.: U.S. Naval Institute, 1987).

5. Ibid., pp. 75–81. SCs converted and designated SCC: SC 504, 514, 521, 630, 631, 632, 636, 667, 668, 686, 712, 724, 727, 729, 760, 999, 1004, 1012, 1018, 1020, 1049, 1052, 1066, 1272, 1273, 1278, 1281, 1298, 1306, 1309, 1311, 1312, 1314, 1315, 1316, 1319, 1320, 1323, 1325, 1326, 1327, 1328, 1338, 1341, 1349, 1350, 1360, 1364, 1365, 1369, 1374, 1375, 1474.
6. Roy Johns, former commanding officer of SC 991, personal communication with author.

Chapter 3. Subchaser Training Center

1. Edward P. Stafford, *Subchaser* (Annapolis, Md.: Naval Institute Press, 1988), pp. 3–4.
2. Commander in chief, Atlantic Fleet, *Fleet Operational Training Command* (Washington, D.C., 1946), 2:7.

Chapter 4. The Battle of the Atlantic

1. "Tenth Fleet Fights the U-boats," in *uboat.net: The U-boat War 1939–1945* [online], cited 13 June 1999. Available from http://uboat.net/allies/ships/us_10thfleet.htm.
2. Capt. Lawrence P. Treadwell, USN, personal war diary.
3. Capt. Donald R. Gustavson, USNR (Ret.), letter to author, 1 January 1996.
4. Daniel V. James, USNR (Ret.), letter to author, 5 February 1996.
5. Tom MacElwee, USNR (Ret.), letter to author, 19 September 1998.
6. Lt. William A. Kruse, USNR (Ret.), letter to author, 30 April 1996.
7. Ed Sullivan, letter to author, 14 December 1995.
8. Judge Allen E. Gramzo, letter to author, 6 January 1996.
9. Lt. H. Nevin Gehman, USNR (Ret.), telephone interview by author, 8 August 1995.
10. Llyle L. Moore, letter to author, 13 December 1995.
11. Cdr. Franklyn B. Zinn, USN (Ret.), "Subchaser," USNI *Proceedings* 118 (April 1992): pp. 82–84.
12. Henry C. Rivers, Boatswain's Mate 2c, USNR, letter to author, 1 February 1996, and letter in *PCSA Newsletter* no. 2 (1995): pp. 2–3.
13. Cdr. Edward P. Stafford, USN (Ret.), *Subchaser* (Annapolis, Md.: Naval Institute Press, 1988), p. 29.
14. Lt. Paul C. Simmons, USNR (Ret.), letter to author, 12 February 1996.
15. Lt. Marion C. Bonham, USNR (Ret.), telephone interview by author, 8 September 1996.
16. Lt. Bernhard Wall, USNR (Ret.), telephone interview by author, 15 December 1995. Also Lt. John Gay, commanding officer, Report to Commandant, Fifth Naval District, 4 March 1943.

17. Office of the Judge Advocate General, Department of the Navy, Report of Investigation and Board of Investigation in Review, Washington, D.C., 8 January 1944, p. 1.

Chapter 5. Her Maiden Voyage

1. Ens. Albert D. Jordan, USNR, wrote a report to his commanding officer, William French, summarizing his role as navigator and executive officer during that fateful voyage. The report is dated 18 March 1943.
2. Harry W. Luessen, Quartermaster 2c, USN, telephone interview by author, 9 May 1996.
3. Lt. W. C. French, USNR to the Secretary of the Navy, "Stranding Report of SC 709," 12 March 1943, pp. 5–6.
4. Ed Levy, interview by Ian McNeil, CBC Radio, Sydney, Nova Scotia, 22 January 1993. The tape was sent to the author by Jean Kyte of the Louisbourg Heritage Society.
5. Walter Boudreau, telephone interview by author, 13 August 1996.
6. Jean Kyte, "Rescued by Gallant Fishermen," *Louisbourg Heritage Society Notes* no. 3 (January 1993): p. 3.
7. Letter, 25 January 1943, from NOIC, Sydney, Nova Scotia, to Commanding Officer, Atlantic Coast, HMC Dockyard, Halifax, Nova Scotia.
8. Kyte, "Rescued by Gallant Fishermen."
9. See George Gagnon's report to his commanding officer, Lt. W. C. French, Jr. This report was included as Enclosure B in Lt. French's "Stranding Report of SC 709."

Chapter 6. The Mediterranean

1. Stafford, *Subchaser,* pp. 45–64. The other four subchasers were the 526, 532, 534, and 535.
2. Ibid., p. 5.
3. Capt. William R. T. Crolius, USNR (Ret.), as recounted by Edward P. Stafford in phone conversation with author, circa December 1995.
4. Stafford, *Subchaser,* pp. 180–82.
5. Lt. P. Rinde-Thorsen, Action Report, 20 February 1944.
6. Lt. H. C. Sumner, USNR, commanding officer, SC 497, Action Report, 19 February 1944.
7. Lt. James A. C. Doran, USNR, commanding officer, SC 638, Action Report, 28 February 1944.
8. Robert Clarkson, Ship's Cook 1c, USNR, letter to author, undated, circa December 1995.
9. Lt. Joseph W. Barr, USNR (Ret.), commanding officer, SC 651; letter to author and telephone conversation with author, both circa February 1995; and "Joseph Barr—A 20th Century Life. World War II, 1942–1945," videotape made by Barr,

April 1996. Also Barr's Action Report, 21 April 1944, "Re: destruction of enemy midget submarine."

10. Clarkson, letter to author, undated.
11. Art Malecki, letter to author, 3 December 1995.
12. Thomas E. Bass, Rear Adm. (Ret.), USN, commanding officer, SC 676, letter to author, 1 April 1996.
13. Henry Serra, Ship's Cook 1c, USNR, interview by author, 13 February 1996.

Chapter 7. Normandy, the Channel, and Southern France

1. The following subchasers participated in Operation Neptune-Overlord: SC 1202, SC 1282, SC 1290, SC 1291, SC 1301, SC 1308, SC 1322, SC 1329, SC 1330, SC 1332, SC 1334, SC 1342, SC 1352, SC 1353, SC 1354, SC 1358, SC 1359, SC 1361, SC 1378. This information comes from E. J. Comeau of the Patrol Craft Sailors Association, memorandum to author, 5 September 1993.
2. I owe this narrative to Lt. Thomas MacElwee, USNR (Ret.), letter to author, 19 September 1998; Floyd Huntington, Gunner's Mate 3c, USNR, letter to author, 15 June 1998; and Lt. Dale Galles, USNR (Ret.), e-mail correspondence with author, 15 May 1999.
3. *Nassau Daily Review,* 15 November 1944.
4. Henry Serra, Ship's Cook 1c, USN, interview with author, 13 February 1996.
5. Paul Kemp, *U-Boats Destroyed,* rev. ed. (Annapolis, Md.: Naval Institute Press, 1997), pp. 244–45.
6. Ibid., p. 255.

Chapter 8. The Shetlands Bus

1. David Howarth, *The Shetlands Bus* (London: Grafton, 1991), p. 251.
2. The 2-pounder pom-pom was later replaced by one 6-pounder Hotchkiss Mk VII semiautomatic gun.
3. Odd Strand, Hitra—*With Engvald Eidsheim and His Men on Wartime Cruises across the North Sea.*
4. R. R. Guest, Lt. Cdr., USNR to Adm. Harold R. Stark, commander, U.S. Naval Forces in Europe, secret memorandum, 13 January 1945.
5. Howarth, *The Shetlands Bus,* p. 14.

Chapter 9. "Greek's" War

1. This ditty came from Al Angelini, pharmacist's mate on SC 744. In an e-mail message to the author, 25 January, 2000, Angelini mentioned that he found it among the papers of a yeoman who had been transferred off SC 744. Angelini was serving as the interim yeoman at the time. The yeoman's name was Robert F. Maire, described by Angelini as "an arty guy . . . who always had some interesting thing

or experience to talk about." Maire may have written the poem or he may have simply collected it. According to Angelini, Maire had "developed quite a library of books of all types and we were sought out by other vessels to trade or update our storehouse of reading material."

2. The account comes from an eighteen-page, handwritten letter to the author from Bill "Greek" Pappas, undated, circa December 1995.
3. Lt. Richard King Johnson, USNR.

Chapter 10. Adventures in the South Pacific

1. F. M. Fisher, member, ship's company, SC 504; e-mail letter to author, 14 December 1995.
2. Lt. Dudley F. Towne, USNR, letter to author, 21 May 1996.
3. From a taped account sent to author by Francis R. Walsh, member, ship's company, SC 505, 29 February 1996.
4. A form of backgammon popular with World War II sailors.
5. Walsh, ibid.
6. For a good description of this voyage and related events, see J. Henry Doscher Jr., *Subchaser in the South Pacific* (Austin, Tex.: Eakin, 1994), pp. 16–26.
7. Ibid., pp. 44–45.
8. Samuel Eliot Morison, *History of U.S. Naval Operations in World War II* (Boston: Little Brown, 1947–60), 6:232.
9. Lt. (jg) J. M. Nagle, commanding officer, SC 505 to Adm. Chester Nimitz, commander in chief, U.S. Pacific Fleet, Action Report, 31 August 1943, SC 505. The quotation comes from a single-page endorsement signed by Adm. T. S. Wilkinson, ComTaskForce 31.0 and attached to the action report.
10. Carl Boyd and Akihiko Yoshida, *The Japanese Submarine Force and World War II* (Annapolis, Md.: Naval Institute Press, 1995), p. 217. See table, "Summary of Japanese Submarine Losses in World War II."
11. Francis E. McMutrie, ed., *Jane's Fighting Ships 1947–48* (New York: Macmillan, n.d.), p. 482.
12. The Australasian Steam Navigation Company vessel, *Kowarra.*
13. Lt. (jg) Albert L. McNomee, USNR, letter to author, 6 January 1996.
14. This name is fictitious.
15. Ens. John C. Stoltz, USNR, third officer.

Chapter 11. Arawe: The Harbor Nobody Wanted

1. The 112th Cavalry, originally used as a horse-mounted security force on the island of New Caledonia, arrived in New Guinea in June 1943 to be utilized as infantry assigned to General MacArthur's Sixth Army.
2. Morison, *History,* 6:373.

3. LCIs were more commonly used as rocket ships.
4. Daniel E. Barbey, *MacArthur's Amphibious Navy* (Annapolis, Md.: Naval Institute Press, 1969), p. 101.
5. For this daring exploit Lieutenant Foristel received the Silver Star.
6. Morison, *History*, 6:375.
7. Ibid., 6:376.
8. For many years Bill Robinson, a crackerjack SC skipper, was the editor of *Yachting* magazine. His book, *A Sailor's Tales* (New York: W. W. Norton, 1978) contains an interesting chapter about Arawe; see "Arawe and the Ghost Ship," pp. 169–72.
9. William W. Kilgore, Sonarman 2c, USN.
10. Landon M. Gentry, Coxswain V-1, USNR.
11. Frank W. Kittelsen, Seaman 1c, USNR.
12. Bill Robinson, *A Sailor's Tales,* p. 176.
13. Lt. (jg) R. B. Woodcock, commanding officer, to Commander in Chief (Readiness Section), U.S. Fleet, "Report of Anti-Aircraft Action." Woodcock's report is in SC 738's file at National Archives II, College Park, Maryland.
14. Morison, *History*, 7:377.

Chapter 12. Dead End for Dead Reckoning

1. Lt. (jg) Bobbie C. Davis, USNR, commanding officer, Action Report, "Narrative of the Grounding and Loss of USS SC 751, 28 June 1943," p. 2.
2. Ibid.
3. Ibid.
4. Ens. Thomas K. Parkison, executive officer; A. R. Del Fattore, Radioman 1c; S. P. Aceto, S 1c; and Joseph P. Cifone, Sonarman 3c.
5. Department of the Navy, Office of the Judge Advocate General, Washington, D.C., Board of Investigation—Grounding of USS SC-751, convened 29 June 1943, file 43416.
6. Lt. William D. Goldfarb, USNR (Ret.), letter to author, 20 June 1996.

Chapter 13. Kwajalein and Eniwetok

1. Bernard M. Hollander, oral history, *Duty on Subchasers (SCs) during World War II, 18 & 22 June 1997,* transcript of interview by David F. Winkler, Naval Historical Foundation, Oral History Program, Naval Historical Center, Washington, D.C., 1997.
2. Morison, *History*, 7:238–39.
3. Ibid., p. 251.
4. The local Japanese commander had ordered his men on no account to disclose their presence during the entrance of the American force. (Morison, *History*, 7:289.)

5. Lt. (jg) Richard H. Cordell, USNR, commanding officer, SC 539, to Adm. Chester Nimitz, commander in chief, U.S. Pacific Fleet, Action Report, SC 539, 20 March 1944, p. 3.
6. The investigation resulted in a thirty-two page transcript of an oral history recorded by Bernard M. Hollander, which is available at the Naval Historical Center and at the Library of Congress in Washington, D.C. This highly articulate account is more than just a vindication; it is an interesting, occasionally humorous, portrayal of life aboard the 1066 as seen by her skipper.
7. Volume 15, the last volume in the history, which was published in 1962 and reprinted in 1984, contains a thirty-page "Cumulative Errata List" which, unfortunately, does not include a correction of the 1066 error discussed here. There have been twelve reprintings of volume 7, the last in May 1984, with no correction to the 1066 story or vindication of her skipper. At the suggestion of William S. Dudley, Director of the Naval Historical Center, Little, Brown & Company has agreed to delete the statements about the 1066 in future reprints. William S. Dudley letter, 10 July 1998 (Department of the Navy, Naval Historical Center, Washington, D.C.); Little, Brown and Company (Boston) reply, 24 July 1998.
8. Currently, Dr. Morison's grandson, Samuel Loring Morison, a journalist, military affairs consultant, and naval historian, is attempting to correct any and all additional errata. He has been generous in issuing a clear statement, which he attached to a memorandum dated 6 August 1998 and directed to Cdr. David Winkler, USN, of the Naval Historical Foundation. Samuel Loring Morison's correction refutes his grandfather's misstatement and apologizes to "Lt. Hollander, his crew, and to SC 1066 for the grievous error."

Chapter 14. This Is No Subchaser

1. An unpopular but effective method of cleaning and whitening wooden decks by hauling bricks of sandstone back and forth.
2. "Negat" is code for the letter *N*. The Negat flag was checkered white and black.
3. Eight men were listed as killed or missing.

Chapter 15. Those Four-Letter Words

1. A good description of the Biak landing appears in Morison, *History*, 8:110–15.
2. Ironically, Hagmann had been transferred only three weeks before from the author's ship, SC 648.
3. Ray Millholland, *The Splinter Fleet of the Otranto Barrage* (New York: Bobbs-Merrill, 1936).
4. Hatsuho Naito, *Thunder Gods: The Kamikaze Pilots Tell Their Story* (New York: Dell, 1982), p. 14.

5. Morison, *History,* 8:383.
6. Rear Adm. Lawrence F. Reifsnider, commander, Task Group 53.2, First Endorsement, 29 August 1944, in which he stated, "Although recognizably small for the duty, the fact that SC 1319 had been trained in control work and had performed a splendid job up to date, determined her selection." Reifsnider's one-page endorsement was attached to a secret letter written by the commanding officer of SC 1319 to Adm. Chester Nimitz, commander in chief, U.S. Pacific Fleet. The secret letter outlined several recommendations regarding duties and procedures for control vessels. The document is in SC 1319's file at National Archives II, College Park, Maryland.
7. Lt. Cdr. H. E. LeBarron, group beachmaster, and his staff of five officers and fifteen men, and Lt. Col. Guy V. Miller, division supply officer for the 77th Division, U.S. Army, and staff of four officers and twelve men.

Chapter 16. Subchasers as Gunboats

1. Morison, *History,* 13:240.
2. An LCI(G) was an LCI converted to a gunboat.
3. Much of this story is based on the Action Report, 26 April 1945, of R. Alexander Pickering, commanding officer, PGM 4, as well as his unpublished personal narrative, "The PGMs in World War II."
4. Friedman, *U.S. Small Combatants,* p. 237.

Chapter 17. Leyte

1. Cdr. Roy Johns, USNR (Ret.), letter to author, 18 May 1998, and personal communication with author.
2. Dinegat and Homonhon Islands, the latter noteworthy as Magellan's first landfall in 1521.
3. Morison, *History,* 12:128.
4. "Flash Red" was a quick radio signal to all ships indicating presence of "bogeys"—enemy aircraft in the area.

Chapter 18. The Subchaser and the Zero

1. Donald S. Stroetzel, Action Report, 30 November 1944.
2. Albert H. Angelini, letter to author, 12 December 1997.
3. Aldine A. Rosser, tape-recorded narrative based on author's questions, 1 November 1994.
4. "The best chicken soup I ever tasted," said Stroetzel fifty-five years later.
5. Dale Lee Brown, Motor Machinist's Mate 3c, USN, survived.

6. Forwarding letter from Vice Adm. James L. Kauffman to Ernest J. King, commander in chief, U.S. Fleet, 2 December 1944. The letter is in the ship's log file for SC 744 at National Archives II, College Park, Maryland.

Chapter 19. The Sea Rover

1. From Chester R. Partridge to Hon. James V. Forrestal, secretary of the navy, "Report on Loss of Ship," 12 July 1945; and letters from Partridge to author, 28 May, 27 August, and 10 September 1996.

Chapter 20. Conrad Young's Secret

1. *Atlanta Journal and Constitution,* 1 January 1995, p. 20.
2. Cdr. Lewis M. Walker, USNR (Ret.), "Remembering a Battle That Never Happened . . . Deception Plan for 'Operation Olympic,'" (paper presented at "A Retrospective Symposium," Trinity University, San Antonio, Texas, 18–19 March 1995). Commander Walker, former commanding officer of SC 1272, had been given command of PCS 1379 late in the war and would have been a part of Operation Olympic had it materialized.
3. The English name for *Ohka,* a Japanese manned glider-bomber launched from the underside of a medium-type bomber. The men who piloted these aircraft received many months of training and, like the kamikaze pilots, believed that to die for their country was an honorable thing to do. The *Ohka* bombers proved to be a dismal failure for several reasons, though they provided plenty of worries for the navy at Okinawa.
4. Piloted, bomb-laden gliders launched from mother planes.
5. The "phantom" landing would have been late in October 1945 in the Kurile Islands.
6. Bureau of Ships, letter to Adm. Ernest J. King, commander in chief, U.S. Fleet, 23 June 1944. From ship's log of SC 449 at National Archives II, College Park, Maryland.
7. Ibid.

Chapter 21. The Western Pacific, 1945

1. Robert C. Achorn, letter to author, 24 January 1996. Achorn was a crew member on SC 1272 for two years.
2. Ibid.
3. J. P. Marquand, as quoted by Morison, *History,* 14:33.
4. Robert Sherrod, *On to Westward* (Mt. Pleasant, S.C.: The Nautical and Aviation Publishing Company of America, 1990), p. 20.
5. For anyone interested in reading more about the adventures of SC 1272, there is a very good book written by one of her former skippers, Lewis M. Walker, Cdr.

USNR (Ret.), titled *Ninety-Day Wonder* (Detroit: Harlo Press, 1989). The book is unfortunately out of print.

6. Morison, *History,* 14:50 n.
7. Ibid., 14:86.
8. Achorn, letter to author.

Chapter 22. Buckner Bay

1. Originally called "Nakagusuku Wan," the name was changed to Buckner Bay in honor of Lt. Gen. Simon Bolivar Buckner, commander, Tenth Army, killed by Japanese mortar fire in the Okinawan campaign.
2. U.S. Naval Communications USS SC 633 Radio Log Sheet; excerpts from seven original pages, various dates and times.
3. Extracted from Robert W. Daly, "Typhoon Louise and Ensign Salinger," *PCSA Newsletter* no. 22. Daly's article is dated 14 April 1993.

Epilogue

1. *New York Times,* 28 October 1945, p. 1.

Appendix A: Postwar Disposition of Subchasers

1. John Lambert and Al Ross, *Allied Coastal Forces of World War II* (London: Conway Maritime Press, 1990), p. 149.
2. Ibid.
3. *Dictionary of American Fighting Ships,* (Washington, D.C., 1977) 6:728–42.
4. Dominique Darcis, Ambassade de France aux Etats-Unis, Mission Militaire, Bureau Chancellerie, Washington, D.C.; letter to author, 21 March 1996, with a table, "Disposition of 50 Chasseurs ex-americaine type SC."
5. *Dictionary of American Fighting Ships,* 6:731–38.
6. E. W. Ramos Liberatti, Brasília Ministerio da Marinha, letter to author, 19 January 1996, with table, "Decommissioning of Units from Brazilian Navy, Ex-USN Ships."
7. J. M. Goicoechea, Captain (Ret.), Cuban Navy, letter to author, 12 October 1997.
8. *Dictionary of American Fighting Ships,* 6:734–38.
9. Ibid., 6:730–33.
10. Ibid., 6:727–41.
11. Ibid., 6:727–42.

Appendix B: Subchaser Hulls Still Afloat

1. U.S. Navy Dept. Chief of Naval Operations, Navy Department OpNav-P33-100 New 5-46, *German, Japanese, and Italian Submarine Losses, World War II* (Washington, D.C., 1946), pp. 22–25.

Bibliography

Barbey, Daniel E. *MacArthur's Amphibious Navy: Seventh Amphibious Force Operations 1943–1945.* Annapolis, Md.: Naval Institute Press, 1969.

Becton, F. Julian, Rear Admiral, USN (Ret.). *The Ship That Would Not Die.* Englewood Cliffs, N.J.: Prentice-Hall, 1980.

Boyd, Carl, and Akihiko Yoshida. *The Japanese Submarine Force and World War II.* Annapolis, Md.: Naval Institute Press, 1995.

Brown, David. *Warship Losses of World War II.* Annapolis, Md.: Naval Institute Press, 1980.

Connell, Brian. *Knight Errant: A Biography of Douglas Fairbanks, Jr.* Garden City, N.Y.: Doubleday, 1955.

Dictionary of American Fighting Ships. 8 vols. Washington, D.C.: Naval History Division, Navy Department, 1977.

Doscher, J. Henry. *Subchaser in the South Pacific.* Austin, Tex.: Eakin, 1994.

Dupuy, Col. Trevor Nevitt. *The Naval War in the Pacific: On to Tokyo.* New York: Franklin Watts, 1963.

Dwyer, John B. *Seaborne Deception: The History of U.S. Navy Beach Jumpers.* Westport, Conn.: Praeger, 1992.

Freuchen, Peter. *Book of the Seven Seas.* New York: Julian Messner, 1957.

Friedman, Norman. *U.S. Naval Small Combatants.* Annapolis, Md.: Naval Institute Press, 1987.

Hagoromo Society. *Born to Die: The Cherry Blossom Squadrons of the Divine Thunderbolt Corps.* N.p.: O'Hara Publications, 1973.

Halpern, Paul G. *A Naval History of World War I.* Annapolis, Md.: Naval Institute Press, 1994.

Hickam, Homer H., Jr. *Torpedo Junction.* Annapolis, Md.: Naval Institute Press, 1989.

Howarth, David. *The Shetland Bus.* London: Grafton Books, 1991.

Hoyt, Edwin P. *The Last Kamikaze: The Story of Admiral Matome Ugaki.* Westport, Conn.: Praeger, 1993.

——. *MacArthur's Navy.* Jove ed. New York: Crown, 1991.

Hunt, Frazier. *The Untold Story of Douglas MacArthur.* New York: Devin-Adair, 1964.

Lambert, John, and Al Ross. *Allied Coastal Forces of World War II.* Vol. 1. Conway Maritime, 1990.

Lorelli, John A. *To Foreign Shores: U.S. Amphibious Operations in World War II.* Annapolis, Md.: Naval Institute Press, 1995.

MacArthur, Douglas. *Reminiscences.* New York: McGraw-Hill, 1964.

Mason, John T., Jr. *The Pacific War Remembered: An Oral History Collection.* Annapolis, Md.: Naval Institute Press, 1986.

McCormick, Harold J., Lt. Cdr. USNR (Ret.). *Two Years Behind the Mast: An American Landlubber at Sea in World War II.* Manhattan, Kans.: Sunflower, 1991.

Miller, David. *An Illustrated Guide to Modern Sub Hunters.* New York: Arco, 1984.

Millholland, Ray. *The Splinter Fleet of the Otranto Barrage.* New York: Bobbs-Merrill, 1936.

Moffat, Alexander W., Captain, USNR (Ret). *Maverick Navy.* Middletown, Conn.: Wesleyan University Press, 1976.

Moore, John, Captain, U.S. Navy (Ret). *Jane's American Fighting Ships of the 20th Century.* New York: Mallard, 1991.

Morison, Samuel Eliot. *History of United States Naval Operations in World War II.* Vols. 6–8, 12–14. Boston: Little Brown, 1950–60.

Naito, Hatsuho. *Thunder Gods: The Kamikaze Pilots Tell Their Story.* New York: Dell, 1990.

National Archives. *Ships' Logbooks, Cruise Books, Special and Classified Records.* College Park, Md.: Office of Naval Records, 1942–45.

Nutting, William Washburn. *The Cinderellas of the Fleet.* Jersey City, N.J.: The Standard Motor Construction Co., 1920.

Roberts, Douglas L. *Rustbucket: A Chronicle of the USS PC-617 during the Great War.* Newcastle, Me.: Mill Pond, 1995.

Robinson, Bill. *A Sailor's Tales.* New York: W. W. Norton, 1978.

Smurthwaite, David. *The Pacific War Atlas 1941–1945.* London: Mirabel, 1995.

Specifications for Building Submarine Chasers Nos. 628 to 675. Washington, D.C.: Bureau of Ships, 1941.

Stafford, Edward P. *Subchaser.* Annapolis, Md.: Naval Institute Press, 1988.

Steinberg, Rafael. *Island Fighting, World War II.* Alexandria, Va.: Time-Life Books, 1978.

——. *Return to the Philippines, World War II.* Alexandria, Va.: Time-Life Books, 1979.

Sternhell, Charles M., and Alan M. Thorndike. *Antisubmarine Warfare in World War II: Operations Evaluation Group Report No. 51.* New York: Columbia University Press, 1946.

Stettinius, Edward R., Jr. "Lend-Lease and the United Nations War Effort." In *United States at War—December 7, 1941–December 7, 1942.* Washington, D.C.: *The Army and Navy Journal,* 1943.

Submarine Chaser Manual. 2d ed. Washington, D.C.: U.S. Government Printing Office, 1942.

Syers, William Edward. THE SEVEN: *Navy Subchaser.* New York: Duell, Sloan and Pearce, 1960.

U.S. Naval Vessels 1943. Arms & Armour edition. Annapolis, Md.: Naval Institute Press, 1986.

Walker, Lewis Midgley, Cdr., USNR (Ret). *Ninety-Day Wonder.* Detroit, Mich.: Harlo, 1989.

Ward, Geoffrey C. "Douglas MacArthur: An American Soldier." *National Geographic* 181 (March 1992): 54–82.

Index

About the Author

When Pearl Harbor erupted in flames on that Sunday morning in December, 1941, the author was strolling into a dining hall in Cambridge, Massachusetts for breakfast. A graduate of Rutgers University, Ted Treadwell was in his second year at Harvard Business School, but suddenly he and his classmates and tens of thousands of young men like them knew their future was not now to be of their own design. Within three weeks the navy offered commissions to the men of his class which would defer their active duty until they graduated. "Active duty" for this class of B-School men meant an administrative job with the Bureau of Ordnance, most likely in Washington, D.C. Mr. Treadwell accepted the commission but vowed he would do everything in his power to avoid a desk job. "Youthful and rash," he says, "I was imbued with the romantic notion that in wartime a respectable naval officer should be assigned to a ship as an officer of the line shooting at enemy ships and planes on the high seas."

It took almost a year for Treadwell to wangle himself onto a subchaser in the South Pacific, and after two years aboard—the last nine months as its commanding officer—his romantic notions about "naval officers on the high seas" had been pretty well laid to rest. When the war ended he left the navy, made a career in the packaging industry, nurtured a family of five children, four grandchildren and two great-grandchildren, and enjoyed the benefits of our free country. Not until retirement did he begin to think back on that very special period of his life on a subchaser. He decided to write a book about the little wooden warships known as SC subchasers—something needed, he felt, since so little is known today about their adventures and exploits. The process took over five years.

Mr. Treadwell and his wife, Elizabeth, live seven months during the year in Danbury, Connecticut and the other five months in Fort Myers, Florida.